"*Church history is one of the most essential studies for the preacher. . . . familiarise yourselves with previous eras . . . and how God has dealt with them.*"

Martyn Lloyd-Jones,
Preaching and Preachers, pp. 117-18

A Mirror for the Church

Preaching in the First Five Centuries

David Dunn-Wilson

WILLIAM B. EERDMANS PUBLISHING COMPANY
GRAND RAPIDS, MICHIGAN / CAMBRIDGE, U.K.

© 2005 Wm. B. Eerdmans Publishing Co.

Wm. B. Eerdmans Publishing Co.
255 Jefferson Ave. S.E., Grand Rapids, Michigan 49503 /
P.O. Box 163, Cambridge CB3 9PU U.K.

Printed in the United States of America

09 08 07 06 05   7 6 5 4 3 2 1

ISBN 0-8028-2866-3

www.eerdmans.com

FOR ELIZABETH,

uxore amicae carissimae

Contents

Acknowledgments

A Mirror for the Church began life as a lecture on early African preachers. It was commissioned for my appointment to a professorship at Kenyan Methodist University and, therefore, I am grateful to Vice Chancellor Prof. Mutuma Mugambi and to my colleagues in the Department of Theology for their initial encouragement.

As the work developed, many writers enlarged my thinking, and I tried faithfully to acknowledge my indebtedness to them. Frequently they opened up fascinating areas which, although relevant, had not been within the immediate scope of this book; these I have indicated in the notes so that others may explore them. During the past fifty years, it has been my privilege to meet, hear, and teach many preachers in several different parts of the world. They have contributed much to my understanding of the preacher's art. I hope that this book will help to repay my debt to them. I believe that there is material here both for those with a general interest in preaching and for those who wish to research the subject in more depth.

I owe special gratitude to Rev. Dr. Martyn Atkins, Principal of Cliff College, England, who read the original manuscript and encouraged me to publish it, and to Mrs. Theresa Philips, Administrator of the College's Department of Postgraduate Studies for her generous technical help. I also record my thanks to my son, Rev. Mark Dunn-Wilson and to my friends Rev. Eddy Roos and Dr. Claire Smithson who, between them, have often rescued me from the dire consequences of my incompetence with computers. I am delighted, also, to pay tribute to the care and expertise of Jennifer

Hoffman of Eerdmans and her dedicated editorial team who have spared no effort in ensuring that the text has been corrected and the book produced on schedule.

Finally, I owe lasting gratitude to my late father who taught me to love preaching well and to regret preaching badly. I hope that he is pleased with the result.

DAVID DUNN-WILSON
Eastbourne, England 2005

Abbreviations

ANCL	The Ante-Nicene Christian Library (Edinburgh: T. & T. Clark, 1867f.)
ANF	The Ante-Nicene Fathers (reprint, Grand Rapids: Eerdmans, 1994-97)
CAH	*The Cambridge Ancient History* (London: Cambridge University Press, 1939)
CEP	*The Concise Encyclopedia of Preaching* (Louisville: Westminster John Knox, 1995)
CH	*Church History*
CUHB	*Cambridge University History of the Bible* (Cambridge: Cambridge University Press)
DBI	*A Dictionary of Biblical Interpretation* (London: SCM Press, 1990)
DCS	*A Dictionary of Christian Spirituality* (London: SCM Press, 1983)
DCT	*A Dictionary of Christian Theology* (London: SCM Press, 1979)
DECB	*A Dictionary of Early Christian Beliefs* (Peabody, Mass.: Hendrickson, 1998)
DIHC	*Documents Illustrative of the History of the Church* (London: SPCK, 1932)
DLW	*Dictionary of Liturgy and Worship* (London: SCM Press, 2002)
DNTB	*Dictionary of New Testament Background* (Leicester: Inter-Varsity, 2000)
DNTT	*The New International Dictionary of New Testament Theology* (Carlisle: Paternoster Press, 1986)
DOTTE	*New International Dictionary of Old Testament Theology and Exegesis* (Carlisle: Paternoster Press, 1997)
DPL	*Dictionary of Paul and His Letters* (Leicester: Inter-Varsity, 1993)

EB	*Encyclopaedia Britannica* (Chicago)
EBC	*Expositor's Bible Commentary* (Grand Rapids: Zondervan, 1979f.)
Eccl.	*Ecclesia: A Theological Encyclopedia of the Church* (Collegeville, Minn.: Liturgical Press, 1996)
ECW	*The Early Christian World,* ed. P. F. Ester (London: Routledge, 2000)
EDB	*Eerdmans Dictionary of the Bible* (Cambridge: Eerdmans, 2000)
EEC	*Encyclopaedia of the Early Church* (Cambridge: James Clarke, 1992)
ER	*The Encyclopaedia of Religion* (New York: Collier Macmillan, 1987)
ERK	*Twentieth Century Encyclopedia of Religious Knowledge* (Grand Rapids: Baker, 1995)
ET	*Expository Times* (Edinburgh: T. & T. Clark)
HTR	*Harvard Theological Review*
IB	*The Interpreter's Bible* (New York: Abingdon, 1954f.)
JBL	*Journal of Biblical Literature*
JEH	*Journal of Ecclesiastical History*
JRH	*Journal of Religious History*
JSNT	*Journal for the Study of the New Testament* (Sheffield)
JTS	*Journal of Theological Studies* (Oxford: Clarendon Press)
LCC	Library of Christian Classics (London: SCM Press)
Loeb	Loeb Classical Library (London: Heineman)
NBC	*New Bible Commentary* (Leicester: Inter-Varsity, 1994)
NBD	*New Bible Dictionary* (Leicester: Inter-Varsity, 1997)
NDCT	*A New Dictionary of Christian Theology* (London: SCM Press, 1983)
NDLW	*A New Dictionary of Liturgy and Worship* (London: SCM Press, 1986)
NIDCC	*New International Dictionary of the Christian Church* (Exeter: Paternoster Press, 1974)
NPNF	A Selected Library from the Nicene and Post-Nicene Fathers (reprint, Grand Rapids: Eerdmans, 1994-97)
NSHE	*New Schaff-Herzog Encyclopedia of Religion*
OIHC	*Oxford Illustrated History of Christianity* (Oxford: Oxford University Press, 1992)
PC	*Peake's Commentary* (London: Nelson, 1975)
PG	*Patrologia Graeca*
PL	*Patrologia Latina*
Sacramentum	*Sacramentum Mundi: An Encyclopedia of Theology* (London: Burns and Oates, 1970)
SBL	*Society of Biblical Literature* (Atlanta: Scholars Press)
SBLMS	Society of Biblical Literature Monograph Series
SCH	*Studies in Church History* (Oxford: Ecclesiastical History Society)
SNTSMS	Society for New Testament Studies Monograph Series

SS   *The Study of Spirituality* (Oxford, 1986)
TDNT   *Theological Dictionary of the New Testament,* ed. G. W. Bromiley
WDCT   *Westminster Dictionary of Christian Theology*
WTJ   *Westminster Theological Journal*

"Pews and Pulpits"

An Introduction

Preaching has never existed as a discrete and separate discipline. It has always functioned in context. Barth may overstate the case when he claims that "preaching can take place, meaningfully, *only in church,*"[1] but there is no doubt that preachers and congregations need one another. Their existence has always been symbiotic, and long before they were segregated in pews and pulpits, a strange, oscillating "love-hate" relationship developed between them. Throughout the centuries, that relationship generated its own inner dynamic as preachers had to adapt their style and themes to congregations' changing needs. Consequently, in every age, the sermons that are preached reveal the preoccupations both of those who preach and those who listen, illuminating the interaction between them.

When we consider the preacher-congregation relationship during the first five centuries of the church's history, we discover that there are significant questions to be asked. Who are the first preachers? What do we learn when we listen to familiar figures of church history functioning *as preachers?* What do they preach about and what methods do they use? What kinds of people form the early congregations? What issues are uppermost in their minds, and how do they relate to the world around them?

The choice of material within such a broad subject must be selective, and inevitably there will be characters and events that remain untouched. Nevertheless, it is clear that besides the common concerns which dominate the preaching of all ages, each ecclesiastical era has its own specific, homiletic priorities. New demands, at first almost imperceptible, grow in force until they bring about veritable sea changes in the church's life. The major sections of our study seek to identify these overarching priorities and to show how preachers respond to them. Of course, such divisions will be somewhat artificial because preachers simultaneously confront many challenges and fulfill many different roles. However, their sermons reveal the particular issues with which they and their churches are struggling. It has seemed right, wherever possible, to allow them to speak for themselves, and as we listen to them interacting with their congregations, we appreciate the variety, the vitality, and the vulnerability of our spiritual ancestors.

1 "No Stone Unturned"

The Missionaries

> They left no stone unturned to spread the faith in all parts of the world.
>
> Origen, *Contra Celsum* 3

Early Christian Preaching

The Importance and Vocabulary of Early Preaching

In an age when even churches feel uncomfortable about using the word, it is hard for us today to appreciate the tenacious hold which *preaching* has upon the first followers of Jesus of Nazareth. They feel an irresistible compulsion to herald the good news that he is the long-awaited Messiah, and nothing can silence them.[1] As his commissioned envoys, they see proclamation as their primary function,[2] and what begins as a local mission *by* Jews *to* Jews is driven on by its own inner momentum until it embraces the Gentile world and reaches out beyond the borders of the Roman Empire.

The birth cry of the infant church is a sermon,[3] and how can it be otherwise when the "foolishness of preaching" is God's chosen instrument of salvation?[4] Preaching is not mere public expression of opinion but an urgent eschatological activity upon which the very consummation of history depends.[5] Miracles attest its supernatural energy,[6] and under its hammer blows, evil powers are vanquished as men and women find faith in Christ.[7]

It wields "the sword of God's Word," bringing salvation to the obedient and terrible judgment upon the heedless.[8] Such is the awesome potency of preaching that it is not to be entrusted to any who lack divine authorization.[9]

In order to do justice to the magnificence of preaching, Christian writers press into service a whole battery of impressive "communication" words. A preacher is an εὐαγγελιστής — a messenger of the good news.[10] The preacher is a κῆρυξ, a divine herald, a term used more than sixty times in the New Testament. Preachers are *proclaimers*[11] of the kingdom and preaching is the divine kerygma in all its fullness.[12] Although κήρυγμα and διδαχή are not synonymous,[13] a preacher is also a διδάσκαλος because he is a teacher of eternal truths. Preachers are μάρτυρες — witnesses to the saving facts of the gospel, often with undertones of suffering for their ministry.[14] In their attempt to do justice to their theme, the writers use their homiletic vocabulary very fluidly, discovering new words and creating different combinations of old ones.[15] All that concerns them is that they find the right words to establish the supremacy of Christian preaching over all its rivals.

The Record of Early Christian Preaching

In giving preeminence to Peter's Pentecost sermon, Luke faithfully reflects the early church's high view of preaching, but how far he offers an accurate account of the *substance* of that preaching is more problematical. The authenticity of the sermons in Acts has long been questioned,[16] and there is no doubt that the original material is edited. The earliest sermons do not appear in the "we" passages,[17] and Luke must depend upon his informants' memories to reconstruct what the preachers probably said.

Nevertheless, Stanton argues convincingly that Luke draws upon material from "a very early period indeed, certainly well before the emergence of any of the gospels."[18] Like Thucydides, Luke can only "record . . . what various speakers would have had to say in view of the circumstances at that time,"[19] but as T. F. Glasson observes, this does not mean that the sermons are figments of Luke's imagination.[20] Like Tacitus, Suetonius, and Josephus, Luke unashamedly takes a polemical view of history, but also like them, he prides himself upon the factual accuracy of his record.

It is reasonable to believe that Luke retains significant elements of primitive homiletic material.[21] Peter's initial sermon, in particular, has been called "the earliest . . . example of Christian preaching," "derived from a very primitive tradition" and "constructed on the basis of a general knowledge of Peter's sermons."[22] Luke promises "Theophilus" "the truth concerning the things of which he has been informed,"[23] and since he regards preaching so seriously,[24] he is likely to ensure that his edition of the sermons is as accurate as possible. C. H. Dodd insisted that Luke provides sufficient material for a reconstruction of the basic content of primitive Christian preaching,[25] and his fundamental thesis still holds good.

The impact of the primitive preaching is remarkable. The first preachers enjoy neither the approval of the empire's intelligentsia nor the protection of its politicians. They face the hostility of religious authorities and the fickleness of mobs as likely to lynch them as to lionize them.[26] Nevertheless, against all odds the gospel spreads. Within the context of the supernatural activity of the Holy Spirit, this is due largely to the creative interaction achieved between preachers and their congregations. Luke brilliantly catches this. His examples of early Christian sermons ring true *as sermons,* so that, by examining them *homiletically,* we are able to enter the world of first-century preaching. To investigate this further, it will be helpful to examine two contrasting examples of the first sermons — Peter's "Pentecost" address and Paul's *Areopagitica.*

Peter and the Crowds at Pentecost

Few congregations have been analyzed more precisely than the largely Jewish gathering which hears Peter's sermon. In declaring that the congregation represents "all the nations under heaven,"[27] Luke intends to demonstrate the variety and reliability of those who witness the birth of the church. Local Jews, many of whom personally witnessed the ministry and passion of Jesus, are joined by pilgrims from every part of the empire.[28] "The devout" are drawn from those very places where Judaism is most intellectual, successful, and influential.[29] Luke insists that the witnesses of the Pentecost phenomenon are not to be dismissed as a motley crew of local, credulous "country bumpkins." They represent Judaism in all its geographical, social, and theological breadth. The flower of Jewry is here, amazed by the Pentecostal events and eager to listen to Peter's words.

The church can scarcely ask for a better audience for the launch of its

preaching ministry, and whatever the exact nature of the Pentecostal experience, it provides an incredibly powerful preparation for Peter's sermon.
The sight of Jews inebriated by religious ecstasy and the sound of glossola-
lia in the very shadow of the temple make the audience eager to hear what
the ecstatics' spokesman has to say.

Peter's sermon bears the marks of rough spontaneity, but when exam-
ined homiletically, it reveals itself as a skillfully judged and potent evangelistic address. Peter understands his hearers very well and relaxes them by
his disarming quip about early morning drunkenness.[30] This earliest sermon is designed simply to recruit "devout" Jews as followers of Jesus, and
Luke's account of the material admirably reflects this primitive mission.

Understanding his audience's enthusiasm for messianic prophecies,[31]
Peter contemporizes Joel's prophecy by prefacing it with his own gloss, "in
the last days,"[32] knowing full well that many believe themselves to be confronted by the eschaton with all its attendant terrors. Then he creates a
special bond with the "eyewitness" section of his congregation by inviting
them to confirm how "men outside the law" — their Roman overlords —
had tried to destroy their promised Messiah.[33] Peter does not shrink from
confronting his hearers with their own shameful involvement in those
scandalous events, but his reference to the Romans softens the blow and he
quickly assures them that, despite such infamy, all is not lost. The claim
that God raised Jesus from the dead, he continues, is incontrovertibly confirmed both by powerful proof texts and by the amazing events his hearers
have just witnessed.[34]

Peter reminds his hearers how Joel foretells the destruction of Judaism's oppressors and the gathering of God's righteous remnant on Mount
Zion to receive the blessings of the last times. That time has come! By repenting of their former treachery and becoming followers of Jesus of Nazareth, Peter's hearers can receive absolution and share the spiritual gifts
they see bestowed upon his followers. It is claimed that over three thousand people respond to Peter's appeal to accept Jesus as the prophesied
Messiah.[35] The secret of Peter's success is that he manages to convince his
hearers of two compelling truths: that eschatological horror is about to
break over the heads of the hated Romans,[36] and that the followers of Jesus
are Joel's prophesied divinely saved remnant gathering on Mount Zion.

Paul and the Athenians

Comparing Peter's sermon with Paul's *Areopagitica*[37] is instructive because it shows how Christian preaching speedily has to adapt itself for different kinds of hearers. It seems unlikely that the setting is spurious or that the address is merely a Lukan summary of Paul's addresses to Gentile audiences. It may not be a verbatim account of Paul's sermon, but it seems faithfully to present his words on that occasion. Therefore, we may ask, is it Paul's "one significant failure" or "a brilliant example of missionary strategy"?[38] An examination of the congregation and the sermon may help to answer the question.

Paul knows that his congregation, having heard the finest Stoic and Cynic street preachers,[39] is largely composed of connoisseurs of good preaching and amateur practitioners of philosophical debate. He knows, too, that since interest in personal religious experience has long been aflame in Athens, he is addressing religiously sophisticated syncretists for whom the Christian gospel is just one more possible solution to their spiritual quest.[40]

Before reaching the Areopagus, Paul has preliminary forays, firstly in the synagogue with the Hellenistic Jews and God-fearers and then in the agora, where discussions with the market philosophers open the way for a more formal presentation.[41] Paul is now confronted by a more formidable congregation which expects him to produce a philosophical tour de force, and it will require all his rhetorical skill to convince them.[42]

He rises to the occasion remarkably well, taking up the charge of "advocating foreign gods"[43] as the obvious place to begin his address. His opening gambit about his hearers' religious fervor has them preening with self-satisfaction, oblivious to the double entendre of the term he uses.[44] His immediate offer to reveal the identity of the "unknown god"[45] tantalizes them, and his championship of monotheism taps a genuine strand of contemporary philosophical thought.[46] His assertion that God has encouraged religious "seeking" sounds like an accolade given to the inquisitive Athenians,[47] and he maintains the goodwill of his hearers by his tactful use of quotations from pagan writers.[48]

Perhaps it is not until Paul exposes the illogicality of identifying the one, true God with the variety of idols cluttering the city of Athens that his hearers begin to suspect a hidden agenda in his sermon. Nevertheless, even his subsequent call for repentance does not necessarily alienate his congregation, since they have heard similar exhortations from Stoic preachers.[49] However, the sympathy of his hearers evaporates suddenly when Paul speaks of the resurrection of the body, which they regard as both gross and superstitious.[50] The meeting apparently comes to an abrupt and inglorious halt, and even Paul's most generous listeners offer him only a half-hearted hearing sine die.

Paul feels that he has failed. He has no opportunity to speak to the people about Jesus.[51] There is no record of the foundation of an Athenian church as a result of his preaching,[52] and compared with Peter's rich haul of converts, Paul's tally of "a woman called Damaris and some others" sounds very unimpressive.[53] It is little wonder that he leaves for Corinth determined, in future, to proclaim only the *scandalon* of the cross.[54] Nevertheless, there is much to admire in Paul's attempted contextualization of the gospel in Athens, and he undoubtedly perceives that preachers will have to take seriously the need to address Greek culture.[55]

The Contents of the Missionary Preaching

Peter and Paul show how the first preachers see themselves primarily as *missionaries* — messengers sent by God to proclaim Jesus the Great Deliverer — and Stanton rightly claims that the speeches in Acts "provide the only explicit New Testament examples of (this) missionary preaching." He makes the point that "a sketch of the life and character of Jesus is an integral part of" the sermons,[56] but the preachers are offering more than a mere rehearsal of interesting historical facts. They are making certain revolutionary theological assertions. They are describing the acts of the promised Messiah, whose coming is the climax of a salvific process and marks the long-awaited moment of deliverance; it is *gospel*.

They develop their theme by confronting their hearers with a paradox. At the moment when humanity's longing has been fulfilled, the opportunity is lost because the Deliverer is crucified by a God-resisting coalition of Jews and Gentiles. The weight given to the crucifixion in the Gospels reflects its prominence in contemporary oral sermons, and the preachers insist that God has incorporated Jesus' death in his plan of salvation. His purposes are gloriously vindicated when he raises Jesus from the dead and exalts him to a position of eternal majesty. Yet, say the preachers, even that is not the end of the story. The work of the living and glorified Jesus is continued through the presence of the Holy Spirit in the world, and it is through his activity that people are admitted to a new and intimate experience of God.

Preachers claim to base their appeal upon historical facts, attested by eyewitnesses and authenticated by miraculous works done in Jesus' name. The death and resurrection of Jesus signal the advent of the last times, and hearers are pressed to prepare themselves for its coming by repenting, believing, and being baptized. The message is aimed initially at Jews awaiting their Messiah, but the eschatological urgency of the gospel appeals also to Gentiles, troubled by presentiments of lowering, cosmic events.[57] They must first be challenged to embrace monotheism,[58] but they too are attracted by the promise of new, supernatural powers available to those who own the lordship of Jesus.

Preachers and Their Congregations

The Constituents of the Earliest Christian Congregations

What kinds of people constitute the earliest congregations among whom the preachers' message takes root? In his thoughtful study of preaching, Le Grys argues cogently that the preachers succeed because they touch "a specialized target audience" of people who are "sufficiently dissatisfied with their current social location to want to move *and* have the freedom to do something about it."[59] Many hearers seek personal identity in the Christian congregations, and when preachers offer a new self-image and powerful life enhancement, congregations gather and individuals respond to the message. Le Grys highlights three groups in particular that respond to the preachers — Gentile adherents to synagogues, former slaves, and women[60] — and although the list is too restricted, it provides a useful tool for examining the earliest Christian congregations.

Many Jews, for instance, experience severe social rejection, and some, hearing the preachers in their synagogues, feel that the call to rally behind Jesus as their messiah gives them a sense of noble purpose. Gentiles associated with Judaism find that the church offers them an alternative monotheistic context for their faith. Often they do not feel fully accepted by their Jewish hosts, but the "earliest Christian proclamation" bestows "a full enfranchisement of Gentile converts into the elect of God."[61] In the Christian communities *God-fearers* are welcomed with "a warmth distinguished from the ambivalence of contemporary Jews."[62] It is the genius of the Christian *koinonia* to draw people within the orbit of the preaching of the gospel so that even slaves feel affirmed.[63] The lowliest hear their owners exhorted to treat them well, and those in positions of influence no longer feel socially superior to other worshipers.[64]

For women in the congregations, a change in social status is especially welcome. Those from a Jewish background find their lives circumscribed in so many ways. The pious Jew may honor his mother, but he fervently thanks God every morning that he is not a woman. For their part, women from pagan backgrounds are often regarded merely as fodder for the sexual appetites of men, and many are driven to exploit their sexuality for profit. The poor join the ranks of the "she-wolves" who haunt the city streets,[65] while so many of the more affluent become mistresses and courtesans that Juvenal quips that a chaste woman is "a prodigy as rare upon earth as a black swan."[66] Although imperfect by more modern standards, the early Christian congregations at least offer such women an opportunity for a vital change of direction in life. Similarly, within the churches humble, pious women feel accepted and are allowed to exercise a valued social and religious ministry.[67] Devout women of more august pedigree are also drawn into the churches, and some, such as Lydia, Dorcas, Priscilla, and Phoebe, become significant leaders.[68]

The presence of "women of high standing"[69] raises the larger question of the social spread represented in the earliest Christian congregations. Meeks is not convinced that *all* strata of Roman society find their way into the churches. While admitting that congregations generally represent "a cross-section of the urban society of the time,"[70] he doubts whether they embrace the very poorest or the most aristocratic strata of Roman society.[71] Paul's assertion that "not many of noble birth" attend the meetings[72] certainly seems to support the idea that the majority of worshipers belong to the middle classes. However, the frequent exhortations to care for the poor[73] and the undoubted size of the pauper segment of urban populations suggest that many poor people attached themselves to the Christian congregations.[74] They come seeking diversion and charity but many become devout supporters of the churches, and their care remains a major theme of sermons in the coming centuries.

The case for the presence of aristocratic and powerful men in the congregations is less sure. Attempts to identify influential Christians in

Romans 16 prove somewhat speculative,[75] and Luke's reference to "men of high standing" among Paul's Beroean converts is equally uncertain.[76] The Christian writers will have wanted to record the names of any notable converts in order to parade them as trophies of grace, but such records are hard to find. Aristocratic ladies might be allowed a few religious eccentricities,[77] but because status requires conformity to social norms, it is unlikely that many public figures would risk their reputations by associating with "a new and mischievous superstition."[78] The number of aristocratic Romans showing anything more than a passing interest in the Christian movement seems small, and typical congregations are probably small groups of urban middle-class and lower-class converts and inquirers. How, then, do they survive and even grow once the dynamic ministries of Peter and Paul are extinguished by martyrdom?

Preachers and Travelers

The years following the era of the apostles, in Henry Chadwick's words, are covered by "a shroud of darkness."[79] Who takes up the mantle of the apostolic preachers and saves Christianity from becoming simply a small and obscure sect? Our knowledge of preachers and congregations during the subapostolic period is uncomfortably speculative. Does Matthew evangelize Ethiopia or Mark found the church in Alexandria?[80] We do not know the names of most of the next generation of preachers, but anonymity is not inactivity and Dargan is wrong to suggest that "the death of the Apostles and their fellow-workers" ushers in "a time of decline" in preaching which lasts for 150 years.[81]

Dodd limits preaching to "the public proclamation of Christianity to the non-Christian world,"[82] but the definition is too narrow, and many of the next generation of Christians become informal "preachers" by testifying to their neighbors. It is no accident that μαρτυρέω has an honored place in the early church's homiletic vocabulary.[83] Christians believe themselves "commissioned to make the faith clear to non-Christians,"[84] and Dargan rightly says "conversational appeal to one or two" is a legitimate constituent of evangelistic preaching.[85] Tertullian commends the evangelizing zeal of Christian women who witness to their pagan husbands and neighbors,[86] and Origen praises the noble example of "workers in wool and leather, washerwomen and persons of the most uneducated and rustic sort."[87]

However, not all the informal preachers are content to stay at home. Many travel the seas and roads of that empire which Gibbon says "comprehends the fairest part of the earth and the most civilized portion of mankind."[88] Conditions favor the preachers' work. They enjoy a degree of safety under what Pliny the Elder calls "the immeasurable majesty of the *Pax Romana*."[89] There are fifty thousand miles of paved road, with maps and itineraries available to help travelers on their way.[90] At the ports, they find ships sailing to the edges of the known world across largely pirate-free seas.[91]

In its earliest form, the "good news" may seem no more than rumors of a religious upheaval in Jerusalem.[92] However, there are travelers who informally carry a distinctively *Christian* gospel, and as a result of their efforts, in many places the church grows more by infiltration than by organized evangelism.[93] However, some Christians travel throughout the empire expressly as missionary-preachers, sent out by their local congregations and honored with the title "apostle."[94] Eusebius describes how "Many of the disciples of that day . . . set out on journeys from their homeland, performing the work of evangelists, making it their aim to preach to such as have not yet heard the word of faith at all."[95] Origen describes the fervor of the street preachers addressing crowds in the marketplace, and he tells how these missionary preachers "left no stone unturned to spread the faith in all parts of the world."[96] Hearers seem to respond favorably to these uncomplicated evangelists who "set forth in an artless way, what they have both heard and seen."[97]

Amongst these missionary preachers, the prophetic group is particularly interesting because, though short-lived, their movement plays an important role in the development of early Christian preaching. Dargan detects a strong prophetic emphasis in primitive Christian preaching, and McDonald places *propheteia* at the head of his list of its constituent elements.[98] It is no accident that Jesus himself is honored as *The True Prophet*,[99] and, whether their roots lie in Judaism or paganism, Christians instinctively respect prophetic preachers.[100] It is significant that prophetic groups comprised both men *and* women,[101] although whether or not prophetesses constitute a recognized order of women preachers is unclear.[102] Congregations marvel at the way even those who are initially "illiterate" and "of no ability in speaking" are "transformed by the power of God" and become potent preachers.[103]

Some prophetic preachers exercise quite a formal role in local congregations, delivering their sermons after the lection,[104] but others, like Agabus, are itinerant, moving from congregation to congregation with their own idiosyncratic form of preaching.[105] By their very nature, prophetic sermons are impromptu and ephemeral so that little remains of them, but they are probably practical and repetitive and given a sharp eschatological cutting edge by their emphasis upon the imminence of the parousia.[106] Prophets often strike an iconoclastic note, and their combination of puritan rigor and ecstatic visions makes them uncomfortable members of their communities of believers. Nevertheless, they seem to fascinate their hearers.

Nowhere are the prophetic preachers received more warmly than in North Africa, where the people seem to be instinctively at ease with the concept of prophecy.[107] Two of Paul's chosen missionary partners are African "prophets,"[108] and prophecy continues to fascinate African theologian-preachers.[109] Africans embrace the Montanist preachers whose sermons are "the new prophecy" because their "combination of prophetic and apocalyptic prediction" satisfies a deep spiritual need.[110]

So it is that the gospel is spread and small groups of Christians gather for worship. Initially, they are largely composed of diaspora Jews and their sympathizers, but gradually the gospel attracts wider Gentile interest. As the groups grow, new problems become apparent. The congregations' underdeveloped theology makes them easy prey for persuasive preachers with unorthodox ideas, and they are under continual pressure from family and friends to revert to their former ways and beliefs. The temptation to apostatize is very great, and it becomes clear that, side by side with evangelistic proclamation, there is a growing need for what may be termed "pastoral preaching" to demonstrate a correct blend of exhortation and education. It is to this pastoral preaching that we must now turn our attention.

2 "Things Written"

The Pastors

These things are written that you may believe . . . and have life.

John 20:31

Pastoral Preaching and the Emergence of Written Sermons

Confronted by complex theological and organizational difficulties, the preachers need to augment evangelism with pastoral guidance, but the nascent congregations are now so widely dispersed that the missionary preachers can no longer give them personal supervision. How are the required pastoral sermons to be preached? Fortunately, a technological tool lies to hand — *epistolary sermons.*[1]

Malherbe explains that "Letters, according to ancient epistolary theory, are substitutes for their writers' 'presence,'"[2] and so, by means of letters, preachers may continue to "visit" their congregations, many of whom have attained "a certain level of literary culture."[3] Since public readings are an accepted aspect of Roman intellectual and social life, congregations find it natural to listen to *and remember* the words of absent leaders.[4] Even the illiterate will attend the public readings and understand the preachers' words.

The obvious place to begin a search for this written, pastoral preaching is the Pauline literature, but Dargan magisterially denies that Paul's letters are written sermons because they lack the qualities of oral discourses.[5]

12

Nevertheless, the evidence supports Dodd's view that they contain genuine homiletic material.[6] It is significant that Paul himself refers to his writings as ἐπιστολαί,[7] a form of literature which Demetrius had defined as dialogues, i.e., written conversations, designed for public proclamation.[8] Epistles are intended to be read aloud to their recipients,[9] and Paul adapts traditional Jewish epistolary sermons to meet the homiletic requirements of the church.[10] The rhetorical elements which have been detected in the epistles support this view,[11] since rhetoric was essentially the "systematic study of oratory" designed to persuade those who read or hear.[12] Bo Reicke argues that large parts of Paul's epistles are influenced by apostolic "oral discourses" designed as "literary substitutes for personal addresses."[13] Paul certainly sees his epistles as an extension of his personal preaching ministry, intended to be read publicly to congregations[14] in order to correct their thinking.[15] Greidanus rightly says they not only "contain the actual preaching of the apostle Paul," but that "all may be characterized as a special form of preaching."[16] They are "long distance preaching"[17] by which distant congregations "hear" Paul's sermons, just as we do today. They are sermons initially sent to specific congregations and then passed on to other churches.[18] They are solemnly read to the faithful so that what P. S. Wilson strikingly calls "the aurality of the Word" is activated.[19]

There is now a widespread conviction that many other New Testament writings were originally intended to be used homiletically.[20] The seven epistolary sermons in Revelation are designed initially for specific churches but the book is destined for *all* Christians, and the concluding warning to lectors not to tamper with the text indicates how seriously the church regarded the reading of its sermons.[21] The Gospels may be viewed in the same light. They are "the preaching, the *kerygma* written down."[22] They are "essentially documents that preach the gospel"[23] by recalling "the words and deeds of Jesus . . . in worship."[24] Each Gospel fulfills its homiletic function in its own distinctive way.[25] In his seminal missiological work, David Bosch demonstrates how the testimonies of Matthew, Luke, and Paul each represent distinctive "sub-paradigms" of the early Christian missionary program.[26]

The Pastoral Preachers and Their Congregations

The Formation of Apostolic Congregations

In their role as pastors, the preachers are committed to what Le Grys calls the "third stage" of missioning — "the successful integration of new re-cruits."[27] The task of forming true, Christian ἐκκλησίαι from the converts gathered by the missionaries is not an easy one. As Malherbe points out, the Christian "communities came into existence in response to preaching" but "social factors . . . contributed to that response,"[28] and these become increasingly important as the complexity of congregations emerges. Major cities probably boast several house churches,[29] and within each there will be different social attitudes and degrees of spiritual maturity. It is difficult to determine the nature of these congregations purely by analyzing the content of the pastoral sermons they receive. It is made even harder be-cause homilies which initially address a specific set of needs are later for-warded to other churches whose situation may be quite different.

Thus it may be helpful to concentrate upon a particular early congre-gation and use it as a basis for a more general examination of the pastoral preachers' task. At first sight, Paul's picture of the Roman church is not an obvious choice because he does not know it personally. However, in pre-paring for his intended visit, he has taken special care to glean as much in-formation as possible about the congregation(s).[30] He understands that Jewish-Gentile relationships are a major issue in the church, and he hopes that by sending a précis of his "preaching . . . at Jewish-Gentile gather-ings,"[31] he will be able to reconcile the conflicting parties. His aim is to "shape a community of the new age"[32] and to enable his hearers to see themselves as part of the embryonic, perfect community of agape which Christ came to establish on earth.

Paul typifies the approach of the pastoral preachers who seek to give their congregations an inspiring self-image. They are to see themselves as the ideal *koinonia*, the hitherto unattained "perfect society" bound to-gether by worship and mutual love.[33] Theirs is the Christian synagogue, the true ἐκκλησία which owes more to the concept of *family* than to Greek civic councils.[34] Its members are *brothers* and *sisters* who acknowledge the same divine Father and own Jesus as their "elder brother."[35]

The popular view of early Christian congregations reflects this ideal. They are seen as gatherings of single-minded saints in which "each member of the community loves every other as his own soul."[36] However, it seems that the reality is often different. Early congregations experience immense internal tensions because they break all accepted social rules by binding together disparate and even hostile groups. The pastoral preachers are involved in a challenging exercise in social engineering — nothing less than the creation of ideal communities in which old enmities and traditional distinctions are laid aside. To illustrate the situation, we return to the Roman congregation.

Tensions within Congregations

The Roman church seems to have had its roots within the city's influential Jewish community,[37] but the congregations also include a significant Gentile element. It is not surprising that there is inner tension[38] because the prejudices with which Jews and Gentiles view one another are traditional and instinctive. Gentiles are brought up to believe that Jews are lawless beggars and predators who deceive respectable Roman matrons and practice disgusting religious rites.[39] It is scarcely necessary to enlarge upon the Jews' hatred of the Gentiles. Postexilic particularism still burned fiercely in the hearts of many Jews living in pagan societies, and they guarded their spiritual superiority with uncompromising zeal.[40] For them, to call people "gentiles" (ἐθνικοί) is to dismiss them with extreme scorn.[41] The affair of the care of widows in Acts 6 shows that such entrenched attitudes do not evaporate overnight simply because Jews and Gentiles encounter each other in Christian meetings.[42]

It is against this background that Paul's epistolary sermon is to be set. Jewish and Gentile believers alike must understand that the gospel institutes a new dispensation in which all are equal in God's sight and must live in harmony.[43] The new situation requires great tolerance for the views of fellow Christians,[44] but nothing less will do because it was to create such a harmonious fellowship that Jesus himself came to "preach peace."[45]

It is not only the Jewish-Gentile divide which the preachers have to bridge. The church cannot avoid involvement with the Roman class system, and the popular antagonism between rich and poor has invaded the congregations. Gerd Theissen's detailed examination of the Corinthian church demonstrates the strains these different social strata create in local congregations.[46] As agricultural land falls into neglect or is seized to reward discharged soldiers, thousands of peasants migrate to the cities in a vain quest for employment. Many of these turn to the wineshops and chariot races to anesthetize their grim existence,[47] but others attend Christian meetings in search of charity, hope, and acceptance. These and the urban poor have every reason to hate the rich. The *Epigrams* of Martial and the *Satires* of Juvenal depict a world in which riches are obscenely flaunted in the face of the poor.[48] For their part, middle-class and aristocratic citizens resent having to provide for the poor whom they regard as a disgusting and dangerous rabble, always erupting in ferocious riots. The policy of "bread and circuses" is the grudging price the rich pay for some degree of peace and quiet.[49]

It is against this background that we set Paul's exhortation, "Live in harmony. Do not be haughty (ὑψηλός) but associate with the lowly" (ταπεινός).[50] Christians have to understand that within their congregations the relationship between rich and poor is completely different from that which obtains generally in society. They serve the One who, "though he was rich, for their sake became poor," and whose poverty makes all Christians spiritually rich.[51] Those who are materially wealthy are to regard their riches as divinely given instruments for the care of their poor brothers and sisters[52] so that the poor may overcome their animosity toward the rich and vice versa.[53]

There is another source of tension. The church's evangelistic success brings together two diametrically opposed attitudes toward women, and few of Paul's teachings arouse more criticism than his attempt to deal with the resulting tension. The life of Jewish women converts is hedged about by limitations and taboos of which many "Jewish" Christians approve, but congregations also reflect the more liberal attitudes of Gentile society.[54] Many Gentile women who join the congregations come from a background in which women can achieve a remarkable degree of personal independence.[55] There is a stark difference between the puritanical strictness of orthodox Jewish tradition and the views expressed in Juvenal's description of the life of Roman women.[56]

In view of the inevitable tensions that ensue, the regulations proposed in Paul's sermon originally must have seemed moderate and sensible. In principle, he stands by his claim that "in Christ there is no male nor female,"[57] but its implementation is difficult, especially since some Gentile Christians probably regard their liberal attitude as a bold attempt to contextualize the gospel to win their pagan neighbors.[58] Nevertheless, Paul needs to lay down some ground rules for the guidance of the Roman Christians, and he begins by insisting upon a clear distinction between the sexes, a necessary precaution in a society which takes a perverse delight in confusing them.[59] Homosexual practices are to be eschewed,[60] and using a sermon illustration, Paul reminds his hearers of the regulations safeguarding the sanctity of marriage.[61] These regulations apply both to husbands and wives, and elsewhere Paul reminds Christian husbands of the respect for their wives and for other women which their faith demands of them.[62] The institution of Christian marriage safeguards the family[63] and excludes the kind of marital infidelity which abounds in pagan society.[64] Paul's hearers are to understand that unlike the Greek ἐκκλησία, the Christian ἐκκλησία does not exclude women but honors them and gives them clear responsibilities within the fellowship.[65] Christians are to blend Jewish respect for women with some aspects of the freedom accorded women in Gentile society.[66] Like all compromises, Paul's plan of pacification has its dangers, but it is a brave attempt to solve a difficult problem.

The Empowerment of the Congregations

Paul's sermon testifies to the fact that the inner tensions experienced by congregations are heightened by external pressures. He is preaching to a persecuted church,[67] and his sermons, like those of other pastoral preachers, show that while varying in intensity the experience of persecution is both widespread and bitter.[68] Paul tells the Roman Christians that the purpose of his intended visit is to "strengthen them,"[69] and the twin concepts of *empowerment* and *encouragement* generally become immensely important aspects of pastoral preaching. Paul represents all those pastoral preachers who see themselves as *encouragers* (παράκλητοι), agents of the "God of all comfort" (παρακλήσεως) who, through Jesus, bestows the Comforter (παράκλητος) to continue the ministry of empowerment within the church.[70] Sometimes this ministry is exercised by personal visits,[71] but more often it is mediated through written sermons and addresses.

Paul represents this ministry of empowerment when he encourages the Roman congregations to generate their own support mechanisms, both within their fellowship and beyond it.[72] One important effect of the epistolary sermons is that, being passed from church to church, they encourage isolated and vulnerable congregations to feel part of a Christian network which spans the empire. Thus the greetings attached to the epistles are not simply polite formalities but theological statements about the interactive nature of the congregations which constitute the church.

The pastoral preachers acknowledge that they have a personal responsibility to reinforce the resources of local churches as they face internal tensions and external persecutions. Paul understands how easily continual external pressure can generate dissension among Christians just when they most need to be united,[73] and his exhortation, "love one another with brotherly affection" (φιλαδελφία), is echoed by other pastoral preachers.[74] However, Christians must not seek unity at any cost, and there will be occasions when unrepentant disturbers must be separated from congregations in order to free them from contagion.[75] Paul believes that the external threat of persecution must be faced squarely, and he shows how pastoral preachers may help their converts approach it positively.

They must tell their congregations that persecution is to be expected because it has always been the lot of the faithful,[76] but they need not fear because persecutors can never separate them from the love and power of their Lord.[77] Thus they may rejoice in their suffering, knowing that God will use it to bless them[78] just as he used Christ's suffering and death to achieve the salvation of the world.[79] Anticipation of future glory also makes present persecution bearable, and since God will ensure that eventually justice is done, Christians may bless and pity their persecutors rather than hate them.[80] However, it is not only the persecutors who need to be forgiven. It is hard for faithful members not to despise those who defect during persecution and subsequently wish to return to the fold.[81] By enabling their people to confront martyrdom positively, the pastoral preachers hope also to remove this further source of tension. Their aim is to make suffering so strong a uniting bond that even the church's fiercest opponents will be compelled to admire the martyrs' joy.

The Instruction of the Congregations

Within the congregations there is a division of another kind, caused by what Paul calls "those who deceive the hearts of the simple-minded."[82] The precise identity of the Roman troublemakers is unclear, but their presence symbolizes the doctrinal tensions which arise within the theologically vulnerable congregations. Imperial policies make the great cities magnets for religious entrepreneurs whose mystical and Gnostic ideas fascinate both Jewish and Gentile converts.[83] Paul's hearers come from many religious backgrounds. Some have only a slender hold upon major Christian doctrines, and he tells them that if they embrace "the doctrine they have been taught,"[84] they will find that "the preaching of Jesus Christ" will hold them steady.[85] Paul exemplifies the pastoral preachers' constant battle against those who corrupt the apostolic gospel and lead their people into apostasy. Christians urgently need to hear doctrinal sermons, both for the sake of their own spiritual survival and so that they may be equipped to win others for the faith before the imminent parousia. Without imposing unwarranted sophistication upon these epistolary sermons by "reading back" into them many of the church's later doctrinal disagreements, it remains clear that the preaching revolves around two foci — Christology and ethics. The preachers are primarily concerned to instruct their hearers with basic beliefs and godly behavior.

First of all, congregations must understand that theirs is a unique faith, distinct from orthodox Judaism and from the popular cults. It is unique because Christ *alone* is the climax of God's self-revelation and *only* those who believe his claims and obey his teaching will be saved.[86] The preachers are careful to ground their christocentric gospel in the historical ministry of Jesus of Nazareth because, as R. H. Fuller says, their Christology is "essentially a response to a particular history" and it is the historical Jesus who is presented as the divinely appointed Messiah.[87] The sermons are saturated with references to Jesus as the *Christ* whose messiahship is divinely authenticated by the resurrection and ascension.[88] It is the preachers' claim that by these supernatural events Jesus has been exalted as the supreme *Lord*,[89] an assertion that, for non-Christians, seems blatantly provocative.

The first recorded Christian sermon boldly declares that God has made Jesus *Lord*.[90] Κύριος Ἰησοῦς becomes the most common christological title and the church's earliest creed.[91] To Jews, this appears as nothing less than insulting, crass blasphemy.[92] Pagan opponents of the church are more accommodating, happily embracing "gods many and lords many,"[93] but the exclusivity of the Christians' claim is intolerable, especially once the divine lordship of the emperors becomes an unquestioned axiom of state policy.[94] Any challenge to the godlike supremacy of the divine emperors is treason,[95] and Christians can expect nothing but undisguised popular hostility and official persecution. Preachers realize that they are putting their hearers at risk but they cannot compromise. Congregations must understand that their Lord accepts no rivals and that they cannot hide behind the accommodating syncretism of the age.

One of the most powerful ways of encouraging faithfulness is to remind congregations of the eschatological significance of their faith. The preachers present Jesus the Lord as God's defining historical act, and they urge their hearers to remember that they are living in the end times, when the return of their Lord is imminent.[96] Paul stresses that because the culmination is incomplete, Christians will continue to be persecuted by the powers of evil and they must do nothing to exacerbate the situation.[97] However, suffering will not last much longer and evil will soon be eliminated by the return of Christ.[98] The imminence of the end has serious implications for those who defect, because while it brings deliverance for the faithful, it means judgment for unbelievers and apostates.[99] Therefore, Christians must think very carefully before they apostatize and seek salvation beyond the church. Only in "the Lord Jesus Christ" is there hope of deliverance.

Once again it is Paul's Romans sermon which makes this point most imaginatively. In the style of a classical rhetorical *diatribe,* he devises two imaginary dialogues to show his hearers that only Christ offers hope of salvation.[100] First, he addresses those who seek salvation by following the steps of "the moralist." He does not belittle the ethical sensitivity of many pagans, acknowledging that if guided by their consciences (συνείδησις), they will be mercifully judged.[101] However, he relegates pagan virtue to a preparatory stage of human spiritual development which is now superseded by the gospel, so that those who still depend upon their own moral rectitude for salvation are "without excuse."[102] Paul handles the case against the salvific claims of Judaism with the same homiletic skill, acknowledging the Jews' special place in God's plan but pointing out that despite all their spiritual advantages, they have fallen into the same sins as the pagans.[103]

Thus God has demonstrated the hopelessness of human attempts to be good, and debates about moral superiority between Jewish and Gentile converts are pointless since *all* claims to human goodness are now obsolete.[104] God's plan of salvation centers exclusively upon Jesus Christ, whose sinless human life and sacrificial death remove the sin barrier separating humans from God.[105] All this owes nothing to previous human pedigrees.

It is a work of divine grace, available only to those who have faith in Christ[106] who have been re-created to begin a new way of life in the Spirit.

Having established the christocentric nature of their congregations' faith, the preachers turn to the practical implications of the Christians' new life. They use dramatic images to drive home the radical nature of the Christlike lifestyle. It is exchanging *death* for *life*, the *old* for the *new*,[107] but the metaphor of moving from the domain of *flesh* (σάρξ) to the realm of the Spirit (πνεῦμα)[108] is particularly powerful because it highlights the difference between the mores of contemporary society and the converts' new life of purity. Σάρξ and Πνεῦμα are totally incompatible, and since any vestiges of converts' former way of life bring shame upon the church,[109] converts may no longer "make provision for the demands of the flesh or gratify its desires."[110]

However, the transition to the new life is complicated by the ethical confusion which many converts have inherited from their pagan families. They have to learn to view their previous existence with revulsion and understand the depravity from which they have escaped. It is for this reason that Paul provides his hearers with such a searching exposé of the moral morass into which the human race has sunk.[111] His litany of social ills is so damning that it might seem to be a pessimistic preacher's exaggeration were it not that pagan writers provide plentiful, if unwitting, corroboration of his diagnosis. The sins Paul lists were still grossly present in the surrounding society, and the danger to converts was all too real.

Paul locates the epicenter of the moral contagion in the pagan addiction to idolatry[112] and false, amoral religion which encourages "all manner of wickedness and evil" and spawns a spirit of ruthless self-centeredness.[113] This represents a genuine threat to converts for whom belief in a multitude of gods is woven into the fabric of everyday life. In the same way, it is difficult for Gentile Christians to shake off society's amoral attitude toward lust (ἐπιθυμία) and the sexual vices Paul says spring from it.[114] Equally, Paul's hearers may indeed be beguiled by neighbors whose endless search for pleasure and desire for possessions (πλεονεξία) drive them to contrive new kinds of evil (ἐφευρετὰς κακῶν).[115] Christian families are not immune from the greed and lust which, in the homes of their pagan neighbors, play havoc with normal marital affection and traditional respect for parents.[116] Converts will envy the self-confident arrogance of the rich and the successful; how can they possibly extricate themselves from the web of gossip and deceit endemic in the society that surrounds them?[117]

Paul continues to alert his hearers by warning them against the mind-less violence which shows itself as much in the ritualized slaughter of the *munera* as in the incessant drunken brawling in the streets.[118] Even worse is the ugly blood lust running through the veins of a society which Paul dubs "pitiless" (ἀνελεήμονας), a society not only hardened to suffering but delighting in devising new ways of inflicting it.[119] How can Christians who frequent the games *not* be caught up in the blood lust of the crowd?[120] How can strong men rid themselves of the "manly" belief that when dealing with enemies, cruelty is a virtue and savage destruction a duty?[121] Before their conversion, they never questioned the acceptability of vice and cruelty, but now they have to understand that the society in which they grew up is totally corrupt and doomed.[122]

The preachers believe that living the new life is possible only by opening one's life to the supernatural power of the Spirit. When their hearers respond to the preaching of the gospel, God himself gives them all the power they require.[123] They are incorporated into God's "family" by the indwelling power of the Spirit who endows them with gifts which enable them to stand fast against all the assaults of ἐπιθυμία.[124] Paul encourages his hearers to seize upon the proffered spiritual riches by the exercise of "constant prayer" so that they may "never flag in zeal, be aglow with the Spirit, serve the Lord."[125]

Paul shows us how the apostolic pastoral preachers serve the needs of the growing churches. By their written words, read to congregations throughout the empire, they bind together the discordant elements of the Christian ἐκκλησία, alert them to the perils that surround them and empower them to maintain their Christian lifestyle against all odds. In this arduous task, they are fortuitously strengthened by the work of the Gospel writers.

Jesus the Preacher

Stanton argues correctly that the story of Jesus is an integral part of the earliest Christian preaching,[126] and Hurtado confirms that when Mark's Gospel appears, it enhances the place of the historical Jesus as part of "the preaching and teaching activity of the church."[127] From the point of view of our study, a significant effect of Mark's work is that it awakens, or at least strengthens, a growing interest in Jesus the preacher.[128] It reminds its readers that Jesus "comes into Galilee preaching the Gospel of God,"[129] so that the people first encounter him *as a preacher*. Later congregations come to understand that Jesus is no ordinary preacher but the One whose "proclamation of the good news" brings universal peace and opens the way to God.[130] He is the preacher whose power cannot be limited by time and space and whose postmortem preaching plucks lost souls from the realm of death and makes the spiritual powers tremble.[131]

The Evangelists reflect this fascination with the preaching of Jesus. They themselves are preachers whose "gospels are preached sermons before they are Scripture,"[132] and they describe, dramatically, how Jesus of Nazareth, "filled with the Spirit," strides on to the stage of history as the self-proclaimed prophetic herald of deliverance.[133] They pile image upon image to draw out the full meaning of Jesus' preaching ministry. He is the human voice of God, the bringer of good news, the long-awaited proclaimer of the kingdom, the eschatological Prophet whose preaching is authenticated by the miracles that attend it.[134]

Christians in churches all over the empire hear how Jesus' preaching grips the minds and hearts of congregations with whom they feel an immediate affinity. The wealthy and powerful have little time for Jesus, for he comes to preach to the poor, the prisoners, the blind, and the oppressed,[135] and the common people hear him gladly.[136] He speaks to the same disadvantaged groups that still constitute later congregations — slaves, children, women, even prostitutes, and social outcasts such as lepers and tax gatherers (τελῶναι).[137]

Jesus knows how to inspire ordinary people, whether he addresses them in the formal setting of their synagogues,[138] during ad hoc meetings in private homes, or in large open-air gatherings.[139] His preaching and teaching are seamlessly joined,[140] and his congregations benefit both from his "preaching of the good news of salvation (and) his instruction regarding discipleship."[141] He rivets their attention by his simple visual and analogical style with its compelling use of narrative. In his hands, parables become a remarkable homiletic tool which establishes a powerful interaction between himself and his congregation. They are confrontational and subversive,[142] challenging the received wisdom of contemporary society and demanding a response from their hearers.[143]

The Evangelists offer the congregations no verbatim accounts of Jesus' sermons. Even the most famous homily, the so-called Sermon on the Mount, is a combination of *verba Christi* and editorial glosses, presenting material drawn from public addresses and private tuition.[144] Nevertheless, scattered throughout the Gospels are enough examples of the things Jesus said to illustrate the practical nature of his preaching. He offers everyday guidance for everyday people under the great overarching theme of the kingdom of God.[145] The kingdom provides the hub of Jesus' preaching from which all the spokes of his teaching radiate. Homiletically, it is inspired because it seizes the attention of every member of every congregation, from the longing peasants and fiery patriots[146] to the apprehensive rulers of the people.

Despite his reluctance to use the term itself, Jesus obviously "thinks of himself, in some sense, as 'messiah' i.e. anointed,"[147] through whom the kingdom "comes upon" his hearers, is "within" them, and "belongs" to them.[148] They are the *kingdom community,* and, however imperfect, the church is the *koinonia* in which the values of the kingdom are being lived out in the period between Pentecost and the parousia.[149] Thus the pastoral preachers take the ethical preaching of Jesus, centered upon selfless love, as the pattern for the conduct of their congregations[150] and hold before them Christ's glorious promise of victory and blessing for the faithful.[151]

For the purposes of our study, there is one particularly important by-product of the congregations' interest in Jesus the preacher. Once the supremacy of his preaching is established, the work of the pastoral preachers becomes irrefutably authenticated. It becomes clear that their authority is not dependent upon the number of their converts, for Jesus himself knows "failure" as a preacher.[152] He is no crowd pleaser, and sermons that "range from scathing invective to tender invitation"[153] are bound to alienate as well as attract. The preachers' authentication arises solely from the fact that, during his earthly ministry, Jesus bestows his own prophetic authority upon his appointed heralds and, finally, commissions the apostolic band to preach throughout the world.[154] It follows that when the apostles speak, Jesus himself is speaking,[155] and preachers who stand in the apostolic line also must be heard with respect, for they utter divine words with power to save or condemn.[156]

3 "After the Apostles"

The Early Fathers

He rejoices in company with the apostles . . . and blesses our Lord Jesus Christ.

Martyrdom of Polycarp 19

The Preachers and Their Sermons

In his *History of Preaching*, Dargan summarily discounts the postapostolic era, saying that "Its homiletical worth is almost nothing,"[1] but this is an overhasty judgment. In their preaching, Clement of Rome, Ignatius, Polycarp, and Papias may not match the majestic sermons of Paul or John, but they do continue the apostolic preachers' work and give valuable practical guidance to their congregations. The early church certainly accepts the "apostolic" credentials of this group of preachers.[2] Polycarp is honored as "an apostolic and prophetic preacher in our own time" with power "to expound deep sayings,"[3] an authority granted to all the others who "speak with God's own voice."[4] The preachers themselves claim their place in the noble succession stretching from the antediluvian Noah through the prophets and the apostles, whose successors still visit the churches.[5]

Armed with this authority, these preachers confidently assert their right to "exhort (παρακαλέω) their congregations,"[6] sometimes by personal contact[7] but more often by widely circulated epistolary sermons.[8] The *Epistle of Barnabas* is one of these homilies widely read in churches, but the chief example of postapostolic preaching is 2 *Clement* or *Pseudo-Clement*, which possibly originates in Corinth (120-49 C.E.). This is considered "the earliest Christian homily extant"[9] and, although mediocre in itself, originally is accorded semicanonical status and is solemnly read after the lection in public worship.[10]

However, these unimpressive sermons are not the only examples of postapostolic preaching. There are other writings which, if not actually called homilies, are homiletic in form and designed for public reading. Ignatius's first seven letters are epistolary sermons which "treat of faith and patience in all things that tend to edification in our Lord."[11] Eusebius affirms that *1 Clement* is "publicly read in very many churches."[12] The *Didache* is read to appreciative congregations throughout the empire, and *The Shepherd* promises blessings to those who listen to it "with pure minds."[13]

Reading becomes increasingly important as a means of sustaining the spiritual life of scattered congregations, and sacred writings are precious.[14] Evangelists also serve as colporteurs, distributing copies of the Gospels, and martyrs even embrace their books as they die.[15] Congregations become protective of their literature,[16] insisting that those entrusted with the task of public reading must be competent and of good character.[17] Similarly they must be trustworthy, neither introducing "spurious books" nor tampering with the received text,[18] since the reading of Scripture is a form of preaching.[19]

The faithfulness of lectors is to be matched by congregational attentiveness. Hearers are not to emulate the dilettantes who idle their time away in the antechambers of *auditoria*, merely pretending to listen to the orators.[20] Congregations must give full attention and "keep those things which they have received, neither adding to them nor taking away from them."[21] Christians have inherited from the synagogue their belief in the importance of the correct reading of Scripture and its close association with preaching, and by the time of Tertullian the lection is regularly accompanied by expositions in public worship.[22] Some of these are informal and impromptu, but congregations take very seriously the more formal, written sermons which are sent for their edification.[23] It is in this context that the pastoral sermons of the postapostolic preachers are to be set.

Judged homiletically, these sermons may seem mundane, but they are lit up by occasional vivid flashes of oratory. For all its excesses, *The Shepherd* is a striking exercise in narrative preaching and fascinates its hearers by its visions, fantasies, and parables. However, it is Ignatius, in particular, who produces memorable word pictures. He likens harmony between bishop and people to the well-tuned strings of a lyre, and heresy to "a deadly drug honeyed with wine."[24] The cross, he says, is "the engine of Jesus Christ" by which the "rope" of the Holy Spirit hauls up the faithful as stones in a living temple.[25] Nevertheless, generally speaking, it is the practicality of these sermons that atones for their lack of eloquence.

The Preachers' Congregations

The aptness of the preachers' sermons becomes clearer when we understand the nature of their congregations, although in some ways they are similar to those addressed by Paul. Some hearers are converted proselytes who arrive in the church via Judaism, and others come directly from paganism, disgusted by the prevailing climate of amorality. Although churches attract a few wealthy members,[26] they are outnumbered by members of disadvantaged classes — women, widows, children, young people, and slaves.[27] Many of the communities are small and vulnerable, and the preachers must help them discover their inner resources. It is interesting that while urging hearers in general to help one another, they present the Christian home as the hub support system, emphasizing the importance of marital faithfulness and the spiritual training of children, young people, and slaves.[28]

It is difficult to resist the feeling that the specter of widespread defection and apostasy hovers over the postapostolic sermons. In many cases, the first ecstatic enthusiasm of the believers has passed and they face the challenge of living routine Christian lives in an unsympathetic world. It is important to remember that for many Christians their new faith involves severing precious human ties. At best, they are dismissed as mad and irreligious, but they may face complete ostracism, shunned by old friends, rejected by former customers, and mocked by once-loving relatives. To their neighbors, their new enthusiasm for honesty, mutual love, and marital fidelity appears eccentric in the extreme, and the attractions of apostasy must have seemed very great.

The spiritual immaturity of many converts renders them ill equipped to resist the confusion wrought by traveling preachers who "pass through, bringing evil doctrine," dividing the faithful by "mingling poison with Jesus Christ."[29] In addition, there is a general feeling of menace in the air. Significantly, Clement's letter of encouragement to Corinth is delayed by the Domitian persecution.[30] Ignatius has to encourage the Ephesians to be patient under persecution, and Hermas prepares the saints for "the great tribulation" (τῆς θλίψεως τῆς ἐπερχομένης).[31]

The preachers' fear of apostasy is not unfounded. The Jewish passion for "rescuing" converted Jews and proselytes has not lessened, and paganism remains a potent and hostile force.[32] Preachers need to warn their hearers against returning to either fold. Ignatius condemns those who flirt with Judaizing notions, and "Barnabas" warns that defectors who seek the comparative safety of Judaism as a *religio licita* will surely join the Jews in perdition.[33] Arrows are also aimed at persuasive paganism, as preachers utter fierce warnings against surrendering to the enticements of pagan life.[34] However, these are only skirmishes before the preachers' main attack.

The Content of the Preachers' Sermons

The Primacy of the Church

The preachers launch their assault by presenting their hearers with a high ecclesiology to show them that defection from the church is no light matter. The church is no mere human organization but a mystical fellowship, "created before the sun and the moon . . . and manifested in the flesh of Christ,"[35] which, though blemished at present, is being perfected.[36] Thus, it is baptism alone which, miraculously, can free neophytes from "this world's bondage" and open them to the joys of the "next world."[37] It follows that separation from the church is self-destructive arrogance, and that Christians must "meet more frequently with an undivided heart" to "gladden Christ" as they gather around his altar.[38] It is by sharing matters of "common welfare" and "hearing the preaching" by which the Spirit "teaches the saints"[39] that congregations discover the strength to resist the disintegrating forces.

The Power of Evil

The preachers' claim that the church offers the only sure refuge from malign supernatural powers is "a palpable hit" in a world where life is short and perilous. Contemporary literature is filled with accounts of disasters[40] wrought by invisible, menacing forces, and it is prudent for people to gain as much control as possible over their uncertain existence.[41] Sinister diabolical forces prey upon human beings from the cradle to the grave, so that doting grandmothers surround babies with magic charms, and funerals are attended by complicated rituals to protect the dead.[42]

Christians face the same problems as their pagan neighbors, and are also tempted to resort to astrology, magic, and incantations.[43] The preachers warn them that Christ has "dissolved every sorcery, every spell" and there is no safety in the stars or in the predictions of the *mathematici*.[44] Preachers take the threat of evil spirits very seriously, believing that the world is teeming with demons who have to be identified and destroyed.[45] Baptism alone offers reliable protection from evil,[46] but cautious believers make doubly sure of protection by regularly seeking the services of exorcists.[47] The matter is rendered ever more urgent because the attacks of evil are increasing as the end draws near and the time for repentance shortens.[48]

The Glory of Martyrdom

The conviction that congregations are living in "the time that remains over until Christ's coming"[49] spurs on preachers to counteract the threat of defection caused by fear of persecution. They placard before their hearers the glories of martyrdom and the blessedness of those who persevere to the end. Ignatius graphically describes the horrors awaiting him as a martyr, and he sets his hearers a brave example by pleading with them not to attempt to save his life.[50] As the saga of Hermas shows, the preachers know the value of narrative preaching, and works such as Ignatius's *Martyrdom of Polycarp* are read publicly to inspire local congregations. They hear how those who are martyred earn the respect of the faithful,[51] and they gather in increasing numbers to honor the heroes of faith.[52]

Doctrinal Guidance

Heick is right when he says that the postapostolic preachers' "doctrinal expression is sporadic and accidental"[53] but they are compelled to offer theological guidance, even if it is of the most elementary kind. Although they know at least some of the New Testament books,[54] the preachers' theology depends heavily on the Jewish Scriptures as "the revelation of the past, present and future."[55] Thus their doctrine of God is cast in a Jewish mold which, homiletically, is valuable since many converts need first to accept monotheism. Nevertheless, their doctrine is trinitarian, in that they speak of the Fatherhood of God and Christ's preexistence, divinity, and humanity,[56] and honor the Holy Spirit,[57] but they make little attempt to discuss trinitarian relationships.

The preachers need their basic doctrinal weapons to counteract the apostasy of educated members of the congregations who are being tempted by esoteric pagan gnosis. It is not enough for preachers to urge them to "forsake false teachings and turn to the word that was delivered from the beginning."[58] They must establish the intellectual superiority of that primal Christian faith[59] and show that, unlike "ignorant" teachers of pagan religions, Christ offers his followers true gnosis.[60] Knowing the accepted maxim that it is the ancients who stand closest to the fountain of truth,[61] Tatian skillfully asserts that Christian *philosophia* antedates by far the depraved and erroneous philosophy of Greece.[62]

Ethical Guidance

The preachers' soteriological teaching is a basic exposition of the vicarious suffering of Christ without any detailed development of the concept.[63] Since their "chief interest" is "the demands of the new Christian life,"[64] it is not surprising that they emphasize Christ's role as a moral reformer who blesses those who fulfill the ethical demands of the new law. If the sermons sometimes have a legalistic flavor, it is because the Christian challenge has to be presented clearly as a choice between blessing and destruction.[65]

Since Christians choose to walk "the high-road of those that are on their way to die unto God,"[66] their moral example must demonstrate the life-changing power of the gospel. Consequently, the preachers take great care in enabling their congregations to avoid the three major pitfalls described by Hermas — sexual sins ("adultery and fornication"), sins of excess ("drunkenness, wicked luxury, many viands and costliness of riches"), and sins of speech ("falsehood, hypocrisy and blasphemy").[67]

The preachers defend their hearers from contemporary society's flippant approach to chastity,[68] marriage, and divorce, asserting that faithful, Christian marriage is a state fit for "blessed saints"[69] and is so sacred that remarriage after divorce is tantamount to adultery.[70] Apart from the procreation of children,[71] sexuality in marriage is tainted with lust, and it is safer to avoid the tentacles of sex altogether. Although Ignatius assures his listeners that he does not "count marriage an abomination," he leaves them in no doubt that virginity is "better."[72] Those who have lost their marriage partners do well to remain single and join the ranks of the godly widows and widowers.[73] The sermons express a sad conviction that *femaleness* itself is sinister,[74] and the preachers appeal to the female members of their congregations to set a special example of holiness so that their purity may openly contradict the pagan view of womanhood.[75]

The preachers' concern for sexual purity sometimes seems paranoid, but it is essential in view of the popular, amoral approach to sexuality.[76] In commanding its listeners not to "corrupt boys, kill newborn babies or permit abortion,"[77] the *Didache* reveals the depravity of a society in which even emperors abuse and mutilate children for sexual gratification.[78] Clement's admonition to avoid "impure embraces" probably is to be viewed in the light of the popular belief in Plato's maxim that "Greek love" between men and boys is nobler than heterosexual affection.[79]

Preachers realize how easy it is for their congregations to be lured into sins of excess, and Hermas solemnly warns them against "all evil desires" which destroy those who seek "extravagance of wealth and many needless dainties."[80] Pagan society idolizes the excesses of the rich and famous,[81] but Christians must think differently and be "content with the provision which God has made."[82] Polycarp reminds his hearers that "the love of money is the beginning of all troubles" and urges them to "refrain from covetousness *(abstineatis ab avaritia)* which is a form of idolatry."[83] Rich Christians are to use their wealth to help the poor and to testify to the community that it is possible to live without covetousness.[84]

The sins of speech belonging to "this age"[85] present the third danger area to be avoided by Christians. Society's highly competitive nature generates the jealousy which ruins human relationships[86] and makes character assassination, gossip, spying, and slander the tools of social success.[87] It seems the infection has touched the churches because they are warned to exclude it as "alien and strange to the elect of God."[88] Christians are not to malign one another to gain positions of power from which they can "exalt themselves over the flock."[89] Rather, they must gladly abandon worldly advancement here so that they may enjoy "the firstfruits of the taste of glorious things future."[90]

In these ways, the postapostolic preachers hold their congregations steady at a critical time when, for many Christians, initial enthusiasm is being tempered by the realities of life in a pagan society. By their practical brand of preaching they add new converts to the churches and sustain many believers who might otherwise be tempted to defect. They do not attain the stature of some of their great apostolic forerunners, but they fulfill a vital function and lay the foundation for the apologists' counterattack upon aggressive paganism.

Fidei Defensores

The Apologists

What is there in common between Athens and Jerusalem?

Tertullian, *De praescriptionibus adversus haereticos* 7

The Church in a Troubled Empire

In the second and third centuries, powerful forces beat upon a Roman Empire often further crippled by incompetent, self-seeking, unpopular emperors and a weakened Senate. It is an "Age of Anxiety,"[1] when even the mighty Hadrian is "so filled with the utmost disgust of life" that he orders his servant to end it.[2] Inevitably, Christian congregations are caught up in the general turmoil. Some churches, on the edges of the empire, suffer cruelly from the incursions of the *barbarians*. Wealthy believers are ruined by a devalued denarius and crippling tax burdens, but it is the "uneducated persons, artisans and old women" who suffer most.[3] In the cities, the poor die of virulent plagues brought by soldiers returning from the wars, and the condition of the rural poor is made yet more wretched by the despoiling of the countryside.

The disasters cause general heart searching, and E. R. Dodds suggests that the empire's multiple catastrophes engender a noticeable spiritual revival among its people.[4] Dodds's thesis has been criticized, but it has much to commend it.[5] W. H. C. Frend observes, "The first decades of the third century saw the Roman Empire as strongly pagan as it had been at any time in its existence."[6] Dodds confirms that as a result of this rejuvenation of contemporary paganism, the empire's decline is seen as a *theological* issue. The affronted gods must be appeased, and initially a *religious* solution to the problem is favored.

Roman religion is a communal matter, designed to assure that the state will enjoy the *pax deorum,* and so it is logical for priests to be state employees and for the emperor to be *Pontifex Maximus.* As the embodiment of the spirit of Rome, emperors, unlike other mortals, may be deified and so become the ultimate arbiters of theological truth, ensuring that only those religions accorded their imperial imprimatur may legally be practiced.[7]

However, the Romans are eager to invoke the support of as many gods as possible by absorbing foreign cults into the state system, and they seem willing to include Christianity in this process.[8] Severus Alexander (222-35) "respects the privilege of the Jews and allows Christians to exist unmolested," erecting statues to "holy souls," including "Christ, Abraham, Orpheus and others."[9] The empress mother eagerly invites Origen to visit her at her court, and Elagabalus (218-22) orders that "the rites of the Christians" be transferred to a new multifaith temple.[10] Eusebius reports popular veneration for a miracle-working statue of Jesus in Caesarea Philippi,[11] and the gnostic Carpocrates instructs his followers to venerate images of Paul and Aristotle.[12]

For some Christians, such inclusive pagan attitudes seem to offer positive opportunities for the contextualization of the gospel,[13] but the apologist-preachers see the dangers of flirting with syncretism, even though they know that rejecting such overtures has serious implications for congregations. Inevitably, the authorities whose olive branches they spurn will infer that their false religion is responsible for the empire's woes and will find fiercer ways of dealing with them. The predictions of the antisyncretists come true. Christians, previously regarded merely as troublesome Jews,[14] are now condemned as being worse than Jews[15] and begin to attract persecution in their own right. Tertullian claims "that the outcry is that the State is filled with Christians" and that there is an officially approved campaign of "hate" organized to destroy them.[16]

Ultimately, the charges brought against the Christians are as much religious as political. Tertullian's view that their "only crime" is "the name of Christian" is illustrated by Justin's claim that a Roman husband has "laid an accusation" against his wife "by saying that she is a Christian."[17] Christian exclusiveness is an affront to the gods, and Porphyry's vitriolic condemnation of Christians as the cause of all the empire's ills gives vent to a long-felt conviction.[18] The people need a scapegoat for their fears and frustrations, and these beliefs cause many local attacks upon Christian congregations. A series of earthquakes in 235 is sufficient to trigger a spate of local persecutions in Asia Minor, and, eventually, in Tertullian's famous words, "If the Tiber has overflowed its banks, if the Nile has remained in its banks, if the sky has been still, or the earth has been in commotion, if death has made its devastations, or famine its afflictions, your cry immediately is, 'This is the fault of the Christians.'"[19] In vain, Justin tries to persuade persecutors that Christians are actually saving the empire from even worse disasters.[20] Feeble official attempts to protect the Christians[21] cannot hide the fact that Christians and the state are on a collision course, and in the period between Marcus Aurelius and Diocletian, congregations are severely tested by official persecution, social ostracism, and domestic violence.[22]

However, despite all opposition, the congregations are swelled by increasing numbers of educated and influential converts. This gives the lie to Celsus's jibe that Christianity attracts only "youngsters and mobs of domestics" and confirms Origen's boast that "an abundance of intelligent hearers" now joins congregations, thirsting for "the noble doctrines of the faith."[23] It becomes clear that the church needs preachers who can meet their congregations' intellectual demands, alert them to the spiritual dangers that threaten them, and convince them of Christianity's eventual triumph.

The Rise of the Apologist-Preachers

Realizing the importance of reliable preaching at this crucial time, Tertullian utters his solemn *praescriptio* that "no preachers other than those appointed by the Church are to be received."[24] It is a time for sound exposition of the faith, and providentially there emerges a group of brilliant apologists who are also significant preachers. Establishing their credentials as preachers is hampered by the loss of many of their sermons, but their other writings are often homiletic in form and intention.[25]

The apologist-preachers themselves make little attempt to distinguish their sermons from their treatises and pastoral epistles.[26] Thus, we may not have any of Irenaeus's actual homilies, but, as he tells "Marcianus," he sends his *Demonstration* "to demonstrate . . . the preaching of the truth."[27] The sermons of Tatian's mentor, Justin Martyr, are lost, but he publishes his apologies so that those who hear or read may be "freed from error,"[28] and they certainly confirm Dargan's view that he "must have been a preacher of some eloquence."[29] Although none of Tertullian's homilies survive, works like *On Repentance, On Baptism,* and *On Prayer* are clearly homiletic in tone and more than justify his reputation as "a man of burning eloquence."[30]

Of the other apologist-preachers, the sermons of Clement of Alexandria that remain[31] demonstrate his preaching skills, and Methodius, although none of his sermons are extant, is reputed to have produced series of homilies and is praised for "remarkable, formal beauty of diction."[32] Melito's *Paschal Homily* is a veritable homiletic tour de force,[33] and if Quadratus's *Apology* is indeed preserved in the *Epistle to Diognetus,* it reveals him as a stylish if not a profound preacher. Hippolytus, with his special interest in the preaching missions of the apostles, uses fragments of his own sermons in his commentaries,[34] and his *Philosophoumena* and sermon *On the Holy Theophany* confirm Jerome's high view of his preaching.[35] *The Apology to Autolycus* by Theophilus of Antioch is the work of a natural orator, and although none of Cyprian's sermons survive, his *Epistles* show him as a pastoral preacher who merits Lactantius's fulsome praise.[36] All this dispersed material is valuable because it gives vital clues to the subjects touched by the apologist-preachers in their formal sermons.

However, there is no shortage of material by the one gigantic figure who towers over all others. Nearly two hundred of his homilies remain, mainly in uneven Latin translations by Rufinus and Jerome, and they reveal Origen as one of that select company of outstanding preachers whose vision and technique are truly innovative. In practice, his preaching is so effective that his enemies drive him from his pulpit in Alexandria, but he pursues his remarkable ministry for another twenty years in Caesarea. For him, preaching is a supernatural exercise in which preachers are "filled with the Spirit of Christ,"[37] and his sermons are the work of a serious and disciplined preacher, finely honed to meet the needs of each situation. They vary in length from the briefest of homilies to sermons lasting more than an hour. By his use of dialogical technique, he personalizes his message as though he is involved in conversation with individuals in his congregation.

Above all else, Origen is the prince of exegetical preachers, the father of the sermon as "a theological-practical exposition of a definite text."[38] As Henry Chadwick observes, "The exegesis of scripture by homily or commentary became Origen's main life's work,"[39] and Gregory Thaumaturgus confirms the contemporary view that the "noblest of all his endowments" is his ability to "be an interpreter of the oracles of God."[40]

Origen introduces exegetical sermons to Alexandria, albeit in the form of lectures, and then transfers them to Caesarea to be incorporated in the Sunday liturgy.[41] In addition to homiletic material in his monumental commentaries on Matthew and John, we have Greek versions of the forty-three sermons he preached on Jeremiah and a sermon on 1 Samuel. He augments his immensely detailed commentaries with copious *scholia* or notes which, although now largely lost, must have been of inestimable value to preachers wishing to follow his exegetical style. Like Clement of Alexandria, Origen draws on the thoughts of other preachers, especially *The Preaching of Peter,* which, Grant observes, demonstrates the use of such sermons "within the church where the 'preaching' might well be read."[42]

The apologetic writing of these preachers displays their intellectual and spiritual ability to meet the challenge of resurgent paganism. The postapostolic preachers wrote mainly for Christians,[43] but these apologist-preachers are also determined to confront *pagan* intellectuals and they are well equipped for the task. Their work is adorned by references to Homer and Virgil drawn from the common educational heritage they share with all the empire's cultivated people, and their training in philosophy and rhetoric enables them to meet pagan intellectuals on their own ground.[44] Clement of Alexandria, an Athenian-trained rhetorician, is immersed in Stoicism. Justin embraces Christianity as "the true philosophy,"[45] and like Melito and Cyprian, Tertullian is expert in rhetoric and an admirer of Stoicism. Such academic expertise is immensely important because, hitherto, the church has produced few intellectual heavyweights to combat the skills of the philosophers.[46] The new preachers are able to meet the needs of the growing number of educated converts and to carry the gospel beyond the boundaries of the churches.

However, the apologist-preachers are by no means unanimous in their enthusiasm for using their scholarly expertise. Generally speaking, the Greek preachers are happy to utilize all available philosophical and rhetorical skills, but their Latin counterparts have serious doubts about using such "pagan" skills in the service of the gospel. Tertullian famously rejects the Christians' use of philosophy, saying, "What is there in common between Athens and Jerusalem? What between the Academy and the Church? . . . After Jesus, we need no subtle theories."[47] He, like Cyprian and Jerome, resists the employment of rhetorical techniques to proclaim the Word. Cyprian opines that whereas "full eloquence might be the pride of vocal ambition" in law courts and public meetings, only "pure simplicity of expression" and clear argument are appropriate when "speaking of the Lord God."[48] Nevertheless, although divided in their methods, the apologist-preachers have no doubt about the nature of the tasks before them.

The Tasks of the Preachers: Practical Guidance

The Strengthening of the Churches

Throughout this period congregations are drawing together in loose diocesan federations, which enables local bishops to preach to groups of believers through their epistolary sermons.[49] They stress the superiority of Christian gatherings over all their rivals and the importance of regular meetings for mutual strengthening.[50] Gregory Thaumaturgus cleverly draws people away from pagan gatherings by initiating new Christian festivals and reminding congregations of their "duty to present to God, like sacrifices, all the festival and hymnal celebrations."[51] Preaching plays an important part in these celebrations, and Justin shows how sermons are also vital in developing the regular liturgy, when, Sunday by Sunday, the faithful "in cities or in the country gather together in one place" for worship and "verbal instruction and exhortation."[52]

The preachers encourage their congregations to stand firm and be confident. By baptism they have "disowned the devil and his pomp and his angels" and have accepted the discipline of their new status in Christ.[53] Their common heritage with Judaism has merely prepared them for the gospel, and now the time has come to make a clear break from the Jewish religion. To drive home their point, the preachers fill their sermons with anti-Jewish diatribes[54] and tell their people that there is little to choose between "stiff-necked Jews" in their "synagogues of Christ-murderers" and "ignorant" pagans in their "houses of demons."[55]

The Authority of Scripture

Such a break with Judaism presents a problem for the preachers because the authority and content of their preaching are largely dependent upon the Jewish Scriptures. They safeguard their position by insisting that the Jewish Scriptures foretell the revelation in Christ[56] and that, since the Jews fail to appreciate the types and symbols by which God protects spiritual truths,[57] their Scriptures have become the property of the church to whom the truth is revealed.[58] Thus the church may gather *testimonia* to support its claims or adjust the text of Scripture to clarify hidden truths,[59] and the preachers produce distinctively "Christian" exegesis of Old and New Testament passages to guide their congregations and other preachers.

The apologist-preachers show how, by the divine use of types, the Old Testament prepares the way for the gospel, foretelling events in the life of Christ and revealing hidden truths to "spiritual believers."[60] For instance, Eve is the type of Mary; Jacob, Joseph, and Noah prefigure Christ; and Psalm 22 sets the pattern for the passion.[61] The complexity of the typological scriptural preaching increases as Clement of Alexandria, Hippolytus, and Methodius all build on Justin's foundation. However, the approach is most refined in Origen's homilies on Old Testament books. It is suggested that he adapts allegorical methods learned from Alexandria's pagan teachers to accommodate different levels of spirituality.[62] He argues that Scripture has cryptic meanings and posits a threefold form of exegesis, explaining that "The simple man has to be edified starting from what may be called the flesh of Scripture, for such we term its obvious meaning. The man who has made some progress may start from . . . [t]he soul, and the perfect man . . . from the spiritual."[63]

Christianity and Philosophy

The preachers realize that if their congregations are to be strengthened, they must understand that their faith has nothing to fear from the assaults of pagan philosophy. As we saw earlier, different preachers approach this task in different ways. In his *Addresses to the Greeks* Tatian pours scorn on the delusions and vices of the philosophers, and Tertullian tells his congregations that pagan philosophy is irrelevant because it is erroneous and, in any case, Christians already possess any useful knowledge that it might offer.[64] Other preachers seek to capture philosophy for the church. Justin declares that Christ was "partially known by Socrates" and that since all true philosophers share the same "spermatic word," Plato's teachings are comparable with those of Christ.[65] Clement of Alexandria tells his hearers that they cannot accept it in toto because it contains errors, but they need not "fear philosophy as children fear a scarecrow" because it is a divinely appointed preparation for the gospel.[66]

Persecution and Martyrdom

The common experience of suffering compels preachers to confront the issues of persecution and martyrdom.[67] Sadly, persecution drives some Christians to defect and even to betray fellow believers, and the deep divisions caused by the return of repentant *lapsi* need to be healed.[68] The preachers seek to steady their people by assuring them that if they make the ultimate sacrifice, they will be honored as faithful martyrs have been in every age.[69] Sermons celebrating the stories of those who have "undergone the baptism of blood"[70] are used to show how the suffering death of Jesus provides the true pattern for all martyrdoms. Like their Lord, Christians must suffer in conformity to the Father's will, for the sake of love alone.[71] Martyrdom is not to be avoided by flight or bribery, but neither is it to be sought as a form of noble suicide or tainted by hatred of its perpetrators.[72]

The preachers applaud those who join the ranks of the blessed and promise great felicity to those who accept Christlike martyrdom.[73] While still alive, they and their families merit the admiring care of fellow believers so that when they face their ultimate test, they may "leap for joy in the presence of death."[74] They die as warriors in the war against Satan, and as they enter Paradise their sins will be absolved by heavenly intercessors for the faithful who will always venerate them.[75] Obviously such preaching succeeds in enabling many believers to overcome their fear of death, because Clement declares triumphantly that "the Church is full" of brave men and women who are ready to "contemplate the death which raises up Christ."[76]

The Moral Distinctiveness of the Church

In his *De idololatria,* Tertullian confronts the issue of the Christian's "daily walk" in a society where even the most casual social contacts are spiritually risky.[77] Stern warnings are required and the preachers often speak severely, believing, as Origen says, that to leave their hearers unrebuked is like "plastering a collapsing wall."[78] Nevertheless, Clement warns preachers to attend to their communication skills, advising a limited use of severity and urging them to favor "mildness" and "persuasion." Cyprian cautions that impatience merely "makes heretics in the church," and he counsels preachers to imitate Stephen who, when preaching, displayed a Christlike patience with his hearers.[79] Nevertheless, all the preachers sound the same note of urgency, being convinced that they must save their congregations from the eschatological attacks of demons who still "struggle to have them as their slaves and servants."[80]

The preachers alert their hearers to the fact that they are locked in moral struggle with a satanic enemy who uses two major weapons with deadly effect. The first is *materialism,* and indeed it is obvious that many of the new, sophisticated converts are finding it hard to slough off their former extravagant lifestyle. The preachers complain that penitents come to their penances dressed in scarlet and purple and that unveiled young women stroll brazenly in the streets, attended by matrons clad in "adornment of vanity" more suited to prostitutes than to godly Christians.[81] Such parading of affluence is an affront to Christian *koinonia,* and even clergy are tainted and have forfeited the respect of their people.[82]

In view of such gross abuses, it is hardly surprising that preachers like Tertullian and Origen urge the greatest austerity upon their congregations. Tertullian praises bishops who make it their "customary practice to issue mandates for fasting to the universal commonality of the Church," since fasting has been divinely sanctioned since the days of Adam and is endorsed by the saints and by Christ himself.[83] Origen, who himself lives a life of extreme asceticism,[84] preaches that since every soul has freewill but is under satanic attack, Christians must "shake themselves free from that burden" and reject the claims of "bodily pleasure and luxury."[85]

However, the finest sermon on this theme is Clement's "Who Is the Rich Man Who Will Be Saved?" and it merits closer inspection. Based upon Christ's meeting with the rich young ruler and memorable for its extended "sermon illustration" about the apostle John, it is a fine example of sensitive, pastoral preaching. Clement begins by condemning those "who bestow laudatory address on the rich," but he calms the fears of wealthy Christians and assures them that "the Lord receives them gladly."[86] He insists that rich converts are not necessarily more evil than poor ones since it is not money itself but the worship of wealth which is sinful.[87] Jesus tries to deliver the rich young ruler from "his excitement and morbid feelings about" wealth by inviting him *willingly* to surrender his riches.[88] Similarly, all wealthy Christians must gladly "love and care for those who believe in" Christ,[89] so that their riches are a blessing to the whole congregation. Almsgiving has always been a special mark of the communal life of Christian congregational life,[90] but Clement realizes that charity is a sensitive matter. In his *Paedagogus,* he judiciously advises that riches are "to be partaken of rationally (and) bestowed lovingly . . . not pompously."[91]

The preachers believe Satan's most potent weapon is *sexuality,* which he seizes and uses for his own malign purposes. It seems they have good cause for concern. Christianity is largely an urban movement,[92] and cities are full of temptations. The preachers may urge their hearers not to allow their "eyes to fall on stews and brothels," but prostitution is a flagrant and accepted aspect of the urban scene.[93] The preachers warn that danger also comes from an unexpected quarter — the very baths which cultured Christians regard as a center of social life.[94] Even poorer members of congregations frequent the public "penny baths,"[95] and yet these glories of Roman civilization have become centers of corruption. Tertullian even tells those awaiting martyrdom that they are safer in prison than in the baths![96] Their function as a focus for homosexual and heterosexual activity is celebrated in an anonymous epigram:

> Balnea, vina, Venus corrumpunt corpora nostra;
> Sed vitam faciunt, balnea, vina, Venus.[97]

It is not surprising that preachers claim that sexual misconduct also infests many churches. Hippolytus thunders at his congregations, "Practise adultery no more!"[98] Other preachers warn of infiltration by "panderers and pimps" who cause believers to "fall into wantonness" and adultery[99] so that their promiscuity leads them into the sin of abortion.[100] In order to limit the damage to the church, the preachers try to create a "safety zone" around sexuality, reminding their congregations that Christ "defines as adulterers" even those who are "contaminated by the concupiscence of their gaze."[101] They have a special word of warning for Christian wives whose pagan husbands may draw them into unchristian practices and, equally, for Christian husbands whose pagan wives may "seduce them into idolatry."[102]

One aspect of the preachers' treatment of sexuality requires further comment, and that is their strangely ambivalent attitude toward women. On one hand they regard femininity as dangerous per se, but on the other they develop an idealistic picture of women as noble, pure, and capable of spiritual perfection.[103] Women have a decisive role in spreading a distinctively Christian approach to sexuality, by being exemplars of the purity of "lady mother the church" who, herself, is the "new Eve."[104] "The holy woman" is a symbol of Christian virtue,[105] and women are taught that they share the victory of the virgin Mary who has "freed the race of women from reproach."[106]

Among the pictures of ideal Christian womanhood, Clement includes his portrait of "the good wife,"[107] since marriage is not despised but, as Tertullian somewhat tactlessly tells his wife, celibacy is better.[108] The theme of virginity inspires the preachers[109] who admire Hermas's vision of the church as "a virgin clothed entirely in white."[110] Because they are "wedded to Christ," virgins must veil themselves.[111] They are "adorned with the Son of God as with a bridegroom . . . (and) clothed in holy light."[112]

The Tasks of the Preachers: Apologetics

The preachers see a close link between behavior and belief, and they realize that if they are to live well, their converts need to understand and spread good doctrine. Many apologetic writings, though primarily directed at nonbelievers, are also available to be studied by educated Christians. Christian congregations resemble pagan study groups "founded under the auspices of professional preachers,"[113] and Daniélou stresses the educative role of the apologist-preachers' "catechetical literature, aimed at expounding the faith to converts."[114] The task is not a simple one because, whereas it is relatively easy to expose the faults of pagan cults,[115] the seduction of believers by heretics is much more subtle. Yet heresies cannot be ignored, for they threaten the integrity of the church and, as Dionysius writes to Novatus, "a man ought to suffer anything and everything rather than divide the Church of God."[116]

The apologist-preachers enthusiastically enter the lists against all heresies, but it is gnosticism in its various forms which proves most dangerous because of its ingenious fusion of paganism and Christianity.[117] Its alluring promise of secret, spiritual gnosis has lurked around the edges of the church from the beginning,[118] but it poses a growing threat as significant gnostics gain positions of influence.[119] Some are persuasive preachers who found their own churches and cause havoc by the use of their own gospels, read to local congregations.[120] The offer of secret knowledge is very enticing, since it bestows spurious kudos on the poorly educated and confirms the sophisticates' sense of superiority. For the average member of any catholic congregation, gnostic ideas seem little different from those proposed in the sermons they hear, but once accepted, those ideas destroy the fabric of traditional Christian doctrine.

The preachers have different ways of meeting the gnostic threat. In his *Praescriptio*, Tertullian uses his legal skills to arraign the gnostics before an imaginary court, while Hippolytus's *Philosophoumena* dismisses gnosticism as pagan philosophy in disguise. The approach of Clement and Origen is interesting because they recognize that their congregations find gnostic ideas attractive and they seek to correct and utilize them. It is said, with some justification, that Origen gives "the catholic church of the first centuries . . . its own Gnostic tradition,"[121] and Clement boldly declares that Christians possess true gnosis and, in *Stromateis,* he draws the portrait of the ideal "Gnostic Christian" to which congregations must aspire.

It is a brave decision to utilize gnostic ideas in this way, but the preachers insist that there are certain nonnegotiable truths, a theological credo by which all other theologies are to be judged. Christians are to believe only those doctrines vested in "churches which the apostles founded by their teaching, by the living voice and, subsequently, through their letters."[122] It is this "apostolic doctrine," scattered throughout the preachers' sermons and treatises, which gives congregations a basic *depositum* of faith. It is based upon the conviction that since Christians believe in one God revealed in Christ the Word and empowered by the Holy Spirit, they cannot compromise with the syncretism of the age.[123]

Grounded in solid trinitarianism,[124] the preachers use all their theological skill to impress upon their hearers that salvation is derived solely from the saving work of Christ. Irenaeus propounds his famous doctrine of *recapitulation* to show how Christ becomes human so that humans may regain "existence in accordance with the image and likeness of God."[125] It seems that congregations warm, especially, to the presentation of Christ as the one who ransoms them and vanquishes the powers of evil.[126] Through the cross and empty tomb, Christ's victory becomes the inheritance of Christian congregations that, consequently, are bound together by his love.[127]

The preachers' sermons and treatises are molded by their conviction that their hearers are living in the last times, when all will go "to eternal punishment" or salvation in accordance with the character of their actions.[128] The time for repentance is short, and only those who are good and faithful can hope for personal resurrection and eternal felicity.[129] Those who heed the preachers' warning will be saved and join their repentant ancestors who were rescued by Christ when he "preached the Gospel to those who were in Hades."[130] The imminence of judgment makes moral reformation vital, and Justin rejoices when the preachers' message strikes home and he sees many in the congregations "who once rejoiced in fornication (and) magic arts" but now "dedicate themselves to the good and unbegotten God."[131]

The Tasks of the Preachers: The Call to Evangelism

Besides strengthening their congregations, the apologist-preachers have a wider task in view. They are to be taken seriously as *missionary-preachers* since, as Danielou perceives, their works "constitute a considerable mass of evidence for a study of Christian missionary preaching."[132] They certainly see themselves as missionaries who must "urge hearers to the utmost of their ability" and "free them from erroneous notions." Since judgment is imminent, they have a duty to ensure that unbelievers are "converted from the error of their ways."[133] Equally, they see their writings as a legitimate form of preaching, an opportunity to "proclaim the faith to all" and compel them "to hear the words that do not pass away."[134] They are called to "expound true religion" and to "persuade by reasonable argument" so that they may lead educated pagans to faith.[135] It is with this task in mind that they construct an appropriate, bold homiletic strategy.

While recognizing the need to discredit pagan errors, the preachers appreciate that they must also establish common ground with pagans[136] in order to show how Christianity is the logical answer to many pagan aspirations. Much in the manner of Aristotle's now lost *Protrepticus,*[137] the preachers invite pagans to "treat with respect" whatever they find "reasonable and true" in their argument.[138]

As part of their strategy, they create a common cultural climate by interlarding their treatises and sermons with hundreds of references to classical writers,[139] and then set about contextualizing the gospel in audacious ways. For instance, Justin cites Odysseus's descent into the underworld as proof of the preexistence of souls and eternal punishment. The hero's encounter with the Sirens prefigures the temptation of Christ, who, without any sense of impropriety, is identified as the "true Orpheus."[140] Hippolytus uses the Odysseus saga differently, urging Christians to reject heresy as Odysseus shut out the sound of the Sirens' song by stopping his ears with wax.[141]

The missionary preaching echoes the foundational theological ideas impressed upon the congregations, presented in a manner designed to appeal to educated minds both within the churches and beyond them. Christian monotheism is shown to be in tune with the views of the best Greek thinkers who, although originally they "spoke of a multiplicity of gods, came at length to the doctrine of the unity of God."[142] In their presentation of Christ, the preachers appreciate the brilliance of the Johannine concept of Logos as a bridge across the divide between Christianity and paganism. They use the idea to demonstrate that because the Logos has become incarnate, all humanity may now be "taught by the divine word."[143]

However, the preachers impress upon inquirers that receiving the Word is conditional upon their renouncing Satan, accepting Christ by faith and accepting a complete moral transformation.[144] By giving human beings freedom of choice, God places an onerous burden on their shoulders since their consequent moral choices are of eternal significance.[145] Such ideas of judgment[146] and human destiny beyond death, in themselves, present few problems to the Greek mind with its belief in Nemesis, Tartarus, and the infernal regions. However, the doctrine of resurrection of the body is a major stumbling block, and it takes the utmost ingenuity on the part of the preachers to prove their point. Tatian tries to persuade his hearers that they "will exist again just as, beforehand, they were born after not having existed," and Theophilus develops a whole series of analogies to demonstrate that resurrection makes perfect sense.[147]

Thus it is clear that the rise of the apologist-preachers initiates an imaginative process of evangelization for educated pagans, using many of the same weapons which sustain their own congregations in the face of destructive doctrinal forces. They present the gospel in a form which commands intellectual respect and offers a clear alternative lifestyle. However, they have set their congregations upon a path of ascetic self-denial and have prepared the way for other preachers who will present an even stronger challenge and commend a way of life that is starkly world-denying and is truly providential.

5 "Immensity of Holiness"

The Ascetics and Mystics

> By abstracting all that belongs to bodies . . . we cast ourselves into
> the greatness of Christ and thence advance into immensity of ho-
> liness.
>
> Clement of Alexandria, *Stromateis* 5.11

The Growth of Ascetic Mysticism

The Apologist-Preachers and Ascetic Mysticism

For many early Christians, the injunction to "please God and mind their
own business"[1] is not radical enough and they turn to the church's inherited ascetic tradition. From the Greeks they learn *self-control* (ἐγκράτεια)
and the sterner *asceticism* (ἄσκησις)[2] by which humans may "become like
God."[3] From the Jews they inherit an admiration for ascetic communities
whose disciplines lead to mystical experience.[4] In practice, the dividing
line between self-control and asceticism is ill defined and oscillating, and
individuals interpret Christ's teaching about self-denial with varying degrees of austerity.[5] However, from its inception the church has encouraged
the ascetics and mystics in its ranks[6] and the apologist-preachers have
given new impetus to the movement, teaching their congregations that
ἐγκράτεια, "temperance and self-restraint,"[7] are necessary parts of Christian living. However, for apologists like Tertullian, that is not enough. He

accepts that "both flesh and spirit are creatures of God,"[8] but still advocates a regime of the strictest self-denial.

Tertullian's ideal congregations are "dried up with fastings and their passion as tightly bound up, holding back as long as possible from all ordinary enjoyments of life, rolling in sackcloth and ashes and assaulting heaven with their importunities."[9] They dress modestly, eat frugally, observe every opportunity for fasting,[10] and if they cannot avoid "falling into wedlock," at least they practice *continence*.[11] Tertullian fulminates against overindulgent church leaders who fail to discipline their people "through the instrumentality of preaching."[12]

Clement of Alexandria sees asceticism, especially, as a means of attaining mystical insight, and he urges his hearers to develop a "faculty of contemplation and self-restraint"[13] and to seek *apatheia*. Thus freed from passions and made "as perfect as they can while abiding in the flesh," they will "imitate God" and eventually be "assimilated into Him."[14] Clement asserts that true gnosis is given only to those who despise "alluring pleasures" and "train themselves to be perfected in the mystic habit."[15] The effect of this teaching is to create a spiritual elite within congregations, distinguishing those who "preach" by their common "piety" from true gnostics whose "impassibility" and "boundless joy of contemplation" render them "perfect" and "godlike."[16]

Origen makes this double standard explicit, arguing that since human souls are "shut in by fetters of flesh and blood," his hearers must use their free will to liberate themselves from all material bondage.[17] Not all can achieve such "perfection," and so Origen discerns two levels of spirituality in his congregations. There are those with "simple faith" who "live a better life as far as they can, and accept doctrines about God, such as they have the capacity to receive,"[18] and there are the spiritual aristocrats, who are "initiated into the mysteries of the religion of Jesus which are delivered only to the holy and pure." These pass through ever more rarefied phases of prayer to attain the beatific vision.[19] For "ordinary" Christians, self-control may be sufficient, but by embracing "the more stringent discipline" of martyrdom even they may hope to join the ranks of the elite who "climb ladders to heaven" and attain an "eternal crown of angelic essence."[20]

The Call of the Desert

Heeding the preachers' words, many Christians live the ascetic life privately, attaching themselves temporarily to groups of like-minded believers.[21] However, others hear the call of the desert. For Jews and Greeks alike, ἔρημος means much more than an uncultivated void. It is the arena of spiritual warfare, where saints see visions and the faithful await the consummation of all things.[22] Ascetics have long lived in the desert,[23] and now many more seek it as a haven from a corrupt society and a contaminated church. The rising sun of monasticism[24] shines brightly upon congregations and preachers, totally committed to an ascetic, world-denying view of Christianity.

The "desert" congregations vary widely in form. For *cenobitic* ascetics, the communal life of worship and prayer naturally dominates their whole existence, but even anchorites and solitaries sometimes leave their *laurae* for worship, preaching, and the Eucharist. In the quest for Christian perfection, social distinctions are largely forgotten and congregations embrace the poor, the wealthy who are seeking "holy poverty," and brilliant, professional men.[25] Women devotees include passing pilgrims like Etheria and aristocratic girls, fleeing forced marriages to join the nunneries of Paula, Melania, and Olympia. In the two great centers of this ascetic revival — Egypt and Syria — congregations coalesce around ascetic preachers, renowned for miraculous powers and their great number of disciples.[26]

Congregations and Preachers in Egypt

First among the "Egyptian" preachers must be Antony, whose extreme asceticism admits him "into divine mysteries."[27] Although reputed to be "cheerful in conversation," he is an awe-inspiring figure, reverentially known as *Abba* by his "many renowned disciples" and by the large congregations that gather to hear him.[28]

The *Twenty Sermons* attributed to him are probably spurious, but his reputation as a preacher is widely affirmed. Athanasius praises Antony's God-given gift "for speech and for exhortation," and his account of one of Antony's sermons reveals a certain rough eloquence.[29] That Antony has "the common touch" is confirmed by Sozomen's statement that "the people listened avidly to his discourses."[30] Ill-educated and passionate, Antony "neither possesses nor admires learning."[31] His sermons are largely practical and pastoral rather than exegetical, but acknowledging the significance of Scripture in his own conversion, he is careful to base his sermons on favorite biblical texts.[32] Congregations are fascinated by accounts of Antony's ecstatic experiences and he teaches them that they too may receive *charisms* from God, but he warns them that they must be on their guard because the devil fabricates illusions to deceive the faithful.

The soldier-monk Pachomius "emulates Elias" and is reputedly a preacher "endowed with apostolic grace in teaching."[33] If his preaching echoes the practicality of his *Rule*,[34] we may assume that it contains little precise exegesis or theological argument but is marked by the asceticism he learned from Palamon the anchorite. Pachomius's preaching is notable because it is deliberately designed to build up the congregational life of the *koinonia* in Tabenisi. He sets individual vocation in the context of a communal life of simplicity and moderate asceticism, teaching his people to see themselves as colonies of heaven, encampments of Christ's army in which each recruit fulfills allotted duties. When Pachomius dies, he leaves about a dozen such monasteries in the deserts, and twice a year his congregations gather together in huge general assemblies.

The third member of the triumvirate is Macarius of Egypt, known as "the Great," an ascetic who reputedly embraces an almost frenetic form of self-abnegation and lives in a perpetual state of ecstasy.[35] Sadly the *Homilies* ascribed to him are probably not genuine, and only his *Letters to His Children* remain to provide clues to the content and manner of his preaching.[36] They suggest that his normal method of preaching is homiletic dialogue. He preaches sermons which offer little systematic theology but are strongly ethical in tone and well suited to guide his congregations of monks following the life of prayer as the path to "enlightenment."[37]

Congregations gather around a number of lesser ascetic preachers. Macarius of Alexandria is author of a strange homily on the eschatology of souls, and his "proficiency in all the exercises of asceticism" enables him to see divine mysteries.[38] The fourth-century *Lives of the Desert Fathers* contains a sermon by another much-admired mystical preacher, John of Lycopolis,[39] a great exponent of *inner stillness*. He calls his congregation to "stand before God with a pure heart and free from all passions," so that in contemplation they may "see" him as far as that is humanly possible. Evagrius Pontus provides biblical commentaries and ascetic texts for his many disciples in Nitria, but his preaching is so esoteric and his "opinions so very obscure" that he can "only be understood by the hearts of monks."[40]

Although they are not strictly speaking "desert" preachers, the Alexandrian anti-Nestorian Cyrus deserves mention as "an expert speaker," as does Antony's mentor, the "persuasive" Didymus the Blind, who is greatly honored by his congregations of Egyptian monks.[41] However, the greatest of all is Athanasius, whom Theodoret reveres as "the right eloquent orator" whose "tongue is adorned by his speech, and his speech by his character, and all about him is brightened by his abundant faith."[42] Having learned his asceticism among the desert monks,[43] Athanasius draws vast crowds in Alexandria where he stands as a rock of apostolic faith in a sea of heresy.[44] He preaches a theology centered upon the incarnate Logos as the One who unites human beings to the Father and restores their lost spiritual union with him.[45] Athanasius bases his call to asceticism on this concept and tells his hearers that, once freed, their immortal souls can know God directly.[46] He encourages individual congregations to feel part of a great multitude of believers throughout the world, all of whom are "overlooking what is temporal and turning their eyes to what is eternal."[47]

Athanasius commends a moderate form of asceticism, telling his people that although the saints extol the virtue of fasting, the Christian life is one of liberty in which sometimes believers are called "to fasting and sometimes to a feast."[48] Nevertheless, when the time for fasting comes, it is to be a fast of body and soul, so that, as the body is disciplined, the soul also is "nourished with divine food."[49] Athanasius does not demand celibacy for all, but he does admire the special "virtue" shown by "the virgins of Christ and the young men that practise chastity," believing that whenever anyone is "called to virginity" Christ empowers that believer to respond.[50]

Most ascetic preachers extend their preaching ministry by means of epistolary sermons. Pachomius's colleague Oresiesis writes "compact dissertations" on "almost the whole Old and New Testaments," and Cyrus the Alexandrian has a reputation as an "elegant and powerful writer."[51] Antony, Pachomius, and his successor Theodore all write letters of guidance to be read to various congregations, and Macarius the Great aims his epistles especially at gatherings of youthful monks.[52] However, the finest of all these written sermons are Athanasius's *Festal Letters,* which are full of wise, pastoral counsel to be read to congregations preparing for the paschal festivals. Didymus the Blind also writes biblical commentaries for the guidance of his congregations, while the irascible Epiphanius of Salamis produces his *Ancoratus* and *Panarion* to provide his people with manuals of sound theology.[53]

It is worth remembering that although these Egyptian preachers devote much energy to the edification of their congregations, they are also eager evangelists. Adrian Hastings nominates Antony and Pachomius as the pioneers of African Christianity[54] who initiate a revival which sweeps through the rural areas of northern Africa and leaves a permanent, monastic mark on the Egyptian church. Antony's pupil, Hilarion, evangelizes nomadic Arab tribesmen, gathering thousands into his Palestinian monasteries, and it is monks from Epiphanius's monastery at Eleutheropolis who fill the deserts of Lebanon with communities of their converts.

Congregations and Preachers in Syria

The Antiochene Congregations

In the second century, the Roman province of Syria centers upon the great city of Antioch and stretches eastward to the Euphrates. Antioch stands at the hub of a network of trade routes, drawing into itself all races and beliefs, and its congregations are a microcosm of that cosmopolitan and cultured city.[55] The first congregations are probably formed of Jews and "Greeks," but eventually Gentiles predominate.[56] From the outset, Antiochene congregations display independence and vigor, quickly establishing their own church order, forms of worship, charitable works, and missionary enterprises.[57] They produce their own coherent theological system and distinctive biblical exegesis.[58] They disseminate didactic and evangelistic written material[59] and send evangelists along the caravan routes so that, by the end of the third century, Mesopotamia boasts twenty or more bishoprics.

The Antiochene Preachers

In their early days, the Antiochene congregations are led by outstanding preachers — Barnabas, Paul, Peter, Ignatius, and Theophilus — but there follows a succession of rather undistinguished bishops.[60] In 260 the episcopate passes into the hands of the pompous and immoral Paul of Samosata. He is a populist, flamboyant preacher who encourages the adoration of women, revels in the adulation of his listeners, and even creates claques in his congregations to applaud his sermons. However, a group of gifted preachers begins to emerge with their own eloquence and tradition of asceticism and scriptural exposition in which theology and homiletics are closely intertwined.

The distinctive theology which undergirds Antiochene preaching favors an Aristotelian, analytical approach to faith which, although friendly to asceticism,[61] has less room for mysticism. It is the creation of a group of brilliant thinkers and orators, including the "literalist" exegete Lucian the Martyr and the rhetorician monks Malchion and Diodore of Tarsus.[62] Diodore is an author of biblical commentaries, but his distinguished protégé, Theodore of Mopsuestia, is the more outstanding exegete in the ascetic tradition. Although little of his homiletic output remains, his erudite exegetical works and baptismal catechism suggest that he preaches careful expository sermons with a penchant for matters of church order. However, it is his illustrious pupil, Theodoret, who earns a greater reputation as a preacher.

Theodoret, trained from infancy in the ascetic tradition, reluctantly leaves monastic retirement[63] for the see of Cyrrhus, a diocese of eight hundred congregations. The reclusive, erudite[64] monk becomes a kindly bishop who cares lovingly for his flock.[65] His writings show a natural eloquence, but his passion when speaking moves his hearers so greatly that they stand and applaud in the middle of his sermons and, afterward, embrace him and fall at his feet.[66] His clergy "listen most gladly" to his pastoral addresses. He urges them to show the "greatest care for their flocks"[67] who are mesmerized by heretical notions, and Theodoret himself uses his pulpit to teach sound doctrines so successfully that "not even one tare is left and the flock is delivered from all heresy and error."[68] He never fails to send his *Festal Letters* to be read to his congregations, and even when his "grief is at its height and his mind seriously affected" by the theological and ecclesiastical wrangles that beset him,[69] he bravely reminds his people of the "celebration, enjoyment and cheerfulness" of their faith.[70]

However, eventually "gloomy and terrible" clouds gather[71] as Theodoret's friendship with Nestorius involves him in the controversy surrounding the virgin Mary as *theotokos.*[72] Bewildered by the hostility suddenly leveled at him,[73] he pleads, "It is not the fame of my sermons to which I am calling attention, it is to their orthodoxy,"[74] but he is exiled by the "Robber Synod" of Ephesus in 449, being reinstated only on condition that he condemn the errors of his friend Nestorius.

It is sad that Theodoret's reputation is tarnished by association with Nestorius, whose condemnation probably owes as much to his prickly personality as to his theological errors. Nestorius himself is an impressive preacher, "a man of natural fluency and readiness of expression,"[75] whose eloquence brings him to the attention of Theodosius II and leads to his elevation to the patriarchate of Constantinople. He soon exploits his influence in his self-appointed role as the scourge of heretics, and his appeal for imperial support well illustrates the extravagance of his style: "Restore unto me, O Emperor, the world, weeded and purged of heretics, and I will render heaven unto thee; aid thou me in foiling the heretics and I will assist thee in overthrowing the Persians."[76]

A passionate man, whose fierce personality gives vigor to his controversial preaching, Nestorius inspires his followers with his own fanatical fervor. Within days of his ordination, he incites a mob to demolish an Arian meeting house, and when his colleague Anastasius is attacked, he leaps to his defense with a whole series of outspoken homilies.[77] His followers believe him to be erudite and well educated, but Socrates asserts that "in reality, he is disgracefully illiterate."[78] Eventually he is banished to die at the Great Oasis in Egypt,[79] but his congregations continue to flourish and it is Nestorian evangelists from Edessa and Nisibis who carry the gospel to the Arabs and, beyond, to India itself.[80]

Finally, brief mention must be made of Simeon Stylites, the greatest of the "pillar saints," who represents the most extreme form of Syrian ascetic preaching. After twenty years in monastic communities, he ascends his "pole" at Telanissus, east of Antioch, and for the next thirty years commands immense crowds, including many influential devotees who carry his words far and wide. Other preachers emulate Simeon, and they too gather their own congregations of adoring disciples and attract passing pilgrims, who listen to their sermons and recount their sayings.[81]

Congregations and Preachers in Mesopotamia[82]

The Ascetic Roots of the Congregations

From its inception in the second century, the rapidly growing Mesopotamian church[83] adopts an uncompromising asceticism and expects its members to be "chaste and circumspect, holy and pure, living like anchorites without spot."[84] Baptismal candidates unfitted for the full ascetic life are received reluctantly because they will be expected to observe strict disciplines.[85]

Mesopotamian priests, themselves expected to "divest themselves of mammon,"[86] instruct their congregations from the *Diatessaron* of Tatian, the leader of the Encratites in the Syrian deserts, and from much-admired apocryphal Acts, especially the ascetic Syriac *Acts of Thomas.*[87] Tatian's conviction, that ascetic Christianity is "fitted to all,"[88] still inspires local congregations who believe that "fasting, pure prayer and virginity" are built into the "house of faith" as naturally as is basic moral living.[89] They are taught to prize martyrdom as the ultimate self-renunciation. They listen to long sermons in honor of the martyrs and readings from *The Martyrdom of Barsamaya of Nisibis* and *The Martyrdom of Habib the Deacon*, the brave "preacher whose mouth was full of faith" and who secretly evangelized his local villages.[90]

Many believers practice asceticism in their own homes. They eat sparingly, dress modestly, practice charity, prayer, and meditation, and meet together under the guidance of chosen teachers. However, for some Christians this is not enough. They aim for that *perfection* which they believe stands at the top of the ladder of faith.[91] Being convinced it is in the solitaries and the monks that "Christ truly dwells,"[92] they totally renounce the world and disappear into the deserts where remarkable preachers await them.

The Preachers

A jewel among these preachers is Ephrem the Syrian, hailed by Sozomen as "the greatest ornament of the catholic church" and a man so devoid of ambition that, as a solitary in Edessa, he reputedly feigns madness to avoid elevation to a bishopric.[93] Above all else, Ephrem is a preacher. He loves "the sweet preaching of the Cross" and deliberately chooses to devote his life to the ministry of preaching.[94]

The *Liber Graduum* shines with Ephrem's "splendid oratory" and reveals a preacher in the grand manner.[95] His erudite, rhetorical sermons are complex in their grammatical structure, but his eloquence and narrative gifts save him from being obscure.[96] As a poet, he sometimes writes in metrical forms, and his sermons run the whole gamut of poetical moods from the frankly maudlin to the mystically ecstatic.[97] In one breath he waxes lyrical about the glories of the virgin Mary, and in the next he mercilessly scourges heretics. He bludgeons sinners into penitence and then woos them with visions of future blessedness. He knows how to evoke memorable, visual images,[98] and he punctuates his sermons with aphoristic sayings which serve as an *aide-mémoire* for his congregations.[99] So stimulating and alluring are his sermons that he has to remind his hearers that he is not preaching merely to entertain them and that "the hearing of the word profits nothing to the man who is busied with sins."[100]

Ephrem's scholarship equips him to range widely in his preaching. His sermons embrace doctrine, exposition, liturgy, and polemic, and they inspire many later Greek homilies on the virgin Mary.[101] Since his debt to Platonism is minimal, his brand of asceticism is not totally world-denying. He teaches his people that because the incarnate Word has restored their lost "robe of glory," they must value themselves and "honour the image of God" within them.[102] The spiritual pilgrimage they begin in baptism will lead to union with God, providing they "set the seal of the living cross on all their doings" and, by constant prayer, discern those divine revelations which will eventually "bring them to the house of the Kingdom."[103]

Side by side with Ephrem we may set Aphrahat, another great preacher and one whose twenty-three *Demonstrations* exude an air of episcopal authority.[104] He not only commends "holy books" to his congregations, but he insists that they read his own works in their entirety and do so without dissension.[105] Kraft has argued convincingly that κηρύσσω signifies "teaching," "argument," "dialogue," and "debate,"[106] and this is how Aphrahat sees his own preaching ministry. He is ready to use every means to gain his hearers' attention because he knows he must compete with the "honeyed words" of the heretics. Earnestly he appeals to his congregations, "Hear then, my beloved, and open the inward ears of your heart to me and the spiritual perceptions of your mind."[107]

Aphrahat firmly links his pastoral preaching[108] to stern asceticism, stressing that baptism is the first step along a "world-despising" path trod by Christian "sojourners" who are ever mindful of the eternal condemnation awaiting "the sons of luxury."[109] They know that only "zeal in fasting and prayer" can overcome "the crafty enemy" who seeks to ensnare them with many devices.[110] Among these snares, none is more dangerous than the sexual laxity which women, those "weapons of Satan," have brought into the churches.[111] Marriage is the refuge of the weak-willed, and the only true defense is "incomparable virginity" which ensures the indwelling of Christ and even "redeems the daughters of Eve from condemnation." However, once achieved, its safety requires constant vigilance, and it is best protected in solitude or in segregated congregations.[112]

Aphrahat's people are being persecuted, and he writes a *Demonstration* especially to comfort "those who today are persecuted for the sake of the persecuted Jesus."[113] He steadies congregations by pointing them to the noble example of heroes of the faith and to the "great and excellent" example of the martyred Christ, urging them to stand firm because "the glorious time of the bridegroom" is near.[114] Then those who remain faithful will rise from their tombs to enjoy eternal bliss while the wicked lie in Sheol with "weeping and gnashing of teeth."[115]

Duschesne calls the Monophysite bishop Jacob Bardaeus "the great celebrity of Edessa in the time of the Christian kings."[116] A courageous man with a restless, inquiring mind, he takes his episcopal role very seriously. Reputedly he is the founder of Syriac literature, which becomes the language of sermons and liturgies in Edessa, and although only fragments of his work remain, his preaching seems to reflect the lyricism of his remarkable hymns.[117] A further clue is afforded by *The Book of the Laws of the Countries,* a dialogical sermon preached to a group of young men and recorded by Bardaeus's disciple, Philip.

In this sermon, Bardaeus's gnostic tendencies are very clear. He tells his hearers that their special relationship with God entitles them to receive true knowledge from Direct Wisdom and they must use their free will "to order their conduct in a godlike manner" by "control of the mind and the will of the soul." However, they cannot liberate themselves completely because they are victims of a conflict between spiritual powers, "the *dexter* and *sinister* in the Zodiac," which will continue until God chooses to bring in "a new world in which all evil commotions will cease." There is no mention of Christian fundamental beliefs and only passing reference to worship and customs of "the new race of Christians." If this is a fair example of his preaching, we can understand why Bardaeus and his followers are eventually accused of heresy.

A very different picture emerges when we consider the work of Pseudo-Macarius, who is active in Mesopotamia in the late fourth century but whose influence is long-lasting and widespread.[118] His *Fifty Homilies* and *Great Letter*[119] provide an unusually large corpus of homiletic material and reveal a preacher of sheer genius whose sermons are brief, uncluttered by verbosity, and perfectly focused upon their "target" congregations. Pseudo-Macarius establishes a close rapport with his "beloved" congregations[120] by dealing with issues that they raise, identifying himself with them, addressing them personally, and openly expressing joy when they respond to his words.[121] It is this emotional quality which gives vibrancy to his preaching.[122] He is a supreme exponent of "heart spirituality," and it is little wonder that a later, distinguished preacher of "the warmed heart" "exceedingly reverences" him and "esteems him very highly in love."[123]

Pseudo-Macarius is a superb evangelist. He sets out clearly the Christian life as a new "world with a special style of living, thinking and acting."[124] This "new world" is entered by *conversion*, "believing firmly in the Lord and giving oneself completely to his commands," and it is continued by *sanctification* "in the assembly of the saints," as believers grow in grace by "continually eating more of the Christian religion as food and drink."[125] Pseudo-Macarius is an outstanding communicator whose visual preaching style abounds in illustrations, metaphors, similes, and narratives derived from his hearers' experience. He speaks to them of the racetrack, flights of birds, surgical operations, fruit trees, the contemporary Persian-Roman wars, and even fire-eating sheep![126]

However, it is as a pastoral preacher that Pseudo-Macarius is supreme, and he urges fellow preachers to embrace God's Word and proclaim it as his "letter to his people" in order to guide and encourage them.[127] Pseudo-Macarius realistically acknowledges that not "all those who live in the church are endowed with a pure and blameless heart" but insists that Christians are to treat even "prostitutes, sinners and disorderly people" with "love and cheerfulness."[128] Instead of condemning weaker members, he assures them that "God does not enjoin the impossible upon his servants." It is Satan who tells them that they cannot "perform anything good," but God compassionately endows them with "nobility and dignity" and gives them free will to do "whatever action they wish."[129] In that confidence, they can begin to take the "twelve steps to perfection" which Pseudo-Macarius prescribes.[130]

The christocentric nature of Pseudo-Macarius's preaching shines in every sermon. He describes how, when Adam's sin renders humanity lost and helpless, "through his goodness" God "diminishes himself" and "comes and suffers the ignominy of the cross" so that humans might recover their "full heavenly inheritance."[131] Thus salvation is all of grace: "The Good Shepherd heals the scabby sheep, but sheep are unable to heal sheep." Like a fifth-century Luther, Pseudo-Macarius declares, "If anyone stands solely on his own righteousness and redemption, he labours in vain."[132] Nevertheless, once individuals "co-operate with grace," they are born again and the Holy Spirit indwells them, uniting them with Christ so that sin is "cut out little by little and diminished."[133] However, Pseudo-Macarius solemnly warns those experiencing this spiritual restoration to avoid three major pitfalls. They must not envy those whose spiritual growth is more rapid than their own; they must expect fluctuations in their own spiritual progress; and they must never allow spiritual pride to rob them of "the goal of things hoped for."[134] Their new life is not easy because they are opposed by "Satan and his powers" who are able to "capture the soul and drag it as a captive to their place," often working so subtly that believers are unaware they "are being moved by a foreign power."[135]

So great a struggle is beyond the capacity of the solitary believers, so Pseudo-Macarius stresses the congregation's role in enabling individual believers to "journey together until they reach the city above."[136] Inspired by heavenly congregations of ministering saints and angels, they must create a holy fellowship on earth in which individuals may grow in grace. They must do everything for the common good and replace pride with a spirit of openness as "the binding force of the community."[137] To help them, they need humble leaders who are "skilled and experienced" in testing the authenticity of their people's faith so that they may be able to enjoy the blessings of their "fraternal love."[138]

Pseudo-Macarius directs his sermons especially at congregations of "those who have chosen the eremitical life," but he advocates a moderate form of asceticism for all believers.[139] He teaches them that their bodies are "the attractive garment" of the soul which must "control itself and the body" by allowing the Holy Spirit to sanctify its "five rational senses."[140] By "tying the passions of sin to the cross" and becoming "strangers to the world," their souls will be released to "pass to the other world and eternity."[141]

However, Pseudo-Macarius warns his congregations that it is not enough to make the "body an altar of sacrifice" because those who "observe only an external purity" gain no benefit from their self-denial. Only those who "under grace ardently seek to observe (God's laws) interiorly" will experience his "holy peace" and achieve the "greatest possession" of perfection.[142] This requires a "zeal for unceasing prayer," offered "in quietness, peace and great tranquillity," which "fills the heart with God's power" and provides "a guiding force for right actions."[143] In the Macarian teaching asceticism and mysticism are intertwined, and he defines a *Christian* as "a person whom Christ, the heavenly Spouse, has asked to be his bride in a mystical and a divine fellowship."[144]

Pseudo-Macarius is probably the greatest pastoral preacher among the ascetics, presenting his congregations with comprehensible and moderate forms of asceticism and mysticism. It is argued that the balance we detect in his preaching is partly derived from his contact with a group of great preachers who will later claim our attention — the Cappadocian Fathers.[145]

"Choirs of Angels"

The Liturgists

Today are strains of praise sung joyfully by choirs of angels.

Gregory Thaumaturgus, *On the Annunciation*

Congregations and Liturgy

At this point, we must turn aside and consider some developments which are affecting the form and nature of preaching. Constantine's accession accelerates changes in the texture of congregational life, as worship becomes increasingly sophisticated and preachers have to take seriously their place within the context of liturgy.[1] Eusebius speaks of "vast congregations flocking to the houses of prayer," specially constructed Christian buildings ranging from modest house churches to "lofty edifices" like that built in the heart of Nicomedia.[2] Often these churches are built "like long ships," reflecting their role as "arks of salvation," crewed by their clergy.[3] About the middle of the third century basilicas are constructed to accommodate the growing congregations,[4] and are later enlarged or replaced by the majestic buildings with which Constantine adorns his empire.

Churches become theaters for ritual, and preaching becomes part of the liturgical drama. Ideally, the bishop is its central player, reigning from his cathedra and flanked by his presbyters,[5] sacrificing priests who are increasingly separated from their congregations. Worship changes its forms to reveal its nature as a glorious foretaste of heaven, its hymns subsumed with the songs of the cherubim and its sermons delivered to "strains of praise sung joyfully by the choir of angels."[6] The antiphonal music of Antioch spreads throughout the church as hymn singing becomes a regular expression of congregational praise.[7] Preachers increasingly become hymn writers,[8] and the music of the chanters suffuses the reading of the Scriptures as taperers accompany lectors to the *ambo*. As kneeling worshipers offer intercessions in a "subdued voice to avoid annoying their neighbours," private devotion is increasingly enriched by sonorous liturgical prayers.[9]

Once fear of official disapproval disappears, church attendance becomes popular. Theodosius claims that even the Roman Senate "hastens to the sanctuaries of the Nazarene."[10] Christianity spreads into the rural bastions of paganism, and since many newcomers "convert" under duress,[11] preachers cannot be sure how many of their hearers are sincere or have any clear understanding of the faith.[12] In the cities, sophisticated pagans attend church to admire the oratory of the Christian preachers,[13] and young hooligans lounge about, "laughing, slumbering and nodding" as boisterously as if they are still in the baths.[14] Preachers recite horrifying catalogues of vices rampant among their congregations, and they have to plead with their people to show a better example to the pagan world.[15]

Consequently, church leaders have no alternative but to dispense with the egalitarian informality of the earliest church gatherings and stratify their congregations. Not only are clergy segregated from the laity but each social group is assigned its own area in churches, with deacons patrolling the boundaries.[16] Men and women enter churches by different doors, and the women are further divided into "dedicated virgins" and older women, younger women and mothers with their children. Young men are watched by stern deacons, and those believers under discipline are banished to the church entrance until their penance is complete.

Upon entering their churches, worshipers face further discrimination in the form of two distinct but interconnected services. The *Missa Catechumenorum*, for all believers, is followed by a eucharistic service, reserved for those who have been baptized. This is increasingly endowed with mystery and awe since consecrated "common bread and wine" which becomes "the flesh and blood of Jesus who was made flesh" must be treated with the utmost reverence.[17]

Preaching and Liturgy

Liturgical developments impel preaching toward greater sophistication as congregations become more aesthetically discerning in their expecta-tions.[18] Even in rural areas, people look eagerly for the coming of clerics who are competent to preach to them, and sometimes they themselves visit the cities to hear great preachers.[19] Bishops are now preachers par excel-lence, and many conscientiously use all "solemn assemblies, auditories, prayers and teachings" to exhort their people.[20] Sermons are often deliv-ered both in the catechumens' service and at the subsequent Eucharist. In the Eastern church, it is decreed that "presbyters, one after another, shall exhort the people, the bishop coming last,"[21] a tedious procedure which provokes complaints that "the delivery of these sermons greatly delays the dismissal from church," sometimes for four or five hours![22]

On festal occasions "crowded gatherings of elevated fervour" converge on churches like "swarms of bees," and preachers use their best eloquence to "open the doors of hearing."[23] The Feast of the Annunciation is de-picted as "the glad spring-time of the soul," and at Whitsuntide, it is claimed, the "trumpet of Gospel-preaching" produces a veritable waterfall of blessings. On All Saints' Day, worshipers are told they may watch "the martyrs disporting themselves," and on Ascension Day they may "pene-trate heaven" itself.[24] The festivals also provide vital opportunities for basic doctrinal teaching of worshipers, many of whom still confuse the church's observances with similar pagan festivities.[25]

Few festivals are more elaborate than those celebrating the martyrs. Although prayers are offered for the dead at every Eucharist, preachers also encourage their hearers to "be continually by the coffins of the martyrs, where there is health of body and benefit of soul."[26] Such apparently noble instructions often compound confusion with similar pagan vigils. More-over, theologically naive converts seize pagan sites and transfer to the mar-tyrs loyalties previously accorded pagan deities.[27] Congregations identify themselves with specific martyrs, consecrating churches in their honor and, in effect, creating subsidiary Christian cults.[28] They adorn the festi-vals with memorable rituals and venerate their heroes in special hymns, pleading with them to exercise efficacious prayers on their behalf.[29] Preachers become principal players in martyrological dramas, arousing the fervor of their congregations by their graphic accounts of the martyrs' torments.[30]

Fasting and prayer usher in Passiontide and Easter when the growing symbiosis of preaching and liturgy is most solemnly displayed. During special Holy Week services, preachers expound the events surrounding Christ's betrayal, trial, and crucifixion, often with disgraceful anti-Jewish polemic.[31] The liturgical pilgrimage moves toward its climax, from the Eucharist on *mandatum* Thursday and the veneration of the cross in the Good Friday Vigil, to the climactic solemnities of the *Great Sabbath*.[32] It is then that, after careful preparation, baptismal candidates receive their final, secret instructions.[33] The preachers complete their catechetical task[34] and beautiful music fills the darkness until, at cockcrow on Easter Day, the newly baptized receive their first Eucharist.[35] The crowds that gather on Easter Day require fine sermons so that the "seed of the Word may grow in the soil of their hearts,"[36] but even this supreme occasion is often marred either because worshipers absent themselves or because those present behave outrageously.[37] Nevertheless, the preachers respond to the church's developing liturgical life, and although the *sermo* or *homilia* has long been an established feature of the rite,[38] it now becomes more firmly embedded in congregational worship.[39] The value of this format becomes increasingly apparent as the church sails into ever more mountainous theological storms, and even the emperor himself, unable to resist joining the preachers' ranks, solemnly delivers his *Oration to the Assembly on the Saints*.

"The Doctrine of the Lord"

The Theologians

We confess that the doctrine of the Lord, which he taught his disciples, . . . is the foundation and root of right faith.

Gregory of Nyssa, *Epistles* 2

THE EASTERN THEOLOGIAN-PREACHERS

The fourth century is dominated by protracted christological controversies, and from the seething cauldron of the Arian conflict emerges a triumvirate of great theologians. Highly educated, the Cappadocian Fathers fine-tune Greek trinitarian doctrine, lead the fight against Arianism, and spread monastic discipline throughout Cappadocia, but they are also fine preachers in the ascetic tradition.

Basil of Caesarea (ca. 329-79)

Basil's Congregations

Basil "keeps his friends in his heart," and as his *Basilead* shows, his love and compassion extend far beyond his circle of friends.[1] Despite ill health, he is always eager to visit those in need, and his copious pastoral correspondence graphically demonstrates his care for his congregations.[2] He rebukes both his own sin and that of others because it damages the church,[3] but his sternness is always tempered by love and exhortations to "make another effort" and to treat the fallen "tenderly and meekly."[4]

Although a towering figure on the stage of global, ecclesiastical politics, at heart Basil is a caring pastor who "holds the society of the saints most useful."[5] He believes that local congregations are God's "lamps set on a lampstand to shine throughout the world," and he is quick to encourage them.[6] He admires the way entire Christian families love their churches and gather for worship even under the most difficult conditions,[7] but it is his admiration for the "constancy, fortitude and endurance" of the women in his congregations which is especially impressive.[8] The women range from godly, aristocratic ladies, respectfully addressed as "your excellencies,"[9] to helpless slave girls and pitiful paupers who expose their children for "want of the necessities of life."[10] Basil has a special word of encouragement for soldiers' wives,[11] and in true ascetic tradition he commends all who "forgo husband and children for the attainment of God's favour."[12]

Basil's congregations include all strata of society, from rich, leisured aristocrats and eminent professional men[13] to those so poor that "a day's labour is hardly sufficient to maintain them" and soldiers, for whom Basil has a special regard.[14] Amongst his most ardent admirers are the "ordinary working people," his beloved "artisans of mechanical trades," who flock to hear him early in the morning. For them, he gladly simplifies and abbreviates his sermons, "so as not to keep them too long from their work."[15] Basil loves the elderly members seated in his congregation who have "passed their prime,"[16] but he retains a particular interest in young worshipers.[17] He covets the "bridle of baptism for them," is delighted when they show "steadiness of character beyond their years" and furious when they are harmed by congregational dissension.[18] He preaches sermons especially for young people, urging them to choose their heroes carefully, to avoid being "bound by the golden fetters" of luxury, and to cherish their Christian homes.[19]

Despite Basil's assiduous care, all is not well in his churches. The men, irregular in attendance, are often to be found among the crowds of unruly idlers, haunting the city streets.[20] Women too bring shame upon the church, and a crowd of tipsy females celebrates Easter Day by dancing and singing indecent songs outside the Basilica of the Martyrs in Caesarea.[21] Congregations are also being "dashed and shattered upon the rocks" by the

Arian controversy, so that "many have reverted to Judaism and paganism" and, among those remaining, "brotherly concord is now destroyed."[22] "Individual hatreds" and "pushing for chief places" thwart every prospect of advance. Families vie with each other in displays of "piety" by forcing their defenseless daughters into bogus vocations, and even monastic communities are infected by the spiritual malaise.[23]

The misbehavior of Christians outside the church is symbolized by their habit of "delaying the *viaticum* of baptism" for as long as possible so that they can indulge in their vices, untrammeled by thoughts of perdition.[24] They wallow in sexual misconduct and luxury, outshining their table companions in lewd conversation and becoming so drunk they are carried home "a laughing stock to the lads in the street."[25] Basil becomes so exasperated that on at least one occasion he prolongs his sermon because, he says, "If I let you go . . . some men will run to the dice, where they will find bad language, sad quarrels and the pangs of avarice."[26]

Basil's commentary on *The Canons* gives a startling picture of the rampant "rebellion and disorderliness" defiling the church,[27] and it prescribes appropriate penances for an incredible array of sins — theft, trigamy, polygamy, murder, abortion, and abduction. The problem is exacerbated by the abysmal example presented by the clergy, some of whom have actually "bought their orders."[28] They are "grievous wolves," locked in "controversies with one another," practicing illicit sexual relations and then daring to sit as "merciless judges" over the sins of others.[29] Confronted by so deep a sickness in his churches, Basil embarks upon a vigorous preaching ministry and reinforces his eloquent sermons by copious pastoral letters.

Basil's Preaching

Basil is not blind to his limitations as a preacher,[30] but his ability to speak extempore enables him to respond quickly to the changing moods of his hearers and to deal speedily with his critics.[31] He displays immense versatility and is equally able to produce densely argued homilies for "the most cultivated minds" and brief addresses for "simple souls" who must shortly hurry off to work.[32] He invites comment from his congregations[33] and constantly watches them so that he can stop in midargument to respond to a questioning look from "the more studious" or simplify his approach when less-academic hearers appear puzzled.[34] He is so committed to his preaching that he often exhausts himself and has to apologize when his sermons are too long.[35] He demands the same degree of commitment from his hearers and reminds them that they are not there to judge the preacher but to "help him as fellow combatants."[36] Basil has little time for "paltry rhetoric" but he is a master of memorable, pithy sayings,[37] drawing illustrations from the natural world[38] and using every device to ensure that his hearers "look at themselves round about from every point of view."[39]

For Basil, exegesis of Scripture assisted by tradition "is the chief way of finding our duty,"[40] and he uses the Bible to purify his congregations' conduct and theology. In his eighteen *Homilies on the Psalms*,[41] he sets about molding his hearers' devotional life but realizes there is little hope of amendment until he has successfully calmed the churches' agitated mood. He needs to ensure that members show "moderation and respect for everyone" and rise "above the waves of feeling" which cause internecine warfare.[42] They need to understand that only by nourishing their baptismal life by regular attendance at the Eucharist[43] can they hope to live uncompromising Christian lives,[44] free from covetousness, domestic strife, drunkenness, and self-indulgence.[45] Their lifestyle must be visibly different from that of their non-Christian neighbors, and they must control their materialistic cravings by "reason, assurance and cheapness."[46] In fact, Basil assures them, it is only dedicated asceticism which offers a sure way to "receive the crown of God's love."[47] It is for this reason that Basil has a special regard for his monastic congregations, "whose bodies are worn away in fasting and prayer," and he preaches to them both personally and by letter.[48] He is distressed that so many believers seek the monastic life and then fall away because they have not counted the cost of the vocation.[49]

Basil believes that asceticism releases the soul's natural desire for God, and as he tries to explain this to his congregations, the mystical element in his preaching becomes apparent.[50] Martyrdom may no longer be available as a speedy path to bliss,[51] but the way of asceticism and mystical contemplation is still open. Basil tells his hearers that they can have profound experiences when "a kind of light falls upon the heart, arousing a multitude of thoughts about God," and have a foretaste of heavenly delights.[52] "Leave your body," he says, "leave your senses . . . and rise above the stars. . . . Soaring at those sublime heights, let the eyes of your soul . . . contemplate the Divine Nature."[53]

Evelyn Underhill declares that "the doctrine of the transcendence of God could scarcely go further" than it does in Basil's writings,[54] and it is from that vantage point that he uses the pulpit to correct false doctrine among his people. He lays a solid trinitarian foundation, safeguarding the divinity of the Son against Arian teachings,[55] and then in response to his congregations' "eagerness to hear something" on the subject, he champions the deity of the Holy Spirit against the *pneumatomachi*.[56]

Basil realizes that his people must understand that they need to be redeemed because their "own self-determining freewill has been . . . brought into captivity through sin" and this has alienated them from God.[57] Thus only Jesus is "able to make atonement" for their sin, and Basil proclaims that he has done this by living a spotless human life and by shedding "his holy and most precious blood . . . on behalf of us all."[58] In Christ alone is there hope of salvation, and therefore commitment to him is an urgent matter. "Hell has different kinds of chastisement" for those who reject him,[59] says Basil, but those who receive him by faith will share in the angelic privilege of "knowing God face to face" in heaven.[60]

Gregory of Nyssa (330–ca. 395)

Gregory and His Congregations

It is a time when "Fashionable people speak . . . almost as enthusiastically about their favourite preacher . . . as . . . of their favourite horse in the races,"[61] and Gregory seems admirably suited to exploit it. Intellectually brilliant, his work sparkles with the sort of inconsistencies native to the innovative mind, but he retains a genuine "shepherd's affection" for his people and preaches to them, both in person and by means of his pastoral letters.[62] Despite often being crusty and difficult, he is received rapturously by congregations who "throng the churches with their families," greet him with "choirs of virgins," and gather "like bees, in undiminished numbers," to hang upon his every word.[63] Nevertheless, his pastoral skills are tested severely. He confesses that there are "many troubles in the churches," which are "distracted by discord," weakened by defection, and shackled by "an accursed chain of vices."[64]

Gregory faces the same congregational scandals that confront Basil, but he seeks to solve them "from the top" by tackling the issue of weak leadership. Gregory recognizes that bishops of "high birth, wealth and distinction" may deal well with affluent and influential members. Nevertheless, he advises congregations to select leaders who are "wise and strong counsellors" so that they may honor their priests as "venerable and separated from the mass of men."[65] Gregory rejoices that "the orthodox faith is preached over the whole world"[66] because he sees preaching as an essential part of the leadership role of bishops, and he himself is a glorious example of the principle.

Gregory's Preaching

As an erstwhile teacher of public speaking, Gregory confesses that he is "filled with wonderful enthusiasm and works with pleasure at his sermons,"[67] and when age and infirmity hamper his preaching ministry, he describes himself as an old racehorse who still has "an eagerness to join the contest."[68] He knows he is called "to announce the glory of God" in every way possible, and he makes little distinction between various forms of proclamation at his disposal.[69] His impeccable style enthralls his hearers with its rhetorical flourishes, especially upon magnificent occasions such as ecclesiastical festivals and imperial funerals.[70] Nevertheless, he retains the common touch, using vivid images and disarming asides. He turns the rhetorical device of verbal illustration to homiletic use[71] and fills his sermons with similes, metaphors, and anecdotes.[72]

Gregory's preaching is founded upon scriptural exegesis,[73] and although he claims to favor a literal approach to Scripture, he finds that, *homiletically,* allegorical interpretations can be wonderfully rich. They render the text a door through which the soul may pass to new awareness of God.[74] Scripture informs Gregory's pastoral preaching, which often reveals an unexpected vein of tenderness in his character. In an age which takes for granted a high rate of infant mortality and the exposing of unwanted babies, *On the Early Death of Infants*[75] is a moving expression of pastoral concern for grieving mothers. Similarly, he does not ridicule young Christians' ardor when they seek the ascetic "life according to excellence," but gently advises them to consult expert guides before they "embrace virginity while young and uninformed in understanding."[76] However, he is far less sympathetic toward those who wish to parade their piety by joining the popular craze for pilgrimages, which he dismisses as unscriptural, morally insecure, spiritually deceptive, and physically dangerous.[77]

It is a time when Christian architecture seeks to outshine the glories of the imperial cult,[78] and Gregory's description of the palatial Church of Martyrs testifies to the impressive ecclesiastical settings and liturgical festivals to which preaching has to be adapted. His liturgical sermons[79] allow him to display his most polished, rhetorical style, but they also reveal him as an outstanding theologian-preacher.[80] His claim that congregations are "encompassed by the war of heresy" is not exaggerated, and Dill observes that "many people of rank and dignity were deserting the Christian fold and lapsing into Jewish or Manichaean or pagan superstition."[81] Therefore Gregory uses his sermons, enlarged by learned treatises, to present his congregations with a clear understanding of the Trinity, set out in his *Not Three Gods*, and to explain the scheme of salvation upon which their faith depends.

The grand sweep of Gregory's theology is beyond the scope of this study,[82] but it is important to consider how he helped his people to understand the divine process of redemption. He shows them that Adam's misuse of his God-given free will infects all humanity with his ignorant disobedience. However, God provides the way of escape by sending Jesus to ransom humanity from the devil. He "repairs the Devil's evil doings by assuming manhood in its fullness" and so "becomes the type and figure of us all."[83] However, each individual, when awakened by "the preaching of the Word," must personally claim the spiritual heritage. In his sermon *Against Those Who Defer Baptism*,[84] Gregory urges catechumens to be baptized at once so that they may be identified with the redeeming work of Christ. Once they receive baptism with piety and faith, its "mighty power" will release them from sin and give them "equality with angels."[85] Their transformed lives will be sustained by the miraculous food of the Eucharist since those who communicate regularly are brought into vibrant contact with the power of the Spirit.[86]

Having established the foundational role of the sacraments in the Christian life, Gregory goes on to explain in more detail the nature of the new life upon which his people have entered. He tells them that God has divided their existence into two interconnected parts, but they must decide whether to indulge themselves here or to "seek the life of blessedness."[87] The "wheat and tares" of good and evil impulses remain within them and, after their baptism, the devil "plots more vehemently" to destroy them and plunge them into the inextinguishable flames which await unrepentant sinners.[88] In the twenty-four elegant, if repetitive, chapters of his *De virginitate*, Gregory explains to his people that their best hope of avoiding satanic snares and inheriting the divine promises lies in treading the path of asceticism.[89]

Gregory uses *virginity* as a rhetorical metaphor for a life without distractions in which "a high strong wall" separates Christians from "the pleasures of the senses,"[90] but he also uses it in its narrow, ascetic sense. He regards sexuality as the main stumbling block in the life of piety. He describes the allures of women with considerable feeling,[91] and urges the "weaker brethren" in his congregations to "fly to virginity as into an impregnable fortress" rather than risk "descending into temptations." Only virginity can offer "complete forgetfulness of natural emotions" and "the thwarting of natural impulse."[92] Although he claims not to "deprecate marriage as an institution," Gregory insists that even those who are married must "close the channel of their senses." He wishes that he himself had remained unmarried, and his tirade against the married state comes periously close to a ridiculous *argumentum ad absurdum*.[93]

Gregory's asceticism melts into his mysticism by which he seeks to lift the Christian life above the daily battle with temptation. He asserts that replacing sexuality by *aptharsia* (incorruptibility) sets the believers' feet upon the first rung of the ladder of mystical ascent because it anticipates heaven itself where there is no marriage.[94] He promises his hearers even more. Those who reject "the noisome effluvia of the flesh" will find their "climbing souls lifted out of themselves by the power of the Holy Spirit" to "be bright and luminous in the communion of the real light," a foretaste of their ultimate condition. However, there is much to be done before they finally "become light in their nearness to Christ's true light."[95] The ascetic way is one of *purgation* which begins in this life but is continued beyond death, to "free the soul from any emotional connection with brute creation."[96] The severity and duration of this ultimate state of purgation are governed by the demands of divine justice, and Gregory is clear that its purpose is remedial rather than retaliatory. It is designed "to get the good separated from the evil."[97]

"When evil passions have been purged by the healing processes worked out by fire," Gregory tells his hearers, the soul moves onward and is reunited with a body made "from the common stock of atoms" to appear before "the divine Judge."[98] Then the souls of the blessed will "return to their pristine state of grace" and, all evil purged away, will receive again the *imago Dei*.[99] By offering them such a glorious prospect of eternal joy, Gregory lifts the hearts and minds of his congregations above mundane matters and mere morality and gives them a beatific vision of the ultimate goal of the Christian life.

Gregory of Nazianzus (330-89)

Gregory's Congregations

The church in Nazianzus, where Gregory helps his aging father, seems to be as unprepossessing as the Roman province itself. Gregory describes it as "woodland and rustic, for the most part grown careless and run wild," and he notes the "littleness of its flock."[100] The commencement of his ministry is inauspicious. Many of his congregation boycott his first service in protest against his apparent reluctance to serve them, and he is deeply wounded when, although it is Easter Day, few come to welcome him.[101] He believes that congregations ought to encourage their preachers, and he is so "filled with despondency" by their careless attitude that he even considers refusing to preach to them.[102] Sensitive by nature and a lifelong "prisoner to ill health,"[103] he is ill equipped for such rebuffs and finds his new congregations miserably unreceptive. He longs to impress truth upon fresh souls like "wax not yet subjected to the seal" but claims he is thwarted by a surfeit of theology which has removed the "boundary between giving and receiving instruction."[104] This strange accusation needs further explanation.

Although remote from most major academic centers, Nazianzus is infected by a passion for ill-informed theological debate, largely stirred up by ignorant and divisive preachers.[105] Gregory complains that "listening to all kinds of doctrines and teachers" turns his congregations "hither and thither by one plausible idea after another" and gives them an illusion of profound theological knowledge.[106] He continues to preach, in the hope that his hearers may permit "a little spark to kindle the torch of truth" within them, only to find that it is the most fervent of his hearers who resist his words most fanatically and refuse to change their opinions.[107]

Despite all this, Gregory cannot simply abandon his people. They are "the Sacred Flock, the praiseworthy nurslings of Christ," and he must not destroy them by overharsh criticism.[108] He begins his ministry by trying to unite them, pleading with them to use the great feast of Easter to "embrace one another and to forgive all offences for the Resurrection's sake,"[109] and he appears to have some success.

Confusion in theology leads to confusion in conduct, and Gregory's congregations adopt the undesirable attitudes of the world around them. Many believers think they have a God-given right to "grow prosperous and luxuriant in the misfortunes of others" by extorting crippling rates of interest and exploiting harsh economic conditions.[110] Pagan attitudes to marriage invade the churches, and Gregory has to remind his hearers that although easy divorce is allowed by Roman law, it is "entirely contrary" to Christian teaching.[111] It is clear that congregations contain many devout, aristocratic ladies because Gregory uses their example of piety to rebuke their erring sisters who "adorn themselves with gold" and refuse to leave "the arts and witcheries of the painter to women of the stage and of the streets."[112] He regards celibacy as "higher and more divine" than marriage and urges his people to embrace the virtues of the ascetic life, to "mortify their earthly members and spend their all on the Spirit," taking "flight to mountains and deserts in order to hold pure communion with God."[113]

In 379, reluctantly, he has to leave Nazianzus for Constantinople, where he finds a church even more dispirited and corrupt. The Arians, ascendant for over forty years, have "drawn many over to their side," fiercely attacking the quarrelsome orthodox congregations, stoning their clergy and insulting their women.[114] Gregory, opposed by the pretender Maximus, is heckled and mobbed by Arians, and hated by the rich and powerful in the church because he refuses to pander to their whims.[115] Nevertheless, within two short years he establishes himself as "one of the great teachers and preachers of the Church,"[116] and his congregation outgrows his private chapel.

In Constantinople, Gregory finds the passion for theological discussion in a flamboyant form, "buzzing in every market-place, boring every dinner-party and throwing women's apartments into confusion."[117] Vividly, he compares the endless theological debates to an "excess of honey that produces vomiting" and wishes his people were as concerned about hospitality, fidelity, and generosity as they are about applauding eloquent sermons.[118] Despite all hindrances, Gregory initiates a magnificent preaching ministry in Constantinople, especially notable for the *Theological Orations,* which earn him the title of "The Theologian."[119] Sadly, that

ministry is cut short by the fracas occasioned by Gregory's nomination as
patriarch, which so distresses him that after preaching a memorable farewell sermon, he leaves the glories of Constantinople for the welcome obscurity of Nazianzus.

Gregory's Preaching

Originally overawed and silenced by his father's "noble utterances,"
Gregory's skills as a preacher are finally released when he sees himself as
"an instrument of God, tuned and struck by that skilful artist, the
Spirit."[120] He never underestimates the task of the preacher since, he
says, "defining God in words is an impossibility," but he believes preachers have to rise to the challenge afforded by their multifarious congregations and learn to "play upon their many strings in various ways" like
skilled musicians.[121] As a preacher he is not faultless, but at least he is
ready to acknowledge it.[122] Sometimes he preaches dry homilies,[123] and
he is fond of complex sentences and "purple passages."[124] Sometimes he
intends to "discourse briefly" on the grounds that "too great a length in
a sermon" produces mental indigestion, but he also delivers long and
heavy discourses, promising to stop long before he finally concludes.[125]
However, generally he is content to speak good, plain Greek and, when
required, he can produce simple sermons, rendered even more "human"
by occasional inaccuracies, illustrations, and memorable phrases.[126]
Sometimes the suppressed emotional power of his *Poemata* breaks
through into his preaching, especially in panegyrics for family and
friends when he weeps openly.[127]

Gregory likens the demands of the pastoral ministry to "walking on a
lofty tight-rope" because shepherds must be balanced in their treatment of
the flock,[128] and he tries to demonstrate this in his pastoral sermons. However, his patience is sorely tried by those who "avoid becoming Christians"
by postponing baptism and refusing to "leave the porch of religion."[129] He
pleads with them to avail themselves of the blessings that baptism brings
and subsequently to live "illuminated lives."[130] However, he realizes that
such triumphant living is impossible while his people's minds are confused by false doctrine.[131] Determined to drive out heresy, he fills his sermons with scriptural references and statements of orthodox belief,[132] rising to a glorious climax in his famous *Theological Orations*.[133]

After using the first of these sermons to prepare the ground, he expounds the theme of "God," acknowledging that here our knowledge must be imperfect but that creation and Scripture reveal enough of God's nature to move his people to praise.[134] In the third and fourth sermons, Gregory cleverly uses the Arians' favorite scriptural texts to refute their attacks upon Christ's deity.[135] The final sermon is concerned with the Spirit, but it is also striking for its discussion of the nature of language and the development of doctrine.[136]

It is significant that Gregory ends each theological sermon on a note of doxology because his festival sermons are filled with spiritual elation and passion. He urges his people to "rejoice and tremble with joy," to "leap before him, joining in chorus with angels and singing with archangels."[137] However, for sheer emotional depth, no sermon surpasses Gregory's *Last Farewell,* preached in 381 to the assembled bishops and his own people at the Council of Constantinople. He reminds them of the "small, poor flock without order" that he had inherited and invites his detractors to see that congregation as it is *now,* "healthy and well-grown, if not yet perfect." Passionately, he turns upon his enemies: "I cannot bear your horse races and theatres and this rage for rivalry in expense and party spirit," and then he bids farewell to his beloved "children" and blesses them.[138]

Seldom has the bond between preacher and people been more movingly expressed. Gregory returns to the comparative obscurity of Nazianzus to write poetry. Only one later sermon remains, delivered in the little village church in Nazianzus. Determined but very sick, Gregory preaches the valedictory sermon of one who, in his own words, longs to "come to the source of the effulgence, when mirrors pass away into the light of truth."[139]

THE WESTERN THEOLOGIAN-PREACHERS —————

Hilary of Poitiers (ca. 315-68)

As the empire crumbles around it, the Western church survives, largely due to leaders who give solidity to its theology and focus to its organization. With the possible exception of Jerome,[140] these leaders are significant preachers and, leaving Ambrose and Augustine to be considered later, we examine the impressive preaching ministries of Hilary and Leo.

Hilary's Congregations

Little is known of Hilary's story except that he is converted in his middle years and is consecrated to his prestigious see in Gaul about 350. Incurring the wrath of Constantius, he is exiled to Phrygia where, although constant traveling renders pastoral ministry difficult, he continues to care for his congregations. His epistolary sermons and letters are fascinating because they reveal both the strengths and weaknesses of their recipients.

It is clear that Hilary's congregations are living out their faith "amidst the persecutions at the hand of man."[141] The divisive religious policies of Constantius and Julian make life difficult for catholic believers.[142] Hilary also suggests that pagan aggression has become so serious that he must prepare his hearers to face "a violent death," assuring them that their souls will "find rest with God their upholder."[143] He adds a warning that they also face internal "dangers to the soul" because, despite persecution, pagans are flocking into the churches and their theological naïveté makes them vulnerable to the "counsels of the ungodly."[144] They also bring with them many pagan attitudes, and in a revealing sentence, Hilary identifies the "sinners *who are abiding in the Church* — the greedy, the drunken, the brawlers, the wanton, the proud, hypocrites, liars, plunderers."[145]

Hilary's personal spiritual pilgrimage has taught him the vanity of riches,[146] and he loses no time in addressing materialism and its attendant vices. He condemns the greed of wealthy believers, noting that they are following the example of decadent clerics.[147] He exposes the popular obsession with frivolous amusement and gaudy display, reminding his congregations that the greed associated with such a lifestyle breeds violence and even murder.[148] His congregations are not immune from the sexual irregularities, marital infidelities and quarreling that plague other churches, and he urges his people to take Christ's "gentle yoke of meekness," for that alone can "press down the adulteries and fornications" and replace strife with peace.[149]

Hilary realizes that renewed life for his congregations must be rooted in dignified and joyous worship. He himself loves singing and is so impressed by the hymns he hears in Constantinople that he determines to write Latin hymns for his own people.[150] He forges a partnership between preaching and liturgy because his hymns make his theology accessible to his congregations as they sing the doctrines he teaches.

Hilary's Preaching

Hilary is not always systematic in his thought, and his great technical knowledge of Latin can produce a rather obscure, rhetorical style,[151] but when he is preaching, a more accessible side of his nature appears.[152] Coming to faith later in life, he still carries the ardor of a recent convert, gladly testifying that he is "inflamed with a passionate desire to apprehend God"[153] and filling his *Tractates on Psalms* with evangelistic fervor. His determination to be clearly understood sometimes renders his style repetitious, but he enlivens his sermons with illustrations drawn from his love of nature and with personal reminiscences.[154]

Hilary is always a *scriptural* preacher. He comes to faith as a result of studying the Bible and never loses his love for it,[155] regarding it as the stairway believers mount to enter the mysteries of God.[156] Before expounding a text, he insists that it be clearly read and firmly grasped even by "inattentive hearers and hasty readers."[157] Whether chosen passages require an "analytical" or "homiletical treatment," Hilary is just as painstaking in his exegesis.[158] Having established the content of the chosen text, Hilary launches into the type of allegorical interpretation of the passage which he has learned from Origen and adapted for his own use.[159] He believes, passionately, that the same Spirit who inspires the Scriptures also equips the preacher, revealing both the literal and mystical meaning of the text. For Hilary, the Old Testament, especially his beloved Psalms, is essentially *Christian* scripture since, as he puts it, "The doctrines of the Gospel were well-known to holy and Blessed David in his capacity as Prophet."[160]

There is a robust practicality about the spiritual guidance in Hilary's pastoral preaching. He has little interest in dividing congregations into "mystical" and "ordinary" believers and is somewhat skeptical about beatific visions of God.[161] He is not concerned with esoteric knowledge, believing that only when their empty philosophizings are "buried with Christ in Baptism" can his people find their "minds rested with assurance."[162] His sermons are intended to lead *all* his hearers to the joys of a fulfilling Christian life. They need to understand that God wants them to be happy and that, if they follow "the promptings of their natural instincts," they will lose true joy, both in this life and the next.[163] Their only hope is to embrace the Savior who has "offered himself to the death of the accursed, that he might break the curse of the Law," and thereafter to "make their lives one long prayer, by works acceptable to God."[164] Hilary is convinced that the clue to such joyous living lies in attaining *humility*, and he admits that he preaches on that theme "in a great number of places." He regards *kenosis* as an essential element of true Christology, and he reminds his hearers that they must emulate the "self-emptying" of Christ which they see paraded before them afresh at every Eucharist.[165]

It cannot be claimed that Hilary is in the first rank of preachers. His influence is probably limited by the late flowering of his faith, which denies the church the full power of a youthful enthusiasm. However, his contribution is far from negligible. His sermons may never achieve popular, lasting acclaim, but many of his ideas germinate in the minds of Ambrose and Augustine and so leave a permanent imprint upon the life of the church in the West.

Leo "the Great" (400-461)

Leo's Congregations

Little is known of Leo's life before his ordination and consecration as bishop of Rome in 440. He enters upon his duties humbly, amazed that "the Lord has been mindful of him," but any sense of personal inadequacy evaporates once he sees himself as Peter's successor with authority to direct the affairs of the whole church.[166] "When . . . we utter our exhortations in your ears, holy brethren," he tells his clergy, "believe that he (Peter) is speaking to us, whose representative we are."[167] He is *pastor pastorum*, and his abundant correspondence indicates the fastidious pastoral care he exercises over his clergy and congregations.

Leo's awareness of his exalted position endows him with a certain lofty aloofness, but in his preaching he works hard to create a bond with his "dearly beloved people," asking them to pray for him and to share important moments in his life.[168] The affection is genuine. Leo loves to see "the whole body of the faithful flocking together in order to give thanks to God," and he cherishes the diversity of "Christ's whole people engaging in the same duties, with all ranks and degrees, of either sex, co-operating with the same intent."[169] The "tears and pity" he feels for those whose "souls have been ruined and cheated" by heresy are real, and he is determined to save his people by the systematic preaching of sound doctrine.[170]

Leo regards his preaching as an extension of his pastoral ministry, and his sermons are carefully suited to the needs of his congregations. He is a popular preacher, whose brief, pithy homilies can attract congregations "too large for one church to hold them all," but he is not always rewarded with "splendid assemblages" of clergy and laity.[171] There are times when he complains that "the fewness of those present causes him much sadness of heart," and on at least one such occasion the assembled few are treated to a very brief discourse by their disgruntled bishop![172] Nevertheless, Leo is always ready to encourage his congregations and to commend "warmness of devotion" whenever he encounters it.[173]

Leo's churches are afflicted by the same sins and confusions with which we are now familiar. However, he plans to deal with them by vigorously enforcing doctrinal and disciplinary uniformity among the clergy so that they may purify the churches under their care. The plight of congregations infected with "the poison of falsehood"[174] is made worse by corrupt clergy who misappropriate church property, abandon smaller churches in search of career advancement, and even use armed force to impose their will upon their flocks.[175] Many clerics are poorly qualified and lack dedication, due, in Leo's mind, to the fact that "the sacred ministry has become polluted" by the ordination of slaves and *coloni*.[176] He is disturbed by reports that many married clergy are unfaithful to their wives and neglect their pastoral duties, and so, while grudgingly permitting his clergy to marry, he decrees that in the future not "even sub-deacons are to marry" and those of higher orders are to "bridle their uxorious desires."[177]

Of particular interest is the way Leo emphasizes the importance of the preaching ministry of his clergy, especially since the Western church appears generally cautious about nonepiscopal preaching.[178] Leo insists that no priest is "free to withhold from the people's ears instruction by sermon."[179] Preaching is to be regarded as a privilege because it is God who "fills the mouth of the preacher," so that faith may be established and mysteries revealed "by preaching the most holy gospel."[180] It is then that the Holy Spirit, "indwelling the saints," uses their "bodily ears" to enable the Word to "reach the inner hearing of their mind."[181] For Leo, preaching is an urgent matter because he believes that his congregations are under con-

tinual attack by Satan and his demons,[182] both by "open and bloody persecution" and by "corrupting" heresy.[183] The devil is trying to shatter the fellowship by infecting its members with spiritual pride, covetousness,
quarreling, and gossip. He distorts Christian fasts with false asceticism and
"mars by his deceitful arts" even the most holy festivals.[184]

Leo's Preaching

The content of Leo's sermons hinges upon his high view of the church and
of himself as the incumbent of Peter's charge. He is determined that his
congregations see themselves as divinely privileged, "remembering of what
Body they are members and to what head they are joined."[185] Before being
baptized, they have been "instructed by frequent sermons" to prepare
themselves for a place among the "innumerable multitude of those born to
God," embraced in "loving harmony" both by their fellow believers and the
blessed martyrs in heaven.[186] They now stand in an "unconquerable
strength of unity," sharing the faith of Peter the Rock, defended by his
prayers and led by his heir — Leo himself.[187]

The centrality of the church in Leo's thought ensures that he regards
the sermon as an essential constituent of the church's liturgy. He has un-
bounded reverence for "what is read in the sacred lections" accompanied
by an expository sermon.[188] For him, the "recurring" festivals are invalu-
able spurs to corporate devotion, and he delivers many of his finest sermons to celebrate the great ecclesiastical fasts and feasts.[189] Every act of
worship unites earthly congregations with "saints and the very angels," so
all may "exult" together, but it is the great festivals that provide the most
glorious opportunities for gladness and rejoicing.[190] By participating in
the feasts, congregations experience anamnesis and "relive" the great
salvific events, rejecting "temporal matters" and "fixing the mind on eternal things."[191]

In his preaching, Leo also links spiritual growth with fasting and self-
denial, the "publicly proclaimed celebrations" of the church's fasts which
offer congregations opportunities for "general purification."[192] He acknowledges that many wealthy members of his churches try hard to "keep
the commands of God," but he believes they stand in spiritual peril and
that fasting affords a most efficacious way of dealing with the dangers of
affluence.[193] However, he urges *all* his people to embrace self-discipline

but to be "reasonable in their fasting" because Lent is a time of increased satanic activity when the devil tries to lead them into spiritual pride.[194] No discipline "beyond their strength" will be asked of them, but they must ensure that their "fast" includes both body and soul and that it issues in godly actions.[195] Christians observe seasons of fasting "not with barren abstinence but in bountiful benevolence," since prayer, fasting, and almsgiving are "the three comprehensive duties of the Christian."[196]

Fasting is the door through which many blessings will flow into the churches, as love for God and others drives out disharmony and vengeance and redeems the communal life.[197] Clergy and laity will no longer indulge in shameful usury, and domestic harmony will be restored as "the lust of the flesh is tamed by chastity" and masters and slaves grow in mutual respect.[198] The Christian life, described in Leo's *Homily on the Beatitudes,* can then blossom in all its fullness, marked by Christlike humility and expressed in personal purity and generosity toward others.[199]

Leo believes that "true and devout worship" is inextricably bound up with godly living and sound doctrine.[200] These are the three principles of his preaching ministry, and he realizes all are necessary if his churches are to be purged. Consequently, he has to deal firmly with heretics, whom he unjustly links with the Jews as "the remnants of those still deceived by Satan," who uses their envy and lies to assault the Church.[201] The preaching of the heretics confuses believers by cunningly counterfeiting true doctrine,[202] and therefore Leo encourages his congregations to inform upon heretics "wherever they be hidden,"[203] not with vindictive fanaticism but with a sense of "religious grief" which mourns their sin and seeks their restoration.[204]

As an antidote to the assaults of false doctrine, Leo seeks to establish in his congregations a sound understanding of the gospel. His credo is set out in his famous *Tome,*[205] which energizes his preaching to produce a splendid blend of theological insight and pastoral guidance. He teaches his people that the equality of the three persons of the Trinity is not merely a matter of esoteric interest because all three are involved in their spiritual "restoration."[206] Christians must not allow themselves to be misled by heretical teachings which misrepresent the twofold nature of Christ, so clearly displayed in his earthly ministry and declared afresh in the church's liturgical cycle.[207] The salvation of Leo's hearers is dependent upon this truth since only by the divine becoming truly human was it possible to rescue humanity "from the Devil's bondage and from the depths of eternal death."[208] For them redemption becomes more than a single, historical act. It is a contemporaneous experience of divine grace, a living awareness of what God has done for them in Christ. It is here that Leo's emphasis upon the work of the Holy Spirit, the third element of his trinitarian teaching, comes into its own. He declares Whitsuntide "one of the chief feasts" because it celebrates the "indwelling Spirit" through whom the faith of the congregations is born and sustained.[209] It is the Spirit who initiates in them the process of spiritual growth, and those of them who "pursue it with eagerness" are assured of eventual "rest in God's peace."[210]

So it is that Leo combines ecclesiastical statesmanship and theological depth with memorable preaching. He establishes the sermon at the heart of the church's liturgy and ensures its place in the pastoral function of his clergy. In doing so, he prepares the way for three great giants of the pulpit who undertake the task of teaching their clergy how to become effective preachers.

"Delightful Persuaders"

The Homileticians

A great orator has truly said that "an eloquent man must so speak as to teach, to delight and to persuade. . . ." To teach is a necessity, to delight is a beauty, to persuade is a triumph.

Augustine, *De doctrina Christiana* 4.12.27

Preachers, Persuasion, and Rhetoric

In what Dudden calls an "age of magnificent preachers,"[1] sermons increasingly become an art form and preaching becomes an acquired skill. Although it is an ugly, clinical word, "homiletician" is the only word adequate to describe the genius of Ambrose, Augustine, and Chrysostom. It is only because they are wonderfully skilled both in the practice *and theory* of preaching that they are able to raise it to new heights.

I. H. Marshall observes that "the Christian preacher is an advocate . . . and, therefore, preaching is a form of persuasion,"[2] and it is the role of the preacher as *persuader* which becomes dominant in the fourth and fifth centuries. The notion of preaching as persuasion is far from new, having its roots in Scripture and tradition,[3] but as preachers' audiences continue to grow in diversity and intellectual discernment, the power to persuade becomes ever more vital. Christian preachers need to outshine their pagan rivals who are schooled in the art of persuasion.[4]

Although the greatest preachers have natural persuasive gifts, they realize that others need to learn the art.[5] The requisite tools for training are already available in classical, oratorical disciplines, since Aristotle has already identified the ability to influence decisions as the most desirable form of rhetorical eloquence.[6] Quintilian defines rhetoric as "the science of speaking well,"[7] and as its importance for Christian preaching gains new momentum, a permanent bond is forged between homiletic and rhetoric.[8] Some Christians distrust the alliance, but for the great preachers who are trained as rhetors, it seems natural to transfer their skills to the pulpit.[9] If they are to interpret Scripture and tradition correctly, preachers must master the discipline of *hermeneutics*,[10] and Augustine recommends the study of the "five offices of rhetoric" set out in Cicero's *Orator*.[11] It is in the work of the triumvirate that stands at the pinnacle of early Christian preaching that the bond between preaching and rhetoric appears in its most polished and persuasive form.

Ambrose (ca. 339-97)

Ambrose and His Congregations

When Ambrose reluctantly becomes bishop of Milan in 374, he gives his wealth to the poor and prepares himself for his new office by daily devotion and study. This symbolizes the dedication of a man who, although he commands the attention of the mighty, never forgets that he is primarily a pastor and preacher to his people.[12] The "great crowds" that gather to hear him may sometimes overawe him by their "immense and unprecedented numbers," but they do not deceive him. He knows that people can display pretended devotion,[13] and he never confuses plenitude with piety.

At first, Ambrose's congregations seem to experience little persecution.[14] They attract the crème of society, to whom Ambrose sometimes fearlessly addresses his sermons.[15] As even vacillating emperors bow to Ambrose's will, many influential people judge that their surest path to advancement is also to be seen in church on Sundays. Consequently, within the congregations there emerge elements of what we may term *pagano-Christians,* spiritual hybrids who flirt with the church and use it for their own ends.[16] Some come with political promotion in mind, others, perhaps less reprehensibly, come to marvel at the glories of the liturgy enriched by the seductive strains of Ambrose's hymns.[17]

Ambrose's former life of affluence, politics, and the law courts has equipped him to analyze his congregations with great skill, and the picture he paints is a revealing one. Before him he sees society ladies, "perspiring beneath loads of jewels and silks," and, nearby, arrogant plutocrats, surrounded by hordes of slaves whom they neglect and even flog to death.[18] He knows the splendid houses from which they come,[19] their lavish feasts of "exquisite viands brought from distant parts,"[20] and his eye searches his congregations for the indolent *parasites* who haunt the feasts in search of *dole.*[21] He has seen how drunkenness "causes the loss of innumerable souls" among his people, turning their feasts into orgies, corrupting soldiers and clerics alike, making tipsy women caper in the streets and so befuddling respectable folk that they cannot say their prayers.[22] He knows he is preaching not only to the bleary-eyed revelers who have just lost fortunes at the gaming tables, but also to the very usurers who have those gamblers in their power. He hears that even his clergy are scanning their congregations for impecunious worshipers to whom they may offer loans at extortionate rates.[23]

Ambrose acknowledges that "even in riches there is a place for virtue,"[24] and he is not sentimental about the "greedy beggars" who crowd the entrances of the churches. However, he also knows that poverty can make parents sell their children and even drive them to suicide, and he is disgusted by rich Christians who refuse to ease the needs of their fellow worshipers.[25] He has overheard their conversation, and incensed by their claim that it is "God's will that the poor should be in want," he bursts out: "a people weeps bitterly and you finger your jewelled goblet. Wretch!"[26]

Ambrose is under no illusion that "pagan-Christians" regard churches as little more than an extension of the bathhouses where they indulge in ribaldry and make their business deals. In church they boast of the rival merits of their prize dogs and horses and plot schemes of "legal robbery," safe in the knowledge that they are probably standing beside the very magistrates they need to bribe.[27] No wonder their behavior in church is disgusting as they disturb the devotions of sincere worshipers by their "groans, cries, coughing and laughter at the Mystery."[28] Such unruly elements will not be controlled without powerful direction by Ambrose and a highly trained corps of preachers.

Ambrose the Preacher

In his short history of preaching, O. C. Edwards incredibly dismisses Ambrose as not "distinctive enough in his preaching to merit extended consideration," but the evidence is on the side of writers who recognize him as "outstanding as a preacher and teacher."[29] Ambrose himself protests that he is "possessed of but moderate ability" but declares that he is driven to preach by "the great necessity laid upon him" to expound "the sayings of God entrusted to him."[30] He champions the preaching office of the bishop, frequently preaching every Sunday, with additional sermons for festivals and numerous courses of addresses.[31] He develops homiletic vocabulary[32] and ensures that his sermons are carefully edited, written down, and expanded for wider and more permanent use.[33]

Augustine's comment that Ambrose's "manner is less winning and harmonious" than that of his hero Faustus may reflect the fact that he has a voice "which a very little speaking will weaken" and that he follows his own advice and refuses to use "a theatrical accent" when preaching.[34] However, Latourette rightly affirms that Ambrose's preaching is both "earnest" and "eloquent." His distinctive and influential style[35] is often deeply emotional and overtly prayerful,[36] and Augustine himself is proof of its persuasive qualities. The young man who initially goes "only to hear how he spoke" is soon persuaded of "how truly he spoke."[37]

The persuasiveness of Ambrose's sermons has much to do with the empathy he has with his congregations. No matter how wicked they are, he never forgets that they too are "preachers of the Lord" to the world around them, and that the less educated among them need simple and direct speech.[38] He has an outstanding ability to "read" his congregations and to turn their moods to good advantage. When they are annoyed, he disarms their hostility: "I see that you are unusually disturbed and that you came closely watching me."[39] He compliments them when they "gather in immense numbers" and deftly touches upon delicate matters "pertaining to human nature" by crediting them with "understanding what . . . I do not want to say."[40]

Ambrose is not too proud to enrich his sermons with thoughts from Basil and Origen, and while claiming to frown upon humor in the pulpit, he enlivens his preaching with sly, comical touches.[41] He can turn a pretty phrase and leaves his hearers with memorable aphorisms. "The Devil's snare does not catch you unless you are first caught by the devil's bait."

"Sin is an old custom — as old as Adam."[42] His preaching pulsates with illustrative material. Pugilists and charioteers, physicians and prostitutes all
find their way into his sermons and jostle there with illustrations taken
from the natural world,[43] popular legends, the saints,[44] pagan stories,[45]
and Ambrose's personal experiences. However, above all, Ambrose is a biblical preacher, and his sermons are saturated in scriptural allusions and
references.

Most of Ambrose's sermons are essentially expositions of Scripture,
based upon minute dissection of the text, but he learns from Origen how
to present weighty material in digestible form by using series of homilies
like his *Hexameron* delivered as Lenten addresses. He arouses his hearers'
interest by selecting little-known texts and seems especially happy when
expounding intriguing themes from the Old Testament,[46] which he sees as
a Christian library, yielding its riches when interpreted *literally, morally,
and mystically*.[47] Ambrose's allegorical approach earns him Dudden's censure for being "too subjective, capricious and arbitrary,"[48] but Simonetti
observes that Ambrose's "exegesis takes the form exclusively of preaching
(and) has pastoral interests," and it is that pastoral concern which saves
him from flights of hermeneutical fantasy.[49]

The clue to Ambrose's pastoral preaching is that he sees churches as
places of spiritual healing where the disease of sin is cured through the
penitential system and sinners are speedily and gently "restored to the
communion of the Church" rather than being excluded and condemned.[50]
He wants his people to know that God "promises His mercy to all," that
even postbaptismal sins are forgiven, and that the worst of sinners may be
restored to their congregations, "washed in the tears of the multitude."[51]
Ambrose's pastoral concern compels him to preach fiercely against the
"hydra" of heresy which is attacking his congregations and "rending the
holy vesture of the Church."[52] Typically, but sadly, he includes Jews with
heretics as threats to the church, but he does urge his people not to retali-
ate against those who attack them.[53]

To counteract the wiles of the heretics, Ambrose produces a remarkable series of sermons and treatises, later developed as the five volumes of
De fide. Although it is a considerable work of trinitarian theology, its evangelistic and pastoral origins frequently reveal themselves. "He took to
Himself my grief. I preach His Cross." "No military eagles, no flights of
birds, here lead the van of our army but Thy Name, Lord Jesus, and Thy
worship."[54] Ambrose uses his sermons to explain the Holy Spirit's involve-

ment in believers' redemption and growth, "burying all wickedness" in their baptism, sealing them to possess Christ's bright image and then feeding them in the eucharistic elements.[55] It is for this reason that penitent sinners must be "at once restored to the heavenly sacraments" which embrace them in the company of those bound together by "communion in the mysteries."[56]

Nevertheless, Ambrose insists that the waters of baptism are "of no avail for future salvation" without "the preaching of the Cross," and he reminds his hearers that the salvation Christ "won for them" by his sacrificial death requires that they live Christlike lives.[57] To help his congregations meet this challenge, Ambrose gives them a simple rule for Christian living, and he bases it upon the notion of *modestia*.[58] This is derived from the Greek concept of σωφροσύνη and is variously translated as "prudence," "reasonableness," and "moderation." It is this quality which is to control every aspect of living, from the way believers say their prayers and exercise their charity to the way they walk and talk.[59] It is to guide the pastoral skills of the clergy and, especially, govern the deportment of Christian women, both within the churches and outside them.[60]

Against this background, Ambrose tackles the two great pastoral issues confronting his congregations — economic disparity among their members and issues of sexuality. He preaches a series of sermons on usury and avarice, stressing that the churches can never be a sign of the "justice and goodwill which holds society together" as long as Christians "extort from one another or gain money unjustly."[61] He claims there is ample money in the pockets of believers, both rich and poor, to "help those of the household of faith" by "tearing up debtors' bonds," caring for the sick, and visiting the impoverished.[62] He instructs his clergy to report cases of need because theirs is an age of "common fear, when everything is dreaded from the barbarian movement," and believers can be carried off by marauders, leaving congregations to care for orphans and raise money for ransoms.[63]

Ambrose hears of antinomians in his churches who "preach pleasure and esteem chastity to be of no use," and he knows they are augmenting those malign pagan influences which create the "rust of wantonness and lust which are dimming the vision" of the people.[64] How is such sexual decadence to be resisted? Although Ambrose protests that he neither "discourages marriage" nor forbids remarriage, he is distrustful of both and commends celibacy and virginity as the only true antidotes to sexual peril.[65] His doctrine of *modestia* seems forgotten as he describes marriage as "a galling burden" and expatiates upon the "painful ministrations and services due to their husbands from wives" which lead to insane extravagance and the sorrows of motherhood.[66] He congratulates "happy virgins" who "know no such torments" since they escape marriage, which, to his mind, is worse than a slave auction.[67]

Some women, like Ambrose's own sister Marcellina, take the veil, and he praises young people who voluntarily choose that path, urging Christian mothers to "avoid nuptial intercourse" except for procreating children who may later embrace celibacy.[68] He challenges the women in his congregation to experience the blessings of celibacy by staying at home and adopting a regular pattern of daily prayer, psalm singing, and meditation. Thus they will avoid the pitfalls of socializing, dancing, and excessive drinking.[69] In fact, they ought never to venture out unaccompanied "except for divine service," and when in church they are modestly to remain silent and to concentrate on "the divine lesson."[70] Ambrose instructs his clergy to set their congregations a good example in such matters. They are to keep themselves "free from the enticements of various pleasures" and to ensure that their ministry is "not defiled by conjugal intercourse" and the "begetting of children," as has happened in "some out-of-the-way places."[71] With the advantage of hindsight, such instructions appear shockingly arrogant, demeaning, and repressive, but Ambrose firmly believes and preaches that only extreme measures can deliver Christian men and women from the tentacles of pagan sexual attitudes.

Ambrose the Teacher of Preachers

Ambrose believes that trained, preaching clergy are pivotal in his plans to purify and invigorate congregational life. He has a very practical approach to the matter, and although probably the simplest of the three great homileticians, he shares with Zeno of Verona the honor of providing "the first major homiletical documents in Latin."[72] While advising young presbyters modestly to make way for their elders, he encourages his clergy to preach[73] with care because, for him, preaching is not a Christian version of pagan rhetoric but the clear communication of the gospel by conscientious pastors. Therefore, he includes homiletics in his *De officiis ministrorum*, amid instructions about obedience to bishops, respect for fellow clergy, prudence in social relationships, and dedication in "reading and prayer."[74]

The practical presentation of the preacher's material is of great importance, and Ambrose insists that his clergy pay proper attention to elocution. Obliquely, his instructions give a picture of the kind of effete oratory to which many congregations are being treated. He insists that his preachers replace "languid, feeble and womanish tones" with "quality, rhythm and a manly vigour." He warns them to avoid "effeminate gestures of the body" and to remember that "what is boorish or rustic" will be quite unacceptable to many in their congregations.[75] He declares his opposition to "theatrical" posturing and humor in the pulpit and condemns "vain persons" who parade their eloquence to earn the applause of their congregations.[76]

Ambrose instructs his clergy to remember that sermons that are too brief leave congregations unsatisfied, whereas overlengthy sermons are "wearisome and stir up anger."[77] He reminds preachers that it is vital to use appropriate language when "speaking of the holy Scripture," and at least in later years he distrusts flamboyant rhetoric, claiming that "the finery and paint of words" simply "weakens the force of what is said."[78] He advises his clergy to follow his example and to deal with difficult subjects in series of sermons, and he applies the principle of *modestia* to their language, urging them to use words that are "plain and simple, clear and evident, not too refined nor rough in style."[79]

Ambrose is not without his faults. His self-confidence sometimes borders on arrogance and his judgment in some areas is far from sound. Nevertheless, he remains a fine preacher and homiletician who still deserves the accolade accorded him by Foakes-Jackson well over a century ago. "Never was an office of such responsibility filled by a man more fitted to wield it for what he considered to be the good of others, than was the see of Milan by Ambrose."[80]

Augustine of Hippo (354-430)

Augustine the Preacher

The Style of Augustine's Preaching

The congregations to whom Augustine preaches are very similar to those described by Ambrose, and there is no need for us to reexamine them. Instead, we may turn immediately to the preacher himself, whose five hundred extant sermons reveal "the inordinate brilliance and penetration of his mind."[81] That is no mean achievement in an age when crowds flock to hear popular orators as if going to the theater, and even fashionable lawyers employ personal claques to enhance their oratorical reputations.[82] Augustine records that in churches too, "great multitudes assemble," their numbers so swollen by ill-behaved "crowds of heathen" that they can scarcely breathe.[83]

The bravura performances of preachers like Severian are legendary among the sermon tasters who appreciate a fine turn of phrase and a polished performance.[84] They come to hear classical rhetoric, perfect as "a seamless robe" and pleasant as "a garden . . . decorated . . . with neatly planted shrubs of digression."[85] To such purists, Augustine must be a disappointment, for he bends and breaks many rhetorical rules in the service of the gospel,[86] but he certainly knows how to hold the attention of his congregations. Like Cicero, he believes that orators must both "teach" *(docere)* and "delight" *(delectare)*, and he is not afraid of his role as an *entertainer.*[87] However, he is not deceived by the plaudits of his congregations, knowing it is "easy to applaud the preacher" and that such exhibitions are no guarantee that "wicked men running to the church" have "heard and obeyed the Shepherd's voice."[88]

Augustine's health is not robust and sometimes his voice is "feeble" and he is "exhausted by the heat."[89] Nevertheless, he often preaches five times a week and twice a day,[90] establishing remarkable rapport with his hearers, even when he has to scold them.[91] The secret of his success is that he makes allies of his congregations, identifying himself with them and addressing them as "we" and "holy brethren."[92] He is realistic about their limitations but he never belittles them, remembering that Christ is at work among them.[93] He commands the respect of intellectuals by his references to classical writers and Roman history,[94] but he also has time for slower learners, using words they can understand, asking them if he has "expounded the text too hastily," and repeating important points.[95]

Possidius says those who hear Augustine "speak in church" receive great blessing,[96] and it is because he has the truly great preacher's gift of making individuals feel that he is addressing them personally. He makes himself vulnerable in their presence, asking for their support and never pretending omniscience,[97] apologizing when he feels he has not done justice to a subject and promising to return to it later.[98] He tries to give his congregations a good self-image, commending them for "intentness of purpose" and "stretching their minds."[99] He constantly monitors their reactions and is ready to change his style and subject if he feels attention is flagging or to call for greater attention if he thinks his hearers have not understood his argument.[100]

Unlike classical rhetors who do not regard brevity as a virtue, Augustine never forgets that his congregations "stand for a long time" and he apologizes if sometimes he "speaks somewhat lengthily."[101] His sermons are recorded in different ways, and the written versions are not an accurate guide to the duration of the originals.[102] Although he sometimes petulantly complains about "the stress of time," he is ready to promise his hearers "few words" if they are too hot or tired to concentrate.[103] He then signals ahead that the end of the sermon is near, although sometimes words such as "To be brief; that I may conclude this sermon, brethren," simply introduce a new and lengthy discourse![104]

Augustine is always trying to seize his hearers' attention with stories, metaphors, similes, and aphorisms. "Hope" is an egg; the Scriptures are "the hem of Christ's garment"; divine correction is "cauterizing a wound"; human life is a leaky ship and human beings "frailer than glass."[105] Rowe rightly refutes Burleigh's claim that there is an "absence of illustrations from life" in Augustine's sermons.[106] They are filled with a vivid array of lawyers, gladiators, circus performers, wrestlers, and beggars.[107] He takes his hearers into doctors' surgeries, farmyards, orchards, and streets where urchins play in the mud.[108] He likens their redemption to being ransomed from barbarian marauders and compares the divine Son to the brightness of the fire burning in their hearths.[109] Like Quintilian, Augustine believes in the persuasive power of humor,[110] and sometimes he enlivens his sermons with mischievous witticisms which probably stir his volatile congregations to raucous laughter.[111] However, if the presentation of Augustine's sermons sometimes has a light touch, their content certainly does not.

The Content of Augustine's Preaching

Augustine declares that "the words of the Lord are always sweet," for he loves to preach from the Bible and never doubts that preaching is, at its heart, pure scriptural exegesis.[112] He decrees that the lectionary "must not be altered" so that the appointed passages are firmly linked to the preacher's discourses, and he chooses his texts and compares translations with great care.[113] He knows his Bible well and generally quotes Scripture from memory when preaching, only calling for the text to be handed to him when passages are very long or total accuracy is required.[114]

Augustine never forgets how, in his youth, Ambrose's allegorical exegesis "drew aside the mystic veil and spirituality, laying open" the Scriptures, but he insists it is important to differentiate between "figurative" and "literal" meanings.[115] Augustine's approach to allegory develops, but Goldinghay grasps an essential point when he says that for Augustine "the importance of allegory lay in its capacity to respect and release scripture's power as God's word."[116] He seizes upon the usefulness of allegory as a homiletic tool, especially in the exposition of the Old Testament, since all "Scripture is written for Christ" and the gospel is essentially the fulfillment of prophecy.[117] The Psalms concern Christ and are written for Christian worship, so Augustine asks soloists to sing appropriate passages before he expounds them. The Song of Songs is a Solomonic prophecy about the coming of Christ and the beauty of his heroine-bride, the church, so Augustine feels free to use it in that way.[118]

Although he utilizes pagan ideas, in his heart Augustine prizes the principle of *sola Scriptura* as the source of pure beliefs and a sure bastion against the attacks of "heretics, heathens and Jews."[119] Rowe points out that Augustine is "one of the few leading figures in Christian history" whose teaching "has come down to us in the form of transcripts of sermons,"[120] because he sees the pulpit as the focus of true doctrine and the scourge of heresy.[121] To survey the doctrine set out in the sermons would be, in effect, to examine Augustinian theology in its entirety, which is far beyond our prescribed boundaries, but we need to consider the pastoral effects of that theology. Augustine's doctrine informs the practical guidance given to congregations, whom he deems to have entered the only sphere of salvation, the body of "the whole Christ" and the sanctuary of true doctrine.[122]

Augustine believes that an important function of his preaching is to alert and encourage his congregations who are facing troubled times. They are still under attack from angry pagans who resent their claim that the empire is being punished by multiple disasters and their refusal to give blind obedience to a state which "enjoins actions against God."[123] Moreover, Augustine believes that the situation is being exploited by the "gospel-hating" Jews who have "made a unity" with heretics and heathens in "the kingdom of the devil" to attack the churches.[124]

The bellicose notes sounded by Augustine give credence to Averil Cameron's accusation that he is among the preachers who foment the fury of monastic extremists and Christian mobs.[125] Although Augustine eschews violence,[126] we know that his preaching is sometimes attended by disorder, especially when he describes the sufferings of the martyrs, and we also know that Christians *did* attack synagogues and pagan temples.[127] In view of the spiritual immaturity of many in Augustine's audiences, it seems quite possible that some are tempted to go out from their churches in a mood of "righteous indignation" to attack the enemies of the gospel.

However, this is not Augustine's intention. He wants to make his people understand that there is a distinctively Christian modus vivendi they must display in the midst of hostility and social disintegration. His series of sermons *De sermone Domini in monte* sets out the moral requirements of this Christian lifestyle, but first the people must understand that the prerequisite of the new life is a radical transformation of their human nature. They have been spiritually mutilated by Adam's fall and are "debtors to God" and deserve punishment here and eternal chastisement hereafter.[128] Their situation is made worse by their total inability to save themselves, but God has offered them hope in Christ. He has achieved their salvation by submitting to unjust death at the hands of the devil, showing his redeeming love upon his cross.[129] He alone is the loving physician who can cure their spiritual ills if only they will commit themselves to him.[130]

Having himself entered Christianity through the door of an intense, personal encounter with Christ,[131] Augustine covets that intimate faith for his hearers. "I plead, I do not discuss . . . give in your name for baptism that you may know with me what is meant; 'Knock and it shall be opened to you.'"[132] This act of repentant commitment will initiate their spiritual pilgrimage. "Walk by humility that you may come to eternity," says Augustine; "Christ-God is the country to which we go; Christ-Man is the way whereby we go."[133] The Christian life is an *imitatio Christi* in which believers walk in Christ's footsteps and take his earthly life and glorification as their model.[134] Some will tread the path of "active" faith like Peter, others will emulate John and progress by the way of contemplation,[135] but through Christ all the redeemed will become "equal to the angels of God."[136] However, Augustine stresses that believers travel, not singly, but in convoy as members of the church of Christ. The congregation is the sphere of spiritual growth within which individual believers are "fed like crying babies at the breast of the catholic church," sustained by the sacraments and cleansed by repentance and absolution until they "arrive at last at maturity and life in perfect happiness."[137]

However, this emphasis upon corporeity presents Augustine the preacher with a problem. He frequently warns his congregations against the "snares" of Pelagianism[138] because it challenges God's sovereign right to apportion his grace as he chooses and to select the redeemed. Since many of Augustine's hearers reject God's gracious offer, he can only conclude that his congregations consist of two preordained groups, the *elect* and the *rejected*.[139] A further complication is that the two groups are not clearly defined, since "many who receive the sacraments" are not of "the number of the elect" and their identity will not be revealed until the day of judgment.[140] The intricacies of Augustine's doctrine of *predestination* cannot concern us here,[141] but in practice he seems to cut the pastoral Gordian knot by treating *all* his hearers as elect until proved otherwise. He concludes that it is not preachers' task to identify the redeemed who, themselves, "sometimes do not know" of their blessings, but to be content with the knowledge that "the Shepherd knows them."[142] Preachers are to concentrate upon guiding *all* believers along the path of salvation, and Augustine turns his mind to the practicalities of this task.

The most obvious way of coexisting with pagan society is to remain aloof from it, and Augustine certainly advises his congregations to "depart from the wicked in heart" and avoid flirting with pagan religion in any guise.[143] However, he knows that in practice Christians' lives are interconnected with the pagan world, and therefore they have no alternative but to seek "the conversion of the carnal" by showing that "the Christian religion is concerned with a just and virtuous life."[144] They are to be visibly different from neighbors whose lives revolve around "sorceries, the stage, the chariot-races, and the wild-beast fight," so that eventually the theaters will empty and "go away for very shame."[145]

Congregations are to distance themselves from the popular worship of power and riches, even though wealthy members may find this difficult.[146] Augustine says that once they have freed themselves by making "God to be the guardian of their gold," they will be able to demonstrate honesty in business and generosity in charity.[147] They will "let their hospitality and good works abound," welcoming the poor to their churches and glorifying God by embracing even strangers in their benevolence.[148] Such continuous, small acts, Augustine whimsically assures them, will keep their lives buoyant, just as constant pumping keeps a ship afloat.[149]

However, it is in the realm of sexual relationships that Christians are to shine most brightly in a dark world. Long before the revelations of Freud, Augustine understands from personal experience that sexuality is a primal force. He tells his congregations that their sexual desires are "the punishment of Adam from whom they spring," a burden to be borne and a temptation to be neutralized.[150] For this reason, voluntary, perpetual virginity is the safest and finest response, and in heaven all kinds of virginity will "shine diversely, their brilliance unequal but the heaven the same."[151] Those already married may seek the haven of "wedded chastity," and if that seems impossible, they must engage in intercourse "regretfully" and only as "necessary for the procreation of children."[152] Once bereavement has freed them from the sexual demands of marriage, women must embrace "holy widowhood" and so attain the third form of blessed virginity.[153]

Thus cleansed, the Christian home will be a public testimony to the purity and power of the gospel. Parents will live in fidelity, mutual affection, and respect, renowned as good citizens and wise guides for their children.[154] The whole household will be so radiant with faith that even the loss of a beloved child will be borne with fortitude and hope.[155]

Augustine reveals himself as a prince among preachers who combines elegance of style with those touches of informality which endear preachers to their congregations. George Lawless rightly judges him to be "conceivably the greatest spokesman for Christianity between Saint Paul and Martin Luther."[156] He is both a towering theologian and a sensitive pastor, and these qualities permeate his sermons, but it is time to turn to another facet of his genius and see him functioning as a homiletician.

Augustine the Teacher of Preachers

Augustine preaches because his own faith was "breathed into him through the ministry of a preacher" and he wants others to reap the rewards of the gospel.[157] "Watering the sheep," he says, is a vital element of "the pastor's office," and clergy must never "defraud" their people.[158] He is "filled with laughter and joy" whenever he thinks of bishops and clergy preaching to congregations throughout the empire[159] — but all is not well.

It appears that bishops and clergy need to be reminded that they are not superior to the congregations.[160] Augustine hears that some exploit their pastoral office for personal gain and in their preaching have become "people pleasers" in their "desire for human applause."[161] They must be taught to preach with "pastoral watchfulness" and to remember that theirs is a humbling, divine office[162] which demands profound inner spirituality and holiness of living.[163] However, even this is not enough. They must also learn to be skillful preachers,[164] retaining the "intimacy and familiarity" of the earliest *homilia*[165] while earning the respect of the most sophisticated congregations. Convinced that sermons need careful preparation, Augustine writes two textbooks, *De catechizandis rudibus* and *De doctrina Christiana* 2-4, in which he shows himself to be the true father of "homiletics seen as a distinct branch of study."[166]

Although primarily designed to help the gifted catechist Deogratius,[167] *De catechizandis rudibus* contains valuable advice for preachers in general who have to address audiences of "of all classes" and establish "a common brotherhood" with them.[168] Augustine admits that he is "almost always displeased with his own discourses," but he reminds preachers that it is their *congregations'* perception of their sermons which is truly important, so they must heed their hearers' reactions, neither being "flattered by reverence" nor angered by "correction."[169] Like Aristotle before him, Augustine urges speakers to study their audiences carefully so that they may address them appropriately.[170] They approach their congregations prayerfully and read their emotions skillfully, sensing when the message has been understood and when it needs further, patient explanation.[171] Augustine warns that people may be "taught and pleased but still not consent," so preachers must know when to persevere until their hearers are "victoriously persuaded" by the indwelling power of Christ.[172]

To assist this process of persuasion Augustine encourages preachers to enrich their sermons with pagan culture. Since *all* truth "belongs to the Master," they may harness pagan insights to the chariot of the gospel,[173] but their main inspiration must always be the Scripture as "received by all the catholic church." Preachers are to understand Scripture thoroughly, memorizing its words and mastering the Greek and Hebrew of its text.[174] To help them, Augustine produces many exegetical aids, and Simonetti rightly describes *De doctrina Christiana* as essentially "a treatise on biblical hermeneutics."[175] In it Augustine deals at length with the figurative and literal interpretation of Scripture,[176] so that preachers may avoid the "wretched slavery" of trying to interpret "figurative expressions" literally. He shows them how to use less obscure texts to illuminate difficult ones,[177] but knowing how easily good homiletic material is ruined by poor presentation, he also sets about improving their practical skills.

Augustine avoids imposing "inflated" Sophist rhetoric upon his preachers because it will hamper their prime task of "speaking so that they will be understood."[178] He wants them to emulate Paul and the prophets rather than Gorgias or Isocrates, even if sometimes that must mean "neglecting a more cultivated language" in the cause of clarity.[179] Nevertheless, his hero Cicero has taught him that rhetoric is concerned with *persuasion,*[180] and he realizes that since preachers are also persuaders, they may have much to learn from rhetors, providing that rhetoric is the servant and not the master.

Aristotle's "three factors of persuasion" plus the insights of Quintilian provide a remarkably useful framework for examining Augustine's blend of homiletics and rhetoric.[181] Aristotle maintains[182] that effective persuasion depends upon three factors — *ethos* (the character of the speaker), *pathos* (the emotions aroused by the speaker), and *logos* (the power of the speaker's speech and argument) — and Augustine adapts these for the guidance of his preachers.

With good reason, Augustine places great emphasis upon *ethos* in the training of preachers. Lucian's satirical tale of the unscrupulous preacher Peregrinus parodies "real life" situations in which "wicked clerics" are causing congregations to reject the ministry of honest preachers.[183] Augustine's solemn admonition is a necessary one. "Whatever may be the majesty of the style," he writes, "the life of the speaker will count for more in securing the hearers' compliance."[184] He also understands the importance of *pathos* and advocates emotional openness between preachers and their congregations who need to be moved as well as instructed.[185] He urges preachers to use "great vigour of speech, emphases and reproaches and . . . all other means of rousing the emotions," and never to forget the power of sermon illustrations.[186] Nevertheless, he knows that sometimes even the appeal to emotion proves insufficient to convince the hearer, and then "nothing remains but to subdue him by the power of eloquence."[187] Therefore, Augustine reserves some of his profoundest thoughts for *logos,* the power of speech. Quintilian has taught generations of orators to study *grammatiae,* "the theory of correct speech,"[188] and Augustine understands that his preachers also need to learn to appreciate the importance of words.

Augustine begins by making the obvious point that preachers must communicate in the correct language, and he rejoices that the gospel is preached "in various tongues to nations far and wide."[189] However, the lingua franca in the West is Latin, and Augustine, who admires "pure Latin," expects his preachers to be competent in the language.[190] Nevertheless, whatever language preachers use, they must use words correctly. Augustine is fascinated by words, explaining their nuances, toying with their meanings, indulging in wordplays,[191] and in a remarkable foray into the world of linguistics, he attempts to analyze the very nature of words. He says they are essentially *signs,* entities which "over and above the impression they make on our senses, cause something else to come into the mind."[192] Being ephemeral, words have to be preserved in writing,[193] but preachers reverse that process by turning written words into speech, and so they must be careful to make correct use of punctuation and pronunciation.[194] Nevertheless, Augustine has something more than correct enunciation in mind.

One of Augustine's most thoughtful contributions to the study of homiletics is his consideration of *style,* which Mary Lyons helpfully defines as the "texture and design" of a sermon in which the "principal element . . . is its language . . . selected by the author."[195] Knowing the value of variety in the pulpit, Augustine instructs his preachers to "vary their speech with all types of style,"[196] and he advocates three main styles of delivery — *submisse, temperate,* and *granditer.*[197] The "subdued tone" *(submisse)* is especially effective when preachers want to "sway their hearers" by using a quiet, confidential approach, and the "temperate style" *(temperate)* is the proper medium for exhortation.[198] However, the "grand manner" *(granditer)* is the style appropriate to "the persuasion of minds." It is "carried along by its own impetus" and, being made "forceful with emotions of the spirit," lays hold of its hearers' emotions and moves them to tears.[199] By using these various styles, preachers find that "the impetus of their speech will ebb and flow like the sea" and so retain the attention of their hearers.[200]

It is estimated that Augustine preached almost eight thousand sermons, and it is not surprising that they are sometimes uneven in content and unfortunate in tone. However, there can be no doubt that he is a truly great preacher. Trevor Rowe observes that Augustine incorporates "the best of the classical rhetorical tradition into the art of the sermon,"[201] and we have seen how this enriches his own preaching and, through his tuition, the preaching of his students.

John "Chrysostom" (ca. 347-407)

Chrysostom and His Congregations

Chrysostom's ministry in Antioch and Constantinople touches two very different communities,[202] and yet there are similarities between their congregations. He claims that in both cities large numbers of Christians attend worship and share in the affluence of the societies which surround them.[203] His sermons reveal much about the social composition of his congregations which, he declares, no longer consist only of "slaves and women, nurses and eunuchs" but now attract "rich men and potentates," society matrons decked in gold accompanied by their delicate teenage daughters.[204] Besides the visiting clergy and monks who come to hear Chrysostom preach, his auditors include a sizable contingent of semipagan "sermon-tasters" and minor imperial officials seeking to enhance their career prospects by ostentatious church attendance. There are dilettante socialites wishing to see and be seen in the latest fashions, and at times of crisis even "whoremongers and effeminate become religious" and join the congregations.[205]

It is suggested that congregations like Chrysostom's are drawn mainly from affluent groups, including the nouveaux riches he mocks for their fraudulent, aristocratic airs.[206] However, he also mentions tradesmen, artisans, merchants and laborers, shopkeepers, cooks and blacksmiths, shoemakers, plowmen, dyers, braziers,[207] and the soldiers, whom he prizes especially,[208] together with multitudes of slaves, ladies' maids and nurses for the children for whom he has particular affection.[209] Sometimes representatives from rural churches visit the cities, and Chrysostom, impressed by their simple lifestyle, welcomes them as "a people foreign to us in language but in harmony with us concerning faith."[210] Notably, many poor people are drawn to the churches, some venturing inside while others beg at the doors, prompting Chrysostom's eloquent appeals for charity.[211]

Chrysostom's ambivalent relationship to the women who throng his churches is especially intriguing.[212] His picture of sin as a hideous woman and assertion that the "sex has incurred blame" by their descent from Eve seem to support Kelly's view that "John is an incorrigible sexist."[213] However, Chrysostom's attitude toward women is complex and deserves more careful consideration, especially since it may be influenced by a disquieting awareness of his own sexuality. His sermons show that he appreciates feminine charms and he holds women in high regard.[214]

Chrysostom clearly enjoys describing beautiful women[215] and notes their flirtatious "trailing garments, tripping feet and drooping necks," honestly admitting that "it is not so great trouble not to look upon beautiful women as it is, while looking, to restrain oneself."[216] One of his sermons contains a minutely observed account of current fashions for young ladies and their passion for golden hair.[217] He describes with obvious pleasure the young women he sees in his congregations, "damsels, not yet twenty years old in inner chambers full of sweet ointments and perfumes, reclining on soft couches, themselves soft in nature,"[218] and he protests that such divinely made creatures need no cosmetics to "besmear them with red and white earth."[219] He fulminates against women who abuse their God-given beauty by making their lips "like a bear's mouth dyed with blood, their eyebrows blackened as with kitchen smut, and their cheeks whitened with dust like the walls of a tomb."[220]

Chrysostom's attitude toward the women in his congregations is profoundly affected by childhood experiences. After his father's early death, young John is raised by his saintly mother Anthusa, who gives him such a noble view of women that he cannot tolerate violence toward them, be they matrons, wives, empresses, or prostitutes.[221] The example of Anthusa, who remains celibate although widowed at twenty, engenders in Chrysostom a special regard for widows. He declares that their tears "can open heaven itself," and he preaches sermons specifically designed to encourage them.[222] By today's standards, his attitude to women leaves much to be desired, but at least he may be given credit for preaching that *all* men are to respect *all* women and that *all* women are to respect themselves. He seems to struggle with the theological fiat that women must be condemned for the sin of their ancestress Eve. He tells women they are "not to be cast down" by this disability since, by "bringing up children," they may receive "another opportunity of salvation."[223]

Chrysostom reluctantly acknowledges that many of the women in his congregations do not live up to his vision but prefer, instead, to indulge themselves like Eudoxia and her licentious ladies at court. He addresses them directly, urging them to rise to his image of the perfect Christian woman and to be wary of pitfalls.[224] He warns "virgins and wives" not to dance at public functions, "leaping and bounding and disgracing common nature." He reminds them that the devil who danced in Salome still enters godly women even if they try to escape detection by pirouetting and singing "love songs instead of psalms" in their own homes.[225] In an attempt to appeal to such women, Chrysostom preaches no fewer than five sermons on the Woman at the Well, presenting her as an icon of women whose past life "makes one blush" but whose conversion changes them into glorious advertisements for the faith.[226]

Chrysostom's sermons may sound sexist and condescending to the modern ear, but within his own lights they are honest attempts to raise the image of Christian women. He commends those who exchange "costly jewellery and anointing with perfumes" for the garments of godliness, and he admires the domestic harmony achieved by wives who "adorn their souls with modesty, piety and the management of their houses." Although he accepts that women live with an inherited spiritual disability, he believes that with determination they are "in no way hindered by their sex in the course of virtue."[227] He rejoices that, once indolent, young women are now so consumed "with Christ's flame" that they accept spiritual disciplines and "labour far harder than their handmaids" at domestic chores.[228] He understands the religious fervor of those whose repentance leads them to "fasting and lying on the ground in ashes," but he is filled with concern for them and warns them that the devil may use such ascetic excesses to unbalance their delicate constitutions.[229]

Chrysostom's concern for women exemplifies his desire to weld all the component elements of his congregations into loving Christian fellowships, regardless of sex or social class. He pleads, "Say not, 'Such a one is a blacksmith, a shoemaker, he is a ploughman, he is a fool' and so despise him."[230] "Do you not see that all of us are in need of each other? The soldier of the artisan, the merchant of the husbandman, the slave of the freeman, the master of the slave, the poor man of the rich, the rich man of the poor, he who has no work of him that gives alms, he who bestows of him who receives."[231] However, in the traditionally stratified society of the empire, Chrysostom's task is a formidable one and his sermons show vividly just how far his efforts are frustrated. His Constantinople sermons are more censorious than those preached in Antioch,[232] but in both places the scandals he observed are remarkably similar.[233]

Chrysostom notes that whenever dangers threaten or the pomp of Christian festivals attracts, "the forum will be empty and the churches full," with congregations "resembling the broad expanse of the sea," but once emergencies and festivals pass, "not even the smallest part of that multitude gathers."[234] Many worshipers' attachment to the church is of the most casual kind. Men who would never miss a meeting of their "club" feel no compunction about absenting themselves from worship,[235] and even neophytes preparing for baptism play truant to attend the hippodrome. Some worshipers make little more than annual appearances,[236] and Chrysostom admits that all his "prolonged discourses" have "done no good" and that any excuse for absence is now deemed acceptable, from complaints about the summer heat to personal dislike of presiding clergymen.[237] Household slaves neglect to evangelize their companions, and their masters, who would disdain to go to the baths or the theater without their retinue, never bother to bring their slaves or even their sons to church.[238]

Irregular attendance at worship is not the only blight upon the life of the churches. Many regular worshipers at the two-hour-long services enter with ostentatious displays of devotion, ritually washing their hands and stooping to kiss the porch as though, says Chrysostom, "constant church-going" in itself is the heart of religion.[239] Once inside, they employ exaggerated "gestures of body and loudness of voice" to display their devotion, some even "throwing themselves prostrate and striking the ground with their foreheads."[240] During seasons of fasting, many who do not observe the required discipline still "wear the masks of those that fast," lest they be accused of impiety, and they ensure that they are seen at the "vigils and holy hymn-singing" associated with great festivals. Such people, complains Chrysostom, "surpass the hypocrisy" of the Pharisees, and since they act "merely out of vanity,"[241] the voluble prayers which issue from their "unwashed mouths" have no "earnestness or inwardness" and simply serve to annoy those around them.[242]

Many worshipers deserve Chrysostom's strictures. He sees them pushing each other aside to be near to the preacher, making churches more like "barbers' shops than places of angels," and then carrying on loud conversations, doing business, exchanging scandal, and discussing politics.[243] Condescendingly, he believes that women behave like this because the "sex is naturally talkative," but he is appalled by the way in which men and women alike "partake of Christ's body lightly, from form or custom," approaching the sacred table dressed as for a dance and still chattering like jackdaws.[244] He accepts that normally "there is no harm in laughter," but he cannot tolerate a "church filled with laughter" by ill-mannered youngsters and "filthy old nuisances" who "giggle, laugh and jeer" throughout the prayers and greet preachers' "verbal thrusts" with "inordinate applause and merriment."[245] He notes that even those who do not chatter, "yawn, stretch themselves and continually fidget" during prayers, and he declares that it is better to say prayers with a handful of worshipers than "sweep together a multitude" of those who behave so abominably.[246] Driven to distraction by people who plague him, he threatens to drive out the miscreants as scabious sheep infecting the healthy flock.[247] "Nothing so becomes a church as silence and good orders," he thunders. "Noise belongs in theatres and baths and public processions and market-place," and even theater audiences have the decency to observe "a great silence" when royal proclamations are read.[248]

Chrysostom disapproves especially of the conduct of affluent worshipers, arriving in style to claim the best seats, with their horses' bridles "spattered with gold" and their women preening themselves "with broidered hair and ornaments of gold."[249] He is not deceived by their ostentatious show of piety, and he says that, in truth, "Christ is less precious" to them "than anything else, servants or mules, or couch or chair or footstool."[250] He has specially hard words for the society ladies who shatter his ideal of *the Christian woman* by coming to church in "courtesans' dresses of gold" so that, when they leave after worship, they are greeted by "countless jeers" in the marketplace.[251]

Behavior between the sexes is scandalous, and many people come to church simply to "gaze at the beauty of women" or "the blooming youth of men," with a brazenness intolerable even in the marketplace. Chrysostom regrets that in "the apostles' time" men and women mingled freely in worship but have now become such "courtesans and frantic horses" that it is necessary to erect "boards to wall off" the two sexes in order to prevent them from ogling one another.[252]

Thus Chrysostom serves churches in which the boundaries between Christianity and paganism, piety and superstition, have become increasingly ill defined. It is inevitable that his attempt to establish a sense of Christian distinctiveness and purity makes him bitter and powerful enemies. Their fury, in itself, is a testimony to the effectiveness of his preaching, and it is to this that we now turn.

Chrysostom the Preacher

The Style of Chrysostom's Preaching

The undoubted greatness of Chrysostom's preaching is enhanced by its grand ecclesiastical settings — Constantine's great octagonal church in Antioch and Constantinople's magnificent, episcopal church where noble architecture and the solemn progress of the liturgical calendar provide an ideal setting for great preaching.[253] Although it is impossible to be sure which of his sermons are preached at Antioch and which at Constantinople, hundreds of his sermons are recorded by scribes with varying degrees of accuracy and are circulated during his lifetime.[254]

Not even layers of editorial encrustation can hide the powerful personality of the preacher himself, although, small and emaciated as he is, with a huge, bald head and straggly beard, initially he must have cut an unimpressive figure. Yet congregations soon discover that the deep-seated, piercing eyes, peering from beneath wrinkled brows, can both charm and transfix. His voice is neither loud nor sonorous and, in order to be heard, he often forsakes his episcopal throne to preach extempore from the altar steps or the *ambo*,[255] and if congregations still complain, he rounds on them grumpily and tells them that they will hear perfectly well if only they stop "making tumult and confusion."[256]

This irascible tone is Chrysostom's famous trademark and needs further exploration in the context of his preaching. Milton refers to his ability "to cleanse a scurrilous vehemence into the style of a rousing sermon," and Kelly rightly describes him as sometimes "blunt-spoken, ill-tempered and harsh."[257] However, Chrysostom's anger is not mere congenital bad temper. It springs from a courageous determination to rebuke sin wherever he finds it[258] and, "with a trumpet's blast," to excommunicate every unrepentant sinner, "be he prince, be he even a crowned head."[259]

Chrysostom is aware of his weakness, and since bishops are expected to be above such displays of passion, he ruefully confesses that he is "a troublesome sort of person and disagreeable," who allows himself to be "hurried away into wrath" even while urging others to be gentle.[260] He warns that Christians who "kick and bite like wild boars and asses" disgrace the church because their anger is an "unmuzzled wild beast" which wreaks havoc on its victims like a public executioner "with red-hot lancets."[261] Having told his hearers that speaking in anger ruins even just arguments, he can scarcely avoid apologizing to them when he has been "needlessly hard upon them" or has "used too sharp language."[262] However, such apologies are seldom fulsome because he believes anger is a legitimate homiletic tool in situations where kindliness "does not so arouse the general hearers" as effectively as "the threat of punishments."[263] Therefore, no matter how much it "wearies him" and "disgusts his hearers," he is ready to return repeatedly to painful issues until he is satisfied that congregations are truly "touched to the quick."[264]

Chrysostom's short-tempered pulpit manner may also be an overreaction to his fear of succumbing to the plaudits of his congregations that he brusquely accuses of listening to sermons "as though they are listening to singers and minstrels." He confesses that preachers collude with this by "acting a preposterous and pitiable part, that they may please, be applauded and depart with praise."[265] He protests that "preaching is not meant just for theatrical amusement," and he frequently chastises congregations that applaud him.[266]

It would be wrong to overemphasize the irascible element in Chrysostom's preaching because he believes that his task is not to berate sinners but to "lower ropes" to those who fall helplessly into the "deep well of sin."[267] Consequently, he often radiates patient good humor, presenting his material "little by little" so that it may be "easily understood" and "not escape the memory."[268] He claims that the popular "demand for rhetorical style and acute sophistry"[269] hinders understanding, but nevertheless the rhetoric he learned from the incomparable Libanius of Antioch is in his bloodstream and "can be seen in every part of his sermons' structure, content and delivery."[270]

However, Chrysostom uses rhetorical devices in new and imaginative ways. His sermons retain a perverse, ad hoc quality which frees him from slavish obedience to oratorical rules, and this makes the rhetor's traditional tools unusually sharp in his hands. He reinforces his arguments by stating them both positively and negatively, and he uses repetition *(panaphora)*, piling image on image.[271] He seizes his hearers' attention by asking rhetorical questions,[272] and while sometimes eschewing digressions that "make the discourse too long and interrupt its continuity,"[273] normally he is happy to digress or return to a theme if he feels he has "left unfinished a necessary point."[274] His use of reductio ad absurdum[275] is often calculated and powerful,[276] and he uses the device of speaking *simpliciter* to good effect, exaggerating to the point of parody in order to drive home his arguments.[277]

Chrysostom's illustrative method and material are major elements of his preaching style. Abundant metaphors and similes bring his sermons to life, and he loves to quote rhymes and to play with words, although many of his sallies are lost in translation.[278] The richness of his illustrative material is breathtaking in both its quantity and its variety,[279] and it is amazing that Schaff can believe that Chrysostom "knew little of the world"[280] when his sermons are full of topical references. It is the fact that Chrysostom's eloquence is grounded in everyday experiences that makes his sermons so accessible. He presses into service every aspect of daily life so that his words may be relevant and vivid.

His description of an imperial procession has the quality of a snapshot, so minutely is it observed and recorded,[281] and as he walks in the marketplace his eye and memory are recording everything he sees. He is insulted by beggars, sees children playing tug-of-war, watches jugglers, pipers, and jesters with their "fringes, cups, bowls and cans," dancing endlessly for a pittance.[282] He picks his way through the gawping crowds gathered around knife throwers, ropewalkers, and lion tamers or watching the public beating of miscreants loaded with chains.[283] A host of familiar characters jostle for place in his sermons: "silk-vendors," "worthless boys, unmarried girls, harlots and effeminate men," "bath-men, street cleaners and runaway slaves," prostitutes lurking in the narrow alleys, drunken wedding-revelers and crowds beaten aside by the lictors of rich courtesans and wealthy aristocrats.[284] The two traditional foci of common life, the forum and the baths, often appear together in his sermons. He has seen the poor "sleep in the ashes of the furnace" outside the baths,[285] and through the doors of the taverns he has glimpsed the gladiators drowning their sorrows in drink.[286]

To this kaleidoscope of everyday sights Chrysostom adds his observation of the lifestyle of the rich. He mocks their pathetic attempts to impress their neighbors by borrowing expensive furniture, hiring "superfluous cooks," and arranging lavish feasts where guests gorge themselves until their "temples throb and their bowels ache."[287] He knows that many worshipers also attend depraved orgies with prostitutes, shaven-headed actors, "stage players," capering "monsters, idiots and dwarves" and foul-mouthed *parasites*.[288] He complains that although unable to "repeat one psalm or any portion of the divine scriptures," they can all roar out the latest and lewdest songs.[289]

Responding to his congregations' love of the bizarre, Chrysostom describes the customs of strange tribes,[290] likens life to the unpredictable sea, and launches out on imaginary voyages to the "desolation, tracklessness and unexplained" terrors of the oceans "beyond Cadiz."[291] Remembering his own childhood terror of magic, he penetrates the miasma of sorcery swirling around a society[292] in which kidnapped children are slaughtered to steal the psychic power of their innocent souls and corpses are exhumed in hideous rites.[293] He describes the cavortings of masked, transvestite flautists during the Saturnalia, jugglers with their trained swallows and sooted comics singing songs to Bacchus as they extort donations from the drunken crowds.[294] All these find their way into Chrysostom's sermons as he tries to deliver his people from lives "filled with all sorts of terror" by dread of bad luck and stupid superstition.[295]

Chrysostom's love of nature fills his sermons with pictures. He likens human souls to hives baited with "perfumes and fragrant wines" to attract the bees but observes that they are often more neglected than caged birds.[296] Sin is likened to "dogs that bite slyly," and dancing to the jumping of skittish camels. Chrysostom compares all human follies to animal counterparts — the viciousness of asses, bears, and wolves; the deceitfulness of foxes and serpents; the shamelessness of dogs; and the haughtiness of peacocks.[297]

Chrysostom speaks too of people and situations he has encountered. He remembers brutal estate-owners mistreating their "wretched and toil-worn labourers," and businessmen, obsessed by "usuries, sureties, securities and bondsmen."[298] He recalls how soldiers who visit his father, Secundus, "burnish their arms and make ready their steeds" as they tell tales of ferocious military punishment and drinking competitions in the mess.[299] Perhaps his vivid illustrations about "wrestlers in dust and oil" and "pugilists drenched in blood" are also based upon youthful memories.[300]

Two occupations in particular seem to fascinate Chrysostom and make their way into his sermons. Unsurprisingly, the first is the law, for which he was trained and still obviously enjoys because he tells preachers that their function is "even more desirable" than that of a barrister in the courts which he still frequents.[301] He confesses that he still "shudders" when he visits prisons and sees the wretched captives, "some squalid, some chained and famishing, some shut up in darkness," and he recalls thieves, grave robbers, and pirates and the hellish servitude of the mines.[302] He describes judicial procedures, the joy of prisoners reprieved, and the awful tortures afflicted by public executioners, all with the accuracy of an eyewitness.[303]

Chrysostom's second enthusiasm, the medical profession, also draws upon personal experience. When his health is broken by extreme asceticism, he needs prolonged medical treatment, and as a young deacon he has many opportunities to watch doctors at work among the poor. Consequently, the medical world often invades his sermons, and he even describes the church as "an admirable surgery for souls."[304] He solemnly warns his people against bogus doctors and relates tales of miraculous cures, descriptions of operations, and accounts of violently "insane" or delirious patients.[305] He deals with all manner of treatments, from correct bandaging and the skills of the "cupping-glass" to the preparation of antidotes and procedures for amputation, cauterization, and lancing.[306] He has seen the contortions of fevered plague victims, and his interests extend even to watching the embalmers at their mysterious work.[307] Thus it is Chrysostom's skillful use of his illustrative material which, in part, makes his sermons pulsate with life and holds his congregations spellbound.

The Content of Chrysostom's Preaching

However, it is the *content* of his preaching which sets the seal on his greatness. His reason for preaching is simple. "If I see you living in piety," he tells his congregations, "I have all that I wish." He seeks to enable Christians to "win others by their lives" and to help them understand that thus, "even the untaught can speak with a voice clearer than a trumpet."[308] However, he faces a major obstacle. Many of his people are so ignorant of Scripture that they "are not even aware that there is such a book,"[309] and he believes they will never fulfill his vision for them until they replace the "useless dogmas" of the philosophers with the pure light of the Word.[310] He pleads with them to "look into the depths of the Divine Scriptures" with "earnest prayer," studying the prescribed passages before coming to worship and, afterward, reviewing the passages again with their families in the light of the sermons they have heard.[311]

In order to help his congregations, Chrysostom undertakes a systematic exegesis of Genesis, Psalms, and much of the New Testament, earning himself a reputation as "the greatest pulpit orator and commentator of the Greek Church."[312] His training under Melitius and Diodorus leaves an "Antiochene" mark on his exegesis, and he favors literal interpretations but is ready to use typology when it enhances his homiletic use of the text.[313] He gives new glory to the genre of expository sermons, preaching series of sermons, preceding each sequence with an introduction and then applying it to everyday life.[314] From Melitius, also, he learns the value of catechesis, and continues the catechetical preaching tradition of Cyril, Theodore, and Ambrose,[315] ensuring that his sermons cover the whole spectrum of Christian belief and living. Although the two elements are often intermingled in the homilies, it is helpful to examine separately the *ecclesiastical* and *ethical* contents of Chrysostom's preaching.

The Ecclesiastical Element in Chrysostom's Preaching   Chrysostom is called to govern his churches in troubled times. His sermon series *On the Statues* shows how ready he is to "spend many days addressing words of comfort" to his frightened flock, despite his conviction that the events are partly divine retribution for "making the body of Christ a corpse."[316] He senses "great despondency" among the faithful and tries to ignite the "courage needed to stand against that feeling" and to show his congregations that God will give them "longsuffering" and "place their souls as in a quiet harbour" even in the midst of the storms.[317]

Chrysostom is convinced that prospects for reformation hinge upon respect for the clergy, and although he accepts that there are "unworthy priests who provoke God," he refuses to listen to anticlerical gossip and calls his people to "reverence" those who instruct and pastor them.[318] Above all, they must honor their bishops, who bear a heavy responsibility as "ambassadors of God" himself, and without whom churches are left "bereft."[319] Congregations must help bishops to maintain the spiritual purity of their churches by following Christ's example and "stopping the mouths of heretics."[320] Chrysostom himself leads the attack from the pulpit, and his attitude toward heretics oscillates between tenderness and severity. One moment he is saying it is possible "to find actual goodness" among them and urging congregations to pray for them, and in the next he wants to "take away their freedom of speech, break their assemblies" — anything short of actually killing them.[321]

It must be admitted that Chrysostom reserves some of his cruelest attacks for the Jews, preaching at least eight sermons specifically against them and sprinkling his writings with countless other hostile references.[322] Jewish worship seems still to attract numbers of Christians and pagans, and Chrysostom is determined to stop this leeching away of church members. His sermons become part of the church's general policy "to put a stop to such mixing between the communities,"[323] and by pillorying those who originally opposed Jesus, he tries to establish guilt by association and heaps every possible calumny upon the Jews of his own day.[324]

Compared with Jews and heretics, Christians stand in such a privileged position with God and must not dream of losing it by defection. At the Feast of Epiphany Chrysostom preaches series of sermons urging his people not to defer baptism since, once "their heads are immersed in water," even the worst offenders' "old self" is "buried" and they "rise as new people."[325] He tantalizes waverers by telling them that there are mysterious truths which will be revealed to them only after baptism and that, above all else, they will be admitted to the wonders of the Eucharist. Then "Christ will enter them" and even the humblest will "soar heavenwards and look on the Sun of Righteousness."[326] Believers must receive the Eucharist regularly, if possible after fasting,[327] but Chrysostom attributes special power to the sacrament when celebrated at the shrines of martyrs where there is "health of body and benefit of soul."[328] He reserves some of his most eloquent sermons for the festivals of saints and martyrs who so gloriously prove the church's supremacy, graphically describing the tortures they endured and the miracles wrought by their relics.[329]

Finally, Chrysostom reminds his people of their responsibility to share in the evangelistic outreach of the church, which is locked in a struggle for the soul of the empire.[330] Instead of indulging in worldly chatter, they must "speak boldly," regard everything as "second in importance to confessing Christ," and emulate their forefathers by setting out as missionaries.[331] At home, wealthy Christians must "cultivate the souls of the poor who cultivate their fields" by establishing churches on their estates and maintaining teachers and clergy to serve them.[332] However, Chrysostom proclaims that there is one method of evangelism in which all his hearers may share. By their distinctive lifestyle, they may influence and convert their neighbors, and so the ecclesiastical element of his preaching merges with the ethical.

The Ethical Element in Chrysostom's Preaching Chrysostom tells his congregations that although they are saved solely "by the grace of God," they have been "created in Christ for good works."[333] Using their lives as a powerful evangelistic tool, they must live nobly "in the midst of the city" where, though "battling billows without number," they may "imitate the self-denial of the monks."[334] Chrysostom preaches passionately on public issues, commending those Christians who make their witness as exemplary citizens by respecting civil authority and rejecting anarchy.[335] He condemns the infuriated worshipers' destruction of the imperial statues as a devilish attack upon the stability of the state. However, he is moved by his people's fear, and the sermons he preaches to comfort the terrified believers also serve to convert pagans who come seeking solace in the very churches they have previously attacked.[336] The cause célèbre of Eutropius, the arrogant, imperial chamberlain and scourge of the churches, affords Chrysostom another opportunity publicly to demonstrate both the power and the mercy of the church. When the desperate Eutropius is driven to seek sanctuary in the church he has ridiculed, Chrysostom preaches two sermons, first humiliating the cowering official and then publicly forgiving him.[337]

Chrysostom's world is both politically turbulent and morally dull. He declares, "fornication seems to be nothing evil, dice-playing is exempt from punishment and drunkenness and gluttony are accounted fine things."[338] He ponders sadly, "When we clean people out, as they come here from the theatres with the filthiness, thither they go again and take in a larger stock of filthiness."[339] Eloquently, he alerts his hearers to the seriousness of sin, depicting it as "a savage beast, breathing flames, hideous, black, with ten thousand hands laying hold of thought and tearing everything in pieces."[340] Though he confesses that the very thought of hell makes him "tremble and shrink through fear," he must continue to preach about it if his hearers are to be saved from being "dragged away into its torture chambers."[341] In a society where life is short and cheap, the ability to "die well" is to be valued, and Chrysostom contrasts the horrors of the Day of Wrath with the bliss of the saints mounting "to the very summit of heaven." He asserts that Christians need not "shudder at death" or employ superstitious rituals to "make the Judge propitious" because they know that the righteous "go forth to a very different light" attended by angels.[342]

However, Chrysostom is equally concerned about the *present* life, and no aspect of everyday living escapes him. For instance, his constant denunciation of swearing may strike us as persnickety, but it is an important issue. The use of oaths, once made solemn by cultic observance, has become so debased that even pagan writers condemn it.[343] Instead of subscribing to the popular view that swearing is "natural," Christians must "expel the evil custom from their mouths" and help others to do the same.[344] Chrysostom preaches a succession of sermons against swearing, stubbornly maintaining that although he "may seem tedious," he will not desist until he sees some amendment.[345]

Chrysostom is equally fervent in his attack upon drunkenness, "a demon self-chosen, a disease without excuse" which takes "wine given for gladness" and "mars its excellence" by excess.[346] He describes vividly the havoc wrought among his people as decent folk are robbed of self-control and fall into "fornication, whoredom and adultery."[347] Drunken men, "ridiculed by their enemies and pitied by their friends," nurse their hangovers and groan, "why does it end like this?"[348] "Handsome girls" are reduced to "ugly women" exhaling "sour whiffs of fetid wine," and inebriated matrons degrade themselves with their own slaves and undergo dangerous abortions simply to remain "objects of longing to their lovers."[349]

Perhaps it is the memory of his own youthful seduction by the stage which makes Chrysostom cry out, "I will not cease till I have scattered the theatre of the devil and so purified the assembly of the Church."[350] Furiously he denounces those who, instead of coming to hear him preach, "take their place in the theatre and look on at the devil's show." When the angry emperor punishes his iconoclastic people by "shutting up the Orchestra and the Hippodrome," Chrysostom prays in vain that the "fountains of iniquity" may "never be opened."[351] His sermons seethe with condemnations of the theater. Its music "teems with fornication" and its "filthy songs" are like "swine grunting on a dunghill." Its lewd plots "pluck up chastity by the foundations and encourage crime." Its "foul speeches," for which the actors merit stoning, are made fouler still by their "gestures, gait, apparel and voice," as they confound "common nature" by playing female roles, while their women stroll half-naked among the audience.[352]

The theater parades the sexual mores of pagan society in most seductive ways. How can Christians who attend the shows remain uncontaminated when theaters are the haunts of criminals and prostitutes of both sexes?[353] How can a husband return home "enfettered by the sight of women" and inflamed by "the words and gestures he sees there," without venting his frustration upon his wife, children, and servants?[354] Chrysostom warns his congregations that such experiences lead husbands to forget the duty of faithfulness to their wives so that they fall prey to the "gestures of the harlot" and taste the "honey that turns to gall."[355] Chrysostom is shocked to learn that worshipers are going out from the churches and "indulging in unlawful love," by which he probably means more than heterosexual infidelity. He finds it necessary to urge his hearers to avoid those who "run after that which is contrary to nature" and even "cohabit with creatures void of reason," warning that such conduct "ruins the soul with the body."[356]

It is against that background that Chrysostom preaches regularly about the "unequalled pleasure" of the Christian home.[357] "There is nothing," he enthuses, "which so welds life together as the love of man and wife ... when they are in harmony, the children are well brought up and the domestics are in good order and neighbours and friends and relatives enjoy the fragrance." Such relationships do not depend upon mere physical attraction which, Chrysostom observes somewhat pessimistically, lasts "at most for a year." They are sustained by a spiritual union which expresses itself in domestic piety.[358] Perhaps the most distinctive aspect of the Christian family is the way in which husbands respect their wives, addressing them "with terms of endearment," never betraying them with prostitutes and never abusing them verbally or physically.[359] As head of the household, the husband must correct his wife's faults, lovingly and patiently, lest she overindulge their children and render their daughters extravagant and idle. The exhortation to gentle correction is necessary to ensure that the "shrieks and wailings" of beaten wives are "borne along the alleys" only from pagan homes.[360]

Chrysostom extends his "marriage guidance" sermons to include children and servants,[361] and since children are often entrusted to servants from an early age, he urges parents to choose their nurses carefully. They must not be allowed to bedeck newborn infants with "amulets and beads" to "turn away the evil eye," nor must they overindulge or corrupt their young charges.[362] Spiritual formation cannot begin too early, so parents must bring young children to church and encourage them to participate in other acts of devotion as far as they are able.[363] Turning to the subject of servants, Chrysostom condemns slavery as "the fruit of covetousness, degradation and savagery," knowing that "herds of slaves" are merely a status symbol for masters who care little for their welfare.[364] He draws a terrifying picture of wealthy women furiously stripping, beating, and torturing their maidservants and insists that in Christian homes, slaves must be treated well and must accompany the family to church.[365]

Of all the ethical subjects treated in his sermons, it is to the theme of affluence and poverty that Chrysostom returns most frequently. As the son of an upper-class family, he knows the comfortable lifestyle of the rich, but when a deacon, he also encountered the horrors of grinding poverty. He concludes that although "neither wealth nor poverty is excellent in itself," the rich stand in special spiritual peril and it is easier for Christians to "shine out in poverty."[366] He does not expect everybody to embrace "entire poverty," but Christians must "cut off superfluities and . . . desire a sufficiency alone." He has seen the havoc wrought by greed, and he likens the affluent to children playing games, becoming so obsessed with amassing "goods without end" that they reduce even marriage to the level of a sordid business transaction.[367] He sees rich women "destroying themselves with continual luxury," and their husbands strutting about, ridiculous in their long robes and "golden trinkets," and he observes that for all their opulence they too are mortal, and when they are swallowed up by death their sycophants simply abandon them to the worms.[368]

However, Chrysostom's real point of contention with the rich is their refusal to share their wealth with the poor, a sin sufficient in itself to "cast a man into hell-fire."[369] Christian businessmen quickly condemn monks suspected of minor self-indulgences, but they themselves are so busy squeezing every penny from their debtors that they make no attempt to "break their bread to the hungry."[370] Chrysostom acknowledges that congregations accuse him of "forever preaching about almsgiving" and plead with him to spare them further sermons on the subject, but he will not relent.[371] He has a passion for the poor and he tells his congregations that they have sufficient resources to help, if only they will create benevolent funds and charity accommodations to augment their personal generosity.[372] Having worked among the poor, Chrysostom knows the sensitivity required of those distributing charity and he tells his people to learn the God-given "art of almsgiving." They must address suppliants with respect, remembering that it is "possible even with words to do alms," and they are to sit at the door of the *xenon* to greet personally those who need help.[373]

So it is that Chrysostom uses his sermons as a powerful instrument of ecclesiastical reform and pastoral care, in order to bring every part of life under the judgment of the gospel. It is a task he cannot undertake alone, and therefore he is anxious to train others to take an effective part in the ministry of preaching.

Chrysostom the Teacher of Preaching

Schaff's convenient fivefold division of Chrysostom's life[374] shows that his main preaching ministry stretches over nearly a quarter of a century, from modest beginnings in Antioch to the glories of Constantinople. History has confirmed his posthumous title of "golden tongue," and he has been lionized as "the greatest preacher of the early church."[375] He himself holds the highest view of preaching, believing that since preachers undeservedly "enjoy the divine grace," they must "use every discourse" to educate the souls of their congregations.[376] He seeks to follow the apostles' example by preaching daily and never "neglecting preaching even in seasons of calamity," and he is passionately concerned that others should take the same path.[377]

Chrysostom is more of a practitioner than a trainer of preachers, and he does not emulate Augustine's careful analysis of style and vocabulary. However, in *De sacerdotio Christiano IV-V* he deals at length with the preaching ministry of his priests. The work reveals a disquieting situation and reads more like a spiritual survival manual for preachers than a homiletic textbook. Instead of concentrating upon the minutiae of technique and material, Chrysostom deals with the context in which his preachers have to function. Gone are the days when all that was required of a Christian preacher was transparency of life and simplicity of faith! Chrysostom describes a contemporary situation in which "a passion for sermons has burst upon the minds" of pagans and Christians alike[378] and the ability to preach well has become paramount. Priests are expected to "apply the Word powerfully," like skilled surgeons excising false notions or brilliant generals outmaneuvering the heretics. Chrysostom warns those who are "destitute of that power" that they must lose no time in "gaining that means of strength," lest they place their flocks in jeopardy.[379]

Chrysostom allows that there are a few men of "great ability" who have natural gifts as preachers, but says that even they cannot be complacent. "Preaching," he warns them, "does not come by nature but by study," and even if "a man reaches a high standard of it," he will lose his gift unless he "cultivates his power by constant application and exercise."[380] Even the greatest preachers need to "expend great labour upon the preparation of discourses to be delivered in public" because congregations gather not as eager learners but as critical assessors, judging sermons as though they were jousts or plays. They will pounce on a preacher who dares to "weave into his sermon any part of other men's work" and pillory him as unmercifully as if he were a robber. They will idolize their favorite preachers just as they praise their favorite gladiators, but they are fickle and will soon change their allegiance.[381] They are so vocal that not even bishops are spared catcalls and jeers if their sermons do not win approval.[382]

Chrysostom presents a disquieting account of bitter competition between preachers in a church which has "become a stable of oxen" rather than an "assembly of angels."[383] Many of its clergy live luxuriously with "spiritual sisters," bartering ecclesiastical promotions and "leaving their prayers" to wheel and deal like "tradesmen."[384] Such is the ferocity of the competition, that Chrysostom acerbically declares that any effective preacher will soon find "rivals springing up against him to revile in private and defame in public." They will stir up "the common herd" who, since few of them "possess the power" to judge sermons correctly, will applaud brash orators and "send home faithful preachers without any praise."[385] Once a preacher's reputation is lost, a new pulpit idol will speedily take his place and nobody will pity the passé preacher's "dejection, pain and anxiety" even though it may plunge him "into the deepest lethargy."[386]

In such an atmosphere, how is a godly preacher to survive and persuade his people to "follow and yield to him"? Chrysostom replies that in order to triumph, it is necessary to learn how to exercise "indifference to praise" and then to cultivate "the power of preaching well."[387] Those who "enter upon the trial of preaching, longing for applause," will soon find their ministry full of "annoyances and pangs."[388] So the secret of success is to receive applause humbly if it is given but never to become resentful if it is withheld. Priests who perfect that art will become loving but firm "fathers" for their people.[389]

Chrysostom teaches that attaining that sort of mental and spiritual equilibrium requires a high degree of self-knowledge. It means acknowledging one's need to learn homiletic skills in order to present material without "stumbling, stopping short and blushing," and above all it means working hard at sermons "so that they may please God" and being determined only to seek his approval.[390] When those sermons prove disappointing, instead of despairing, preachers must understand that, "being human," they cannot possibly "acquit themselves successfully at all times." There must be occasions when they "naturally fall short of the mark" and preach "at a lower level of ability than usual."[391] Perhaps Chrysostom speaks from personal experience when he says that such self-knowledge is especially important for famous and successful preachers. They require particular "forbearance" to deal with failure because they can be sure that their rivals will be especially eager to announce that they can no longer fulfill their congregations' "great expectations."[392]

How far Chrysostom is successful in galvanizing his clergy into action is unclear, but there can be no doubt that his impact as preacher and teacher is sufficient to render him intolerable to many powerful people. Bettenson neatly observes that in a situation which requires "more diplomatic tact than eloquence," Chrysostom fails because he "has those qualities in inverse proportions."[393] Even his admirer Socrates admits that he can be "stern and severe, prone to irritability rather than modesty,"[394] and smarting under his scathing criticism, many of his clergy hate him cordially and give willing support to Eudoxia and her wealthy clique.[395] Together they consign Chrysostom to oblivion in humiliating exile, but over thirty years later his body is brought back in triumph to Constantinople and his ministry is finally vindicated. His last recorded words provide a fitting obituary for "John Golden-Mouth" — "Glory to God for all things! Amen."

Epilogue: "Whither the Great Ship?"

Preachers, Congregations, and Pluralism

When thou callest an assembly of the Church as a commander of a great ship, appoint the assemblies to be made with all possible skill.

Apostolic Constitutions 7.57

In conclusion, it is fitting to use the patristic metaphor of the church as a ship, for we have watched congregations and preachers voyaging together, like crews with their officers, often uncomfortably and sometimes downright mutinously. Our study has shown how, from time to time, innocuous wavelets have grown into gigantic tidal waves threatening to engulf the church and that, at such times, it has been the preachers who have had to steady "the great ship" in the ensuing storms.

We have seen how, after the first heady days of primary evangelism, preachers have to *pastor* apprentice-believers who might otherwise be swept overboard. As the church launches out into the pagan world, the apologist-preachers struggle to keep their congregations on course and, when the ship nearly founders under the weight of worldliness, the ascetic preachers ruthlessly lighten the vessel. It is the liturgist-preachers who have to refurbish the ship for imperial service and the theologians who provide it with the charts for future voyaging. Finally, the majestic homileticians inspire the crew and train its officers to keep the church afloat as the western empire sinks into the "Dark Ages."

In the light of our explorations, one cannot help but wonder what future writers will discern as the "tidal waves" threatening the church in this new millennium. What are the issues which now appear only as sinister eddies but whose growth preachers should already be anticipating? The question is not an easy one because reading the "signs of the times" is like viewing an impressionist painting with one's nose pressed against the canvas. Without benefit of "the distant view," it is hard to discern any pattern in the daubs of apparently random events, but we must try to do so.[1]

It seems likely that, of the many challenges which will confront the global church, few will be more pressing than those associated with *pluralism*. Of course, this will not be an entirely new situation. There is a mysterious circularity about the course of history by which past events seem to reemerge in the present, and when we look back we see that the church has always existed in a pluralist context. It has always been a minority movement, proffering just one of many faith options, and it has always manifested plurality within itself. We may refer to "the early church" as though it were monochrome, but we know that its congregations have always been a maelstrom of conflicting theologies, liturgies, and customs. So, what has changed?

Surely the new factor is the growing immediacy of contact produced by contemporary communications technology. There are no longer any secrets. Already the kaleidoscopic variety of the church is universally accessible. Preachers cannot keep their hearers immured in safe, denominational ghettos when, at the flick of a switch, they can join affluent congregations in North America, hear African evangelists in Nairobi, or experience Pentecostal rallies in Bogota. It is true that preachers can now command unprecedented audiences and that global congregations are a reality, but there is a price to be paid. Preachers and congregations are increasingly stripped of their privacy and can no longer function in cozy anonymity. Their successes and their scandals now belong in the public domain, and there are no longer any ecclesiastical hiding places. The same communication systems which permit Christians to disseminate their faith worldwide also bring *non-Christianity* into their homes. The "person in the pew" cannot be protected from the voracious threat of secularism or the attractions of rival faiths and alternative lifestyles.

Pluralism is thrust into the faces of local congregations, shattering any illusion that their personal version of Christianity represents a majority view. Their sense of unease is increased as tourism and migration bring them into personal contact with those who differ from them. Christians who once sang, comfortably, about "heathen lands afar,"[2] now find themselves living and working with "heathens" who often outshine them in spirituality and rebuke them by the purity of their morals. Faced by such evidence, how can Christians maintain their traditional claim to spiritual supremacy? On the other hand, when confronted by the fanatical ferocity of some religious fundamentalists, how can Christians simply pretend that it does not matter what faith-beliefs are held?

There is another aspect of pluralism which proves increasingly bewildering. How are Western congregations to react to the "supermarket spirituality" which offers beliefs like rival brands of detergent? In the aftermath of postmodernism with its massacre of metanarratives, what are Christians to believe? Their faith, once ridiculed as unscientific and naive, is now often received with kindly indifference by non-Christians for whom beliefs are simply matters of personal whim. When a mantra is as valid as a Mass, and a prism as a prayer, why bother to seek converts? Evangelism seems little more than a pillow fight between soft options. It is not surprising that many sincere Christians feel an oppressive confusion settling upon their souls.

If the eddies are already so disturbing, how long will it be before they become a veritable tsunami to sweep the church away? What are preachers to do when, as we have seen, they must often fulfill many roles simultaneously? How are they to steer their congregations between the Scylla of mindless conservatism and the Charybdis of spineless liberalism? The inscrutability of the future denies us any simple answers to the question, but we must make some calculated guesses about the way ahead.

There can be no doubt that, as in the past, preachers will need to use every possible means of communication and that this will mean taking seriously the demands of inductive homiletic.[3] However, that will be mere technical tinkering unless they are able to proclaim a new, persuasive apologetic which functions successfully within a pluralist context. Such a hazardous venture will require serious questions to be asked. How far can the new apologetic be determined by creeds forged of ancient theological squabbles? What is to be the place of Scripture? Is the new theology to be confined within the safety of a sort of Tertullianesque legalism or will the free-floating ideas of an Origen or a Clemens Alexandrinus prove more profitable? Is there still a nonnegotiable corpus of Christian dogma and are there theological "iron rations" upon which Christian congregations must always be sustained? None of these questions will yield their answers to the fainthearted.

What will be the focal point of this new apologetic which will provide the nexus of faith for future congregations? Perhaps Jürgen Moltmann gave a vital clue when, writing under the shadow of the Vietnam War, he declared that even in "an alienated and alienating society," Christians can rediscover the liberating joy of their faith if only they will rediscover their Christ.[4] One suspects that insight will hold firm for the future. Primarily, the new apologetic must be a fresh Christology. Origen, Tertullian, Athanasius, and Leo all grasped the truth that Christology must be plastic enough to fit new situations. As churches see their imperialistic powers crumble and their protected status fade, they will be driven to experience the vulnerability of Christ. They will be compelled to ask how he will be "transfigured" again to reveal himself afresh *from within a pluralist context.*

What form the new Christology will take is a matter for theological theorists to discover, but there is no reason to doubt Schleiermacher's seasoned contention that whatever the outcome may be, preachers will play a major role in communicating it to their congregations. He argued that it is the preacher's task constantly to revitalize the church's consciousness of God and to reassert the charismatic leadership of Christ.[5] Dawn de Vries aptly observes that for Schleiermacher, "An effective sermon is an epiphany: an appearance of Christ in the community of faith."[6] It is the preacher who must be the *herald, proclaimer,* and *interpreter* of any new Christology.

Although it may change dramatically, the office of the preacher will not become obsolete. Indeed, it is likely to become more demanding. In an earlier age when churches struggled with the challenges of pluralism, both without and within, the golden-tongued Chrysostom identified the leaders needed for such an hour. He wrote, "Bring forward those who . . . surpass all others and soar . . . above them in excellence of spirit."[7] Such are the preachers whose continuing task it will be to enthuse their congregations with a new, exhilarating understanding of what it means to be a follower of Jesus Christ. It will be they who must ensure that when the "great ship" finally comes to its port, it may scarcely be recognizable as the vessel that originally set sail but it will be decked with the banners of joy.

Endnotes

Introduction — "Pews and Pulpits"

1. K. Barth, *Homiletics*, trans. G. W. Bromiley and D. E. Daniels (Louisville: Westminster, 1991), p. 58, italics mine. He goes further and suggests that since preaching is God's work, it actually creates congregations since, "wherever the Word of reconciliation creates human hearers for itself, there is the church, the congregation of those whom the Lord has called" (p. 57).

Chapter 1 — "'No Stone Unturned': The Missionaries"

1. 1 Cor. 9:16; 2 Tim. 4:2.
2. Matt. 28:19; Acts 1:8; 10:42.
3. Acts 2:14ff.
4. 1 Cor. 1:21.
5. Matt. 24:14. Schnackenburg (*The Church in the New Testament*, trans. W. J. O'Hara [London: Burns and Oates, 1981], p. 118) insists that his "eschatological attitude" is an "essential feature" of early Christianity, and Alan Richardson believes this is a clue to understanding the primitive view of preaching. It is "one of the signs of the Age of Fulfilment" (*An Introduction to the Theology of the New Testament* [London: SCM Press, 1958], pp. 25-26). Hurtado (*At the Origins of Christian Worship* [Carlisle: Paternoster Press, 1999], p. 48) comments that in preaching, "eschatological salvation" is at hand.
6. Acts 2:43; 6:8; Rom. 15:18-19. It is made clear that the authority of preaching is not dependent upon human gifts (Gal. 1:11ff.; 1 Cor. 1:18-25; 1 Thess. 1:5). Paul claims

that his preaching ministry is divinely bestowed and must have absolute priority (Rom. 1:1; 1 Cor. 9:16; Gal. 1:15-16; cf. Acts 20:24; 1 Cor. 1:17).

7. Rom. 10:14; cf. 1 Cor. 15:11; Gal. 3:2.

8. Eph. 6:17; 1 Cor. 1:21ff.; 2 Cor. 4:2ff.; Col. 1:21ff.

9. Acts 6:4; 2 Tim. 1:1.

10. Although ἀγγέλλω itself is not common in the New Testament, its derivatives occur almost eighty times and are frequently used of "announcing" the Christian message. E.g., καταγγέλλω (Acts 4:2; 13:5; 16:10; 1 Cor. 2:1; 9:14), ἀναγγέλλω (Rom. 15:21; 1 Pet. 1:12; 1 John 1:5), ἀπαγγέλλω (Acts 4:2; 13:5; 26:20; 1 Cor. 2:1; 9:14), εὐαγγελίζω (Acts 16:10; 1 Cor. 1:17; Gal. 1:11; 1 Pet. 1:2), and εὐαγγέλιον (Rom. 1:1; 15:16; 1 Cor. 9:12; 2 Cor. 2:12; 8:18; 11:7; Gal. 1:11) have religious origins in Jewish and Greek thought, and so it is natural for Christians to apply them to the act of Christian preaching. See further U. Becker, *DNTT,* 2:107ff.; D. E. Demaray, *CEP,* pp. 119ff.; G. W. Grogan, *NIDCC,* pp. 361-62.

11. E.g., Acts 8:5; 9:20; 20:25. See further J. W. Thompson, "Preaching, Proclamation," in *EDB,* p. 1079; D. Buttrick, "Proclamation," in *CEP,* pp. 384-85. Barth (*Homiletics,* trans. G. W. Bromiley and D. E. Daniels [Louisville: Westminster, 1991], p. 50) stresses the authority and responsibility implied by using the term "heralds." See further U. Becker and D. Müller, "Proclamation, Preach, Kerygma," in *DNTT,* 3:44ff.; R. H. Mounce, "Preaching, Kerygma," in *DPL,* pp. 735ff.

12. E.g., 1 Cor. 2:4; 15:14; 2 Tim. 4:17. See further C. Brown, "The Structure and Content of the Early Kerygma," in *DNTT,* 3:57ff.; C. H. Dodd, *The Apostolic Preaching and Its Development* (London: Hodder and Stoughton, 1950), pp. 1ff.; Becker and Müller, 3:5ff.; C. F. Evans, "The Kerygma," *JTS,* n.s., 7 (1956): 25ff.

13. J. I. H. McDonald (*Kerygma and Didache: The Articulation and Structure of the Earliest Christian Message,* SNTSMS 37 [Cambridge: Cambridge University Press, 1989], p. 5) sees them as being "broadly complementary." See his discussion of the terms (pp. 1ff.), and see R. MacMullen, *Christianizing the Roman Empire: AD 100-400* (New Haven: Yale University Press, 1984), pp. 1ff.; J. H. Westerhoff, "Teaching and Preaching," in *CEP,* pp. 467ff.; K. Wegenast, "Teach, Instruct," in *DNTT,* 3:759ff.

14. The Johannine writings show a preference for μαρτυρέω (e.g., John 3:11; 1 John 1:2; Rev. 1:2), although ἀναγγέλλω is used of the revelation of mysteries (e.g., John 4:25; 16:13-14). See further, L. Coenen, "Witness, Testimony," in *DNTT,* 3:1038-39; D. Dunn-Wilson, "The Biblical Background of Martys and Its Derivatives, with Special Reference to the New Testament," pp. 186ff.

15. E.g., Paul overlaps the use of κηρύσσω and εὐαγγελίζω (Rom. 16:25; Gal. 2:2; Col. 1:23; 1 Thess. 2:2), and in 1 Thess. 2:2 he uses both λαλέω and κηρύσσω. On one occasion, Luke deliberately replaces Mark's κηρύσσω with εὐαγγελίζω (Luke 4:43; 9:6; cf. Mark 6:12), but on another occasion he uses both words side by side (Luke 8:1).

16. Their authenticity is doubted notably by Dibelius in his *Studies in the Acts of the Apostles,* ed. H. Greeven, trans. M. Ling (London: SCM Press, 1956), pp. 138ff.; cf. E. Schweitzer, who claims to identify "a far-reaching identity of structure" in the ser-

mons and speeches, which proves they "are basically compositions by the author" ("Concerning the Speeches in Acts," in *Studies in Luke-Acts*, ed. L. E. Keck and J. L. Martyn [London: SPCK, 1968], pp. 210, 208).

17. Acts 16:10-17; 20:5-15; 21:1-18; 27:1–28:16. However, the address in 20:17-35 does fall within a "we" passage.

18. G. N. Stanton, *Jesus of Nazareth in New Testament Preaching*, SNTSMS 27 (New York: Cambridge University Press, 1974), p. 84. See his consideration of an underlying Aramaic source for Acts 1–13.

19. Thucydides, *History of the Peloponnesian War* 1.22.

20. T. F. Glasson, "The Speeches in Acts and Thucydides," *ET* 76 (1965): 165ff.

21. See I. H. Marshall, *Luke: Historian and Theologian* (Exeter: Paternoster Press, 1988), pp. 21ff. C. F. Evans believes that Luke reproduces "something of the form and contents of the general run of preaching in his day" and that he places the speeches and sermons strategically throughout Acts to give a general overview of primitive preaching ("The Kerygma," p. 41). See also confirmatory views in F. F. Bruce, *The Acts of the Apostles: The Greek Text with Introduction and Commentary* (London: Tyndale Press, 1952), pp. 18ff.; C. S. C. Williams, "The Speeches and Theology of Acts," in *A Commentary on the Acts of the Apostles* (London: A. & C. Black, 1957), pp. 36ff.; R. N. Longenecker, "The Speeches in Acts," in *EBC*, 9:229ff.; G. W. H. Lampe, "Acts," in *PC*, pp. 884-85.

22. J. Lebreton and J. Zeiller, *The History of the Primitive Church*, trans. E. C. Messenger, 2 vols. (New York, 1947), 1:168; G. H. C. Macgregor and T. P. Ferris, "The Acts of the Apostles," in *IB*, 9:41; J. Munck, *The Acts of the Apostles* (New York: Doubleday, 1967), p. xliv.

23. Luke 1:4.

24. See H. Conzelmann, *The Theology of Saint Luke*, trans. G. Buswell (London: Faber and Faber, 1960), pp. 215ff.

25. Dodd, pp. 17ff.; cf. C. S. C. Williams, p. 41; R. P. Martin, *Worship in the Early Church* (Grand Rapids: Eerdmans, 1974), pp. 73ff.

26. E.g., Acts 4:21-22; 6:12; 7:57-58; 21:30-31. For the complexity of these relationships, see R. L. Brawley, *Luke-Acts and the Jews: Conflict, Apology, and Conciliation*, SBLMS 33 (Atlanta: Scholars Press, 1987), pp. 133-34.

27. Acts 2:5.

28. Pentecost provides the most suitable travel conditions for such pilgrimages, and vast crowds attend the feasts in Jerusalem. Diaspora Jews tend to be more influenced by Hellenism than their Palestinian counterparts, and possibly are more open to Peter's appeal. See W. W. Tarn, *Hellenistic Civilization* (New York: World Publishing, 1971), pp. 210ff.

29. Luke begins with representatives of the millions of Aramaic-speaking Jews living among the Medes, the Elamites, and the Parthians, followed by Cretan Jews from the West and those living in Arabia, and finally the Libyan Jews. Of special importance are pilgrims from the significant Jewish colonies in Alexandria, Rome, and Antioch.

For the Jews in Rome, see Tacitus, *Annals* 2.85; Suetonius, *Tiberius* 36; Josephus, *Antiquities* 18.3, 5; J. M. G. Barclay, *Jews in the Mediterranean Diaspora from Alexander to Trajan, 323 BCE–117 CE* (Edinburgh: T. & T. Clark, 1998), pp. 282ff.

30. Excessive drinking is not unknown at festival times as pilgrims themselves join their religious duties with seven days of socializing and feasting.

31. Early Christian preaching stands firmly in the prophetic tradition. See J. I. H. McDonald, pp. 28ff.; D. S. Long, "Prophetic Preaching," *CEP,* pp. 385ff.

32. Acts 2:16ff.

33. Acts 2:23.

34. Acts 2:24ff.

35. Acts 2:41. Luke's use of the imperfect (προσετέθησαν) may indicate that Peter's sermon triggers a process of conversion as those who are present communicate their newfound conviction to friends and neighbors.

36. Perhaps this is "the crooked generation" to which Peter refers (Acts 2:40; cf. Joel 3:2). See R. Morgenthaler, "Generation," in *DNTT,* 2:36. Roman literature frequently reflects the traditional hatred of Jews; e.g., Juvenal, *Satires* 5.184; 6.542ff.; 14.96ff., 100; Martial, *Epigrams* 7.30; Suetonius, *Tiberius* 36; *Domitian* 12.2. Philo (*Embassy to Gaius* 18.120) records that "a vast and truceless war was prepared against the nation."

37. Acts 17:16-34.

38. G. H. C. Macgregor and T. P. Ferris, "The Acts of the Apostles," *IB* 9:238; C. Gempf, "Acts," in *NBC,* p. 1092.

39. See J. I. H. McDonald, p. 40. Origen (*Cont. Cels.* 3.50ff.) describes the activities of the Cynic preachers. Philostratus (*Vita Apolloni* 4.19, 41, 35ff.) records Apollonius's most weighty sermons for posterity and describes Nero's angry reaction to the religious revival initiated by philosopher-preachers in Rome.

40. Athens is a significant center for mystery religions. The cult of Eleusis originated nearby in the time of Alexander the Great and, as Paul speaks, still attracts many pilgrims.

41. Acts 17:17.

42. The presence of women (Acts 17:34) suggests that Paul is not addressing the formal council. Tarsus is a renowned center of rhetorical studies. In vv. 17-20, Luke reflects the flexibility of Paul's homiletic approach. He "argues" (διελέγετο) in the synagogue and agora (v. 17), but he is brought to the Areopagus to "proclaim" (καταγγέλλω), to "preach" (εὐαγγελίζω), and to "teach" (λαλουμένη διδαχή).

43. Acts 17:18. Socrates was executed for this crime, 450 years earlier.

44. Acts 17:22. δεισιδαιμονεστέρους means both "religious" and "superstitious."

45. The existence of altars to "unknown gods" is confirmed by Pausanius, *Descriptions of Greece* 1.4; 5.14, and Philostratus, *Vita Apolloni* 6.3.5. Diogenes Laertius (*Lives of Philosophers* 1.110) says they were erected on Mars Hill to avert a plague.

46. F. J. Foakes-Jackson (*History of the Christian Church to 460 AD* [Cambridge:

J. Hall, 1905], p. 185) quotes part of a monotheistic Eleusian hymn: "Go on in the right way and contemplate the Governor of the world, He is the One and of Himself alone, and to that One all things owe their being. He worked through all, was never seen by mortal eyes but doth himself see everyone." The Stoics teach that God is "the Soul of the World," and J. Weiss (*Earliest Christianity: A History of the Period, AD 30-150*, trans. F. C. Grant, 2 vols. [New York: Harper, 1959], p. 241) detects a strongly Stoic element in Paul's thought. See pp. 239ff. for Weiss's general consideration of the Areopagus speech. Like Paul, Euripides (*Heracles* 1345-46) asserts that "God, if he be truly God, needs nothing," and Plato (*Euthyphro* 14c) makes the same point.

47. The use of ψηλαφάω (seek) in 17:27 is subtle because it can also signify the blind groping of the lost rather than the dedicated search of honest seekers.

48. A hymn to Zeus attributed to Epimenides the Cretan and Aratus (*Phaenomena*, line 5), the latter an astronomer and fellow countryman of Paul. See on this passage Bruce, pp. 338ff.

49. E.g., Philostratus, *Vita Apolloni* 4.2. See also Weiss, p. 233, where he mentions especially the *Sermon on Repentance* from the hermetic tractate *Poimandres*.

50. E.g., "Once a man dies and the earth drinks up his blood, there is no resurrection" (Aeschylus, *Eumenides* 647-48). D. G. Bostock favors the view that Paul reorganized his own teaching about resurrection in the light of the Osiris myth in order to steer a middle way between Jewish and Greek thought ("Osiris and the Resurrection of Christ," *ET* 112, no. 8 [May 2001]: 265ff.).

51. Stanton explains this strange omission by suggesting that the address is intended to be only "a pre-evangelistic attack upon idolatry" (Stanton, p. 2), but it is possible it was a homiletic decision. Remembering that his critics seem to regard Jesus and Anastasis as proper names of two "foreign gods" (Acts 17:18), Paul decides to discard both words and to replace the name Jesus with "the man from God" and *anastasis* with the more explanatory "resurrection of the dead" (ἀναστήσας αὐτὸν ἐκ νεκρῶν) (17:31).

52. There is little historical evidence for the claim that Paul's convert Dionysius becomes the first bishop of Athens (Eusebius, *HE* 4.33.3).

53. Acts 17:34.

54. 1 Cor. 1:17ff.

55. Although the word φιλοσοφίας only appears in Col. 2:8, as a warning against syncretism, Paul does not seem to dismiss philosophy itself as useless or to suggest that it is impossible to preach the gospel in philosophical terms.

56. Stanton, pp. 13, 67. This questions the view set forth by Bultmann in *The Historical Jesus and the Kerygmatic Christ,* ed. C. E. Braaten and R. A. Harrisville (Nashville: Abingdon, 1964), that the primitive preaching was primarily concerned with "the Christ of faith."

57. Natural and human disasters spawn widespread dissatisfaction with the status quo, and the preachers' claim that the present world is in the grip of evil powers seems eminently reasonable (e.g., Rom. 8:19ff.).

58. E.g., Acts 16:16ff. Here Christian preachers find allies in the philosophers who ridicule the gods of popular pagan religion; e.g., Paul's contemporary Seneca in *On Superstition* (see Augustine, *De civ. Dei* 6.10) and Juvenal (*Satires* 6.51.1ff.). Weiss (p. 238) comments that the evangelists "borrowed their armour from this Greek-Jewish arsenal."

59. A. Le Grys, *Preaching to the Nations: The Origins of Mission in the Early Church* (London: SPCK, 1988), p. 114. He skillfully uses the insights of Erikson, Gerd Thiessen, and Peter Berger to support his thesis.

60. Le Grys, pp. 117-18.

61. Hurtado, p. 48.

62. M. Goodman, *Mission and Conversion: Proselytizing in the Religious History of the Roman Empire* (Oxford: Clarendon, 1994), p. 105.

63. For a useful review of the complex Roman system of slavery, see C. Wells, *The Roman Empire* (London: Harper Collins, 1992), pp. 197ff.

64. It is possible that one of these appears in Rom. 16:11. It is suggested (e.g., E. F. Harrison, "Romans," in *EBC*, 10:165) that Narcissus is Tiberius Claudius Narcissus, the wealthy freedman who serves both Tiberius and Claudius.

65. Juvenal, *Satires* 3.65-66; Martial, *Epigrams* 1.34.

66. Juvenal, *Satires* 6.165.

67. At least six women merit mention in Paul's special greetings to the Roman congregations (Rom. 16). Perhaps some are already involved in mystical rites of the Great Mother cult which dominates vast areas of the empire. Some are serious seekers, but others are simply curious to explore a new, bizarre religion.

68. Acts 16:14, 40; 9:36, 39; 18:26.

69. Acts 17:12; e.g., Priscilla possibly belongs to the noble *gens Prisca* (Acts 18:2; Rom. 16:1ff.; 1 Cor. 16:19). For a further consideration of the social composition of the early Christian communities, see E. W. Stegemann and W. Stegemann, *The Jesus Movement: A Social History of Its First Century* (Edinburgh: T. & T. Clark, 1999), pp. 288ff. D. E. Watson ("Roman Social Classes," in *DNTB*, p. 1003) also favors the idea that Christians are drawn from a wide cross section of the population.

70. W. A. Meeks, *The First Urban Christians: The Social World of the Apostle Paul* (New Haven: Yale University Press, 1983), p. 157.

71. Meeks, pp. 155ff.

72. 1 Cor. 1:26.

73. E.g., Rom. 15:26; 1 Cor. 13:3; Gal. 2:10; James 2:1ff.

74. In its earliest days, Christianity was essentially an urban movement. It is claimed that over a third of the population of Rome lived on public charity and the streets were filled with thousands of unemployed people. See J. Carcopino, *Daily Life in Ancient Rome: The People and the City at the Height of the Empire,* trans. E. O. Lorimer (London: Penguin Books, 1991), pp. 78-79.

75. E.g., Paul's "dear friend" Ampliatus bears a name often found in the imperial

household, and Aristobulus may be a confidant of emperors (cf. Philo, *Embassy to Gaius* 203ff.). See Harrison, 10:160ff., for a useful summary.

76. Acts 17:12: εὐσχημόνων may signify character as much as wealth or social status.

77. Although even this is not always acceptable. Under Flavius, Pomponia Graecina, wife of the consul Aulius Plautus, is executed for indulging in "criminal religion" (Tacitus, *Annals* 13.32).

78. Suetonius, *Nero* 16.

79. H. Chadwick, *Alexandrian Christianity* (Philadelphia: Westminster, 1954), p. 15.

80. Mark's association with the Alexandrian church (Jerome, *De vir. illus.* 8; cf. Eusebius, *HE* 2.16) has gained some acceptance (H. D. McDonald, "Alexandrian Theology," in *NIDCC*, p. 26). According to Coptic tradition, Mark comes to Africa after disagreeing with Paul at the beginning of the second missionary journey and is martyred in Alexandria in 68 C.E. See the review of traditions regarding the missionary activities of "the twelve" in J. Foster, *After the Apostles: Missionary Preaching of the First Three Centuries* (London: SCM Press, 1951), pp. 13ff.

81. E. Dargan, *A History of Preaching* (London: Hodder and Stoughton and G. H. Doran, 1905), 1:35-36.

82. Dodd, p. 7.

83. Personal testimony becomes a vital means of preaching the gospel; e.g., Tatian, *Address to the Greeks* 29; Theophilus of Antioch, *Autol.* 1.14; *Clementine Recognitions* 1.6.

84. G. H. Williams, "The Ancient Church AD 30-313," in *The Layman in Christian History*, ed. S. C. Neil and H. R. Weber (Philadelphia: Westminster, 1963), pp. 28ff. For more about the importance of lay witness, see W. H. C. Frend, "The Church in the Roman Empire, 313-600," in *The Layman in Christian History*, pp. 57ff.

85. Dargan, 1:36.

86. Tertullian, *Ad uxor.* 2.2.

87. Origen, *Cont. Cels.* 3.4.

88. E. Gibbon, *The Decline and Fall of the Roman Empire*, ed. C. A. Robinson, abridged ed. (London: Penguin Books, 1980), p. 27.

89. Pliny, *Natural History* 17.3.

90. E.g., the third-century *Antonine Itinerary.*

91. See Strabo, *Geography* 1.45. On trade in general, see Tarn, pp. 239ff. Five major fleets are stationed at strategic points around the Mediterranean to keep the seas free from pirates. Augustus, *Res gestae* 5.25; cf. Philo, *Embassy to Gaius* 21. For a traveling preacher's experience with pirates see Philostratus, *Vita Apolloni* 2.24.

92. Peter's "Pentecost" converts will return home as supporters of a Jewish reform movement. If Eusebius is right (*HE* 2.2.1; cf. Irenaeus, *Adv. haer.* 3.12.8) and Philip's converted eunuch returns home to preach, his version of the gospel is likely to contribute to the essentially "Jewish" nature of the Ethiopian church.

93. E.g., the church in North Italy grows little until the third century, and then its

development is sporadic because it depends upon the work of traveling Christian merchants from the East.

94. See D. Müller, "Apostle," in *DNTT*, 1:132ff.

95. Eusebius, *HE* 3.37.2f. He notes especially the brilliant Pantaenus, head of the school in Alexandria, who takes the gospel "to the natives of Asia" (5.10).

96. Origen, *Cont. Cels.* 3.9, 52.

97. *Clementine Homilies* 1.9. Of the preaching of Barnabas the twenty Greek homilies purport to be an account of Clement's association with the apostle Peter.

98. Dargan, 1:18ff. He identifies Greece and Rome as the other sources of Christian oratory. J. I. H. McDonald, pp. 12ff., 28ff., 31ff.

99. E.g., *Clementine Recognitions* 1.16, 45. See further D. Hill, "Jesus, a Prophet Mighty in Deed and Word," in *New Testament Prophecy* (Basingstoke: Marshall, 1985), pp. 48ff., and C. H. Peisker's useful summary ("Prophet," in *DNTT*, 3:83).

100. Paul places prophets second only to apostles in importance (1 Cor. 12:28), and "Hermas" (*Herm. Man.* 11) places them above priests. J. Broadus (*Lectures on the History of Preaching* [New York: Sheldon, 1886], pp. 102ff.) finds the roots of Christian preaching in the Jewish prophets, and John the Baptist is a major figure in the Jewish-Christian line of prophetic preachers. (See Peisker, 3:82ff.) The sermons of Jewish prophets are retained as Christian Scripture; e.g., Ezra's sermon in Neh. 8, and in Jude 14-15. Jewish prophets such as Enoch are honored as preachers, and even pagan prophecies of the Sybil are used as Christian material; e.g., Theophilus, *Autol.* 2.36.

101. E.g., Acts 13:1; 15:32; 21:9.

102. Paul's prohibitions about women preaching (1 Cor. 14:34ff.) indicate serious limitations upon the ministry of prophetesses. However, R. P. Martin (*The Spirit and the Congregation: Studies in I Corinthians 12–15* [Grand Rapids: Eerdmans, 1984], p. 87) suggests that the women are silenced because of "a wrongful aspiration to be charismatic teachers." See further C. Brown, in *DNTT*, 3:1066.

103. Justin Martyr, *Apol. I* 1 and 39.

104. E.g., Acts 13:1ff.; 15:32; Rom. 12:6; 1 Cor. 11:4; 12:28. See further P. K. Jewett, "Prophecy," in *NIDCC*, p. 806.

105. Acts 11:28; 21:10. The *Didache* (11-12) gives instructions about the reception of these itinerants. See also H. von Campenhausen, "Prophets and Teachers in the Second Century," in *Ecclesiastical Authority and Spiritual Power in the Church of the First Three Centuries* (London: A. & C. Black, 1969), pp. 178ff.

106. A. von Harnack, "The Religious Characteristics of the Mission Preaching," in *The Mission and Expansion of Christianity in the First Three Centuries*, trans. J. Pelikan (New York: Harper, 1962), pp. 86ff.

107. Contemporary African Christianity retains its respect for prophetic preachers. See A. Hastings, "Independence and Prophetism," in *The Church in Africa, 1450-1950* (Oxford: Oxford University Press, 1996), pp. 493ff.

108. Acts 13:1.

109. E.g., one of Clement of Alexandria's last works was *On Prophecy*, and Tertullian wrote a seven-volume defense of Montanist prophecy, now lost (Jerome, *De vir. illus.* 53).

110. R. M. Grant, *Augustus to Constantine: The Thrust of the Christian Movement in the Roman World* (New York, 1970), p. 132. The excesses of the Montanist prophet-preachers probably hasten the demise of the prophetic movement in the African catholic churches (Jerome, *De vir. illus.* 40). For the decline of the prophetic movement see B. H. Streeter, "The Rise of Christianity," in *CAH*, 11:253ff.

Chapter 2 — "'Things Written': The Pastors"

1. The work of preachers as writers is assisted by amanuenses (e.g., Rom. 16:22; 1 Cor. 16:21) and the use of various forms of shorthand which have existed ever since its invention by Cicero's freedman, Tiro (Cicero, *Epistulae ad Atticum* 13.22).

2. A. J. Malherbe, *Social Aspects of Early Christianity* (Baton Rouge: Louisiana State University Press, 1977), pp. 15ff.

3. Malherbe, p. 43. He supports his view by locating "classical allusions and quotations" in New Testament material.

4. E.g., the building of *auditoria* and the public readings arranged by Nero, Domitian, and Hadrian (Suetonius, *Nero* 10; Aelius Spartianus, *Hadrian* 14.6; Aelius Lampridius, *Severus Alexander* 35.1-2). Thus an old Latin tag is fulfilled — *littera scripta manet* — "What is written remains."

5. E. Dargan, "Preaching," in *NSHE*, 3:158.

6. C. H. Dodd, *The Apostolic Preaching and Its Development* (London: Hodder and Stoughton, 1950), p. 8.

7. E.g., 1 Cor. 5:9; Col. 4:16; 1 Thess. 5:27.

8. Demetrius, *On Style (Idem typos epistolikai)* 3.223ff. As a student of rhetoric, Paul studied the epistles of famous writers and knew they were more than personal notes. Ever since the days of Plato and Isocrates, they had been instruments for communicating important information to wider audiences than their original recipients. Deissmann (*Biblical Studies* [Edinburgh: T. & T. Clark, 1901], pp. 3ff.) rejects the idea that Paul's writings are epistles in this classical sense, but they display both the dialogical form (Rom. 2:1-7; 16:1-27) and formal salutations of the epistolary style (e.g., Rom. 2:1ff.; 6:1ff.).

9. E.g., some of Isocrates' epistles are speeches and Plato's *Seventh Epistle* is a spirited defense of his philosophical ideas. Emperors communicate their wishes by epistles declaimed before the Senate; e.g., Julius Capitolinus, *Opellius Macrinus* 6.1; Trebellius Pollio, *Claudius* 7.1. F. C. Schale claims that the custom of "silent reading" is a modern phenomenon which does not become common until the 1920s ("Reading," in *EB* [1970], 19:9c).

10. See R. J. Bauckham, *Jude, 2 Peter* (Waco: Word, 1983), p. 3.

11. E.g., H. D. Betz, *Galatians* (Philadelphia: Fortress, 1979); G. A. Kennedy, *New Testament Interpretation through Rhetorical Criticism* (Chapel Hill: University of North Carolina, 1984); G. W. Hansen, "Rhetorical Criticism," in *DPL* (1993), pp. 822ff. Rhetorical and epistolary disciplines are not identical. See *The Thessalonians Debate: Methodological Discord or Methodological Synthesis?* (Grand Rapids: Eerdmans, 2000), edited by K. P. Donfried and J. Beutler, for various views on the rhetorical and epistolary approaches to Paul's epistles.

12. R. Bolger, "Rhetoric," in *EB* (1970), 19:257; P. E. Satterthwaite, "Acts against the Background of Classical Rhetoric," in *The Book of Acts in Its Ancient Literary Setting,* ed. B. W. Winter and A. D. Clarke (Carlisle: Paternoster Press, 1993), p. 338. "Rhetoric" is derived from ῥῆμα, which Souter (*A Pocket Lexicon to the Greek New Testament* [Oxford: Clarendon, 1953], p. 227) defines as "the concrete expression of logos." Aristotle (*Rhet.* 1) defines rhetoric as "the faculty of discovering in the particular case what are the available means of persuasion."

13. B. Reicke, "A Synopsis of Early Christian Preaching," in *The Fruit of the Vine,* ed. A. Friedischen (Westminster: Dacre Press, 1953), p. 145.

14. E.g., Philem. 2; 1 Thess. 5:27.

15. E.g., Rom. 2:21ff.; 1 Cor. 15:1-2; 2 Cor. 1:13-14; Gal. 1:16; Col. 1:23, 28; 1 Tim. 2:6ff.; Titus 1:1.

16. S. Greidanus, "Preaching from Paul Today," in *DPL,* p. 737.

17. Greidanus, p. 738; cf. Bauckham, *Jude, 2 Peter,* p. 3.

18. E.g., Col. 4:16; 2 Pet. 3:15ff.

19. P. S. Wilson, *A Concise History of Preaching* (Nashville: Abingdon, 1992), p. 19.

20. Both James and 1 John have long been identified as "homilies" (L. E. Elliott-Binns, "James," *PC,* p. 1022; C. H. Dodd, *The Johannine Epistles* [London: Hodder and Stoughton, 1947], p. xxi). For Hebrews viewed homiletically see F. F. Bruce, *The Epistle to the Hebrews* (London: Marshall, Morgan and Scott, 1987), p. xlviii; R. McL. Wilson, *Hebrews* (Basingstoke: Marshall, Morgan and Scott, 1987), p. 16.

21. Rev. 1:3; 22:18-19.

22. J. G. Davies, *The Early Christian Church* (London: Weidenfeld and Nicolson, 1965), p. 16. Millard ("Reading and Writing in the Time of Jesus," *JSNT* 69 [2000]: 12) suggests that even before the Gospels were written, "notes and reports" of Jesus' words and activities were circulated and used homiletically. See further R. Bauckham, ed., *The Gospels for All Christians: Rethinking the Gospel Audiences* (Edinburgh: T. & T. Clark, 1998), for the argument that the Gospels were originally written to be circulated generally around the churches for homiletical use.

23. I. H. Marshall, "Jesus in the Gospels," in *EBC,* 1:518.

24. C. F. D. Moule, *The Birth of the New Testament* (London: A. & C. Black, 1973), p. 29; cf. R. P. Martin, *Worship in the Early Church* (Grand Rapids: Eerdmans, 1974), pp. 72ff.

25. See further R. H. Mounce, *Matthew* (Carlisle: Paternoster Press, 1995), p. 2; D. E. Nineham, *Saint Mark* (London: Penguin Books, 1963), p. 34; E. E. Ellis, *The Gospel of Luke* (London: Nelson, 1966), pp. 7ff., where he likens Luke's method to that of *pesher* and *midrash*. I. H. Marshall, *The Gospel of Luke: A Commentary on the Greek Text* (Exeter: Paternoster Press, 1989), p. 35; J. Marsh, *The Gospel of St John* (Harmondsworth: Penguin Books, 1968), p. 80.

26. D. J. Bosch, *Transforming Mission: Paradigm Shifts in Theology of Mission* (New York: Orbis, 1991), pp. 54-55.

27. A. Le Grys, *Preaching to the Nations: The Origins of Mission in the Early Church* (London: SPCK, 1988), pp. 119-20.

28. Malherbe, p. 11.

29. Malherbe, p. 70.

30. J. D. G. Dunn ("Romans, Letter to," in *DPL*, p. 839) observes that Paul "knew enough of the people and their circumstances to frame his teaching and paranesis accordingly."

31. J. Longnecker, "On the Form and Function and Authority of New Testament Letters," in *Scripture and Truth*, ed. D. A. Carson and J. D. Woodbridge (Grand Rapids: Zondervan, 1983), p. 104.

32. J. C. Mille, *The Obedience of Faith, the Eschatological People of God, and the Purpose of Romans*, SBL Dissertations, no. 177 (2000), pp. 238ff.

33. See further J. Schattenmann, "Fellowship," in *DNTT*, 1:639ff.

34. See W. A. Meeks, *The First Urban Christians: The Social World of the Apostle Paul* (New Haven: Yale University Press, 1983), pp. 277ff., and more generally, J. Y. Campbell, "The Origin and Meaning of the Christian Use of *Ekklesia*," *JTS* 49:130ff.; J. Coenen, "Ecclesia," in *DNTT*, 1:291f.

35. Rom. 16:1; 1 Cor. 7:12; Heb. 2:11; 1 John 3:1. See further J. H. Hellerman, *The Ancient Church as a Family* (Minneapolis: Fortress, 2001).

36. J. Wesley, *Notes on the New Testament* (London: Wesleyan Conference Office, 1887), see Acts 2:45.

37. Josephus (*Antiquities* 17.299ff.) speaks of the power and influence of the Jewish community in Rome. See H. Leon, *The Jews in Ancient Rome* (Philadelphia: Jewish Publication Society, 1960), pp. 135ff.; J. Carcopino, *Daily Life in Ancient Rome: The People and the City at the Height of the Empire*, trans. E. O. Lorimer (London: Penguin Books, 1991), pp. 152ff. In his *Commentary on Romans*, "Ambrosiaster" writes that the Roman Christians "embraced the faith of Christ according to the Roman rite," and Paul's salutations suggest that the church has attracted some significant members of the city's Jewish community (Rom. 16: for the originality of these greetings, see J. G. Dunn, *Romans 1–8* [Dallas: Word, 1988], p. lx; J. Zeisler, *Paul's Letter to the Romans* [London: SCM Press, 1990], p. 25).

38. Rom. 1:13f. See J. D. Kim, *God, Israel, and the Gentiles: Rhetoric and Situation in Romans 9–11*, SBL Dissertations 176 (2000), pp. 176ff. Cullmann suggests that the seeds

of Jewish-Gentile distrust in congregations have been present ever since; "first the Hellenists, then Peter and finally Paul were more or less abandoned by the inflexible Jews" ("Dissensions within the Early Church," in *New Testament Issues*, ed. R. Batey [London: SCM Press, 1970], p. 121).

39. Suetonius, *Claudius* 25; cf. Juvenal, *Satires* 14.100; 6.542-43; Martial, *Epigrams* 7.30; Persius, *Satires* 5.184.

40. This aloofness earns them a reputation for "regarding the rest of mankind with all the hatred of enemies" (Tacitus, *Annals* 5.5).

41. E.g., Matt. 18:17.

42. It is possible that in the case of the Roman congregations, relations are especially strained because Jews returning to the churches after the Claudian expulsion resent the fact that "Gentile" influences have become stronger in their absence.

43. Rom. 1–4.

44. Rom. 12; 14:10ff.

45. Eph. 2:17; cf. Rom. 15:5ff.

46. G. Theissen, *The Social Setting of Pauline Christianity*, trans. J. H. Schütz (Edinburgh: T. & T. Clark, 1999), pp. 69ff. See also A. Chester's article on the Pauline communities, "The Pauline Community," in *A Vision for the Church: Studies in Early Christian Ecclesiology*, ed. M. Bockmuehl and M. B. Thompson (Edinburgh: T. & T. Clark, 1997), pp. 105ff.

47. Ammianus Marcellinus, *Rer. gest.* 14.6.25-26.

48. E.g., Juvenal, *Satires* 7.178ff.; 8; Martial, *Epigrams* 3; cf. Suetonius, *Vetellius* 13.

49. "Duas tantum res anxius optat, Panem et circenses" (Juvenal, *Satires* 3.182-83). The hatred of the poor is particularly strong among the nouveaux riches, whose sense of insecurity is increased by having to live above their means in "pretentious poverty" *(ambitiosa pauperate)* (3.182-83).

50. Rom. 12:16.

51. 2 Cor. 8:9.

52. Rom. 12:13; 15:26; 1 Cor. 13:3; cf. Gal. 2:10.

53. The new relationship between rich and poor is most clearly set out in James 1–2, which shows how their roles are not merely emended but actually reversed.

54. See further Meeks, pp. 361ff.

55. See Carcopino, pp. 98ff.

56. Juvenal, *Satires* 6.

57. Gal. 3:28.

58. Bruce Winter in *After Paul Left Corinth: The Influence of Secular Ethic and Social Change* (Grand Rapids: Eerdmans, 2001) argues that this is particularly the case in the Corinthian church with its general enthusiasm for *Romanitas*.

59. E.g., Martial, *Epigrams* 1.96; Juvenal, *Satires* 6.246ff.; 2.93ff. Paul's apparently persnickety regulation about the length of hair (1 Cor. 11:6ff.) touched upon the same issue (Juvenal 6.501ff.; Martial 8.37).

60. Rom. 1:26-27. Roman society accepts lesbianism as normal (e.g., Martial, *Epigrams* 1.90, 92; 7.67), and in 1 Tim. 5:2 Paul stresses that Christian young women are "to live like sisters" but *"in all purity."*

61. Rom. 7:1ff.: the ensuing spiritual application of the regulations loses its power unless the regulations themselves are regarded as sound.

62. E.g., Eph. 5:23ff.; 1 Cor. 7:11; Col. 3:19. This is in marked contrast to the attitude of many pagan men who kept harems of slave women, freeing their favorites and declaring them *liberta*. Martial (*Epigrams* 12.56) playfully rebukes an unfaithful husband with the words: "Your wife calls you an admirer of servant-maids, And she herself is an admirer of litter-bearers. You are a pair!" (Matt. 19:13ff.; Mark 9:36-37; 10:13ff.).

63. The care of Jesus for children (Luke 2:40ff.; 9:38ff.; John 4:49) is reflected by the early church, and its concern for them as part of the Christian congregations is significant (Eph. 6:4; 1 Tim. 3:4, 12; 5:4). Pagan society pays comparatively little attention to children. Rich children are often shamelessly indulged (Martial, *Epigrams* 3.10; Pliny the Younger, *Epistles* 3.2), poor children are often mistreated (Quintilian, *Orat.* 1 and 3.14; Juvenal, *Satires* 14.15ff.) and exploited for sexual gratification (Martial, *Epigrams* 8.87), and "inconvenient" children are exposed at birth or later poisoned (Juvenal 6.602ff., 627ff.).

64. Juvenal, *Satires* 6.0.1-25 (so numbered in the Loeb edition because it was once thought to be a later addition); 6.38ff. 1 Cor. 5:1ff., Titus 2:4 suggest that such irregularities are also present in the churches.

65. Rom. 16:1ff., 6. Elsewhere (1 Tim. 5:2) Paul considers the beneficial role of older women in the congregations in contrast to the corruption spread by many Roman matrons (Juvenal, *Satires* 6.398ff.; 14.25ff.). He also stresses the care of the church's widows (1 Tim. 5:3ff.) and calls for the guidance of young widows in the congregations to prevent their becoming involved in the sexual merry-go-round adopted by their pagan counterparts (1 Tim. 5:6, 14; cf. Juvenal 6.300ff., 420ff.). See further B. W. Winter, *Seek the Welfare of the City: Christians as Benefactors and Citizens* (Grand Rapids: Eerdmans, 1994), pp. 61ff.

66. Perhaps the dissatisfaction of some Gentile women with the limitations applied to their new role and their inexperience in exercising their newfound freedom lead Paul to limit their participation in the assemblies (1 Cor. 11:5; 14:34; 1 Tim. 2:11).

67. Rom. 12:14. The Claudian expulsion, caused by the supporters of *Chrestus*, takes place in 50 C.E. (Suetonius, *Claudius* 25.2). If Romans was written 57-59 C.E., the Neronian persecution still is in the future. It is possible that both Mark and Hebrews are also epistolary sermons designed to sustain persecuted Roman congregations. See further W. Lane, *The Gospel of Mark* (Grand Rapids: Eerdmans, 1988), p. 15; V. Taylor, *The Gospel according to Mark* (London: Macmillan, 1952), p. 32; R. McL. Wilson, "Mark," in *PC*, p. 799; Bruce, *Hebrews*, pp. xxxiv-xxxv; L. Morris, "Hebrews," in *EBC*, 12:5.

68. E.g., 2 Cor. 1:3ff.; 4:9; Gal. 1:23; 1 Thess. 2:14; 2 Tim. 3:12; James 1:12ff.; 1 Pet. 1:6ff.

See generally, W. H. C. Frend, *Martyrdom and Persecution in the Early Church* (New York: New York University Press, 1967); H. B. Workman, *Persecution in the Early Church: A Chapter in the History of Renunciation* (London: Epworth Press, 1923); S. G. Hall, "Women among the Early Martyrs," *SCH* 30 (1993): 1ff.

69. Rom. 1:11. It is interesting that in Acts 4:36, "Barnabas son of consolation" (υἱὸς παρακλήσεως) may equally be rendered "son of exhortation," i.e., "the preacher."

70. Rom. 15:5; cf. 2 Cor. 1:3; 7:6; 2 Thess. 2:16-17; John 14:16, 26; 15:26. J. G. Davies ("The Primary Meaning of *Parakletos*," *JTS*, n.s., 4 [1953]: 35ff.) argues forcefully that "Comforter" is the initial meaning of παράκλητος (2 Cor. 7:4, 13; Phil. 2:1; Col. 1:11; Heb. 13:6).

71. E.g., Acts 16:40; 2 Cor. 7:6; 2 Thess. 3:2.

72. Rom. 12:10; cf. 1 Cor. 14:3-4; 3:1; Col. 2:2; 1 Thess. 4:18; 5:12ff.; Luke 22:24ff.; 1 John 4:11f.

73. Rom. 16:17ff. Perhaps he is warning against στεναγμός, the grumbling and censorious spirit which can arise amongst Christians and lead to disobedience and dissension. Cf. James 5:9; Heb. 13:17.

74. Rom. 12:10; cf. Heb. 13:1; 1 Pet. 2:17; 1 John 4:7.

75. Rom. 16:17ff.; cf. 1 Cor. 16:22; Gal. 1:8ff.

76. Rom. 8:36, quoting Ps. 44:22. Elsewhere it is made clear that suffering is not meritorious per se and Christians should not seek martyrdom (1 Pet. 4:15ff.; 1 Cor. 13:3).

77. Rom. 8:35ff.; cf. Phil. 1:28ff.; 1 Pet. 2:21; Heb. 2:17-18, which suggest that by his example of suffering Jesus identifies himself with his persecuted "brothers." He sympathizes with them and will not allow them to be "tested beyond their endurance" (Heb. 2:18; 1 Cor. 10:13).

78. Rom. 5:3ff.; cf. 1 Pet. 1:7ff.; Heb. 5:8.

79. Rom. 5:1ff.; cf. Acts 17:3; Heb. 2:10.

80. Rom. 8:18; 12:14ff.; cf. 2 Cor. 4:17; 1 Pet. 1:6ff.; Rev. 6:9ff.

81. The uncompromising words of Heb. 6:4ff. indicate the bitterness generated by those who defect (παραπίπτω — "fall away," only here in the New Testament). Later the issue of the *lapsi* becomes a major cause of division in congregations.

82. Rom. 16:18.

83. Caligula and Claudius reverse Tiberius's hostility to "foreign rites" (Suetonius, *Tiberius* 37; Josephus, *Antiquities* 18.3.4-5; Tacitus, *Annals* 2.85). Claudius reforms the liturgy of Cybele and Attis, and Domitian rebuilds the temple of Isis which was destroyed in 80 C.E. Gnosticism is present in congregations in Corinth, Colossae, and elsewhere in Asia Minor (e.g., 1 Cor. 1:17ff.; 2:4ff.). See further J. D. Douglas, "Gnosticism," in *NBD*, pp. 415ff.; A. R. C. Leaney, "Gnosticism," in *DCT*, pp. 133ff.

84. Rom. 16:17, 25.

85. Rom. 16:25; cf. Gal. 1:6ff.; 3:1; 1 Tim. 6:20; Heb. 13:7ff.

86. Rom. 1:1ff.; cf. Heb. 1:1ff.

87. R. H. Fuller, *The Foundations of New Testament Christology* (London: Collins,

1972), p. 15; Rom. 1:3; cf. Acts 2:23ff.; 9:22; 17:3; 18:5, 28; etc.; on early Christology and soteriology generally see also W. Pannenberg, *Jesus: God and Man,* trans. L. L. Wilkins and D. A. Priebe (London: SCM Press, 1968), pp. 38ff..

88. E.g., Rom. 1:4; 1 Cor. 15:1ff.; Eph. 2:6; Heb. 13:20; 1 Pet. 1:3, 21; Rev. 1:17-18.

89. Phil. 2:9ff.

90. Acts 2:36.

91. E.g. Rom. 1:4 (Ἰησοῦ Χριστοῦ τοῦ κυρίου ἡμῶν); cf. Acts 1:21; 1 Cor. 11:23; 12:3; 2 Cor. 1:14; Gal. 6:17; 1 Thess. 2:15; Heb. 13:20; 2 Pet. 1:2; Rev. 22:20. See further H. Bietenhard, "Lord," in *DNTT,* 2:510ff.; Pannenberg, pp. 365ff.; Fuller, pp. 67-68.

92. Bietenhard, 2:512, notes nearly ten thousand instances of the term in LXX and observes that "In the overwhelming majority of cases (some 6156) . . . *kyrios* replaces the Hebrew proper name for God, the tetragrammaton YHWH."

93. 1 Cor. 8:5. Vespasian gladly consults "the god of Carmel" when he is in Judea and Serapis when he is in Egypt (Suetonius, *Vespasian* 5; 7). The well-meaning Severus Alexander places Christ's statue beside those of Abraham and Orpheus and regrets that he is unable to build a temple solely for Christ's worship (Aelius Lampridius, *Severus Alexander* 39.2; 43.6-7).

94. After the postmortem deification of Augustus, emperors accepted their divine role with varying degrees of seriousness, but the imperial office becomes truly theocratic when Domitian insists on being addressed as "Lord and God" (Suetonius, *Domitian* 13.2).

95. Ammianus Marcellinus (*Rer. gest.* 14.1.5) writes bitterly of the way in which the most terrible excesses of Gallus are implemented because "whatever the implacable Caesar has resolved . . . is determined to be right and lawful."

96. Rom. 7:18ff.; cf. Acts 2:17; 1 Cor. 16:51ff.; 1 Tim. 4:1ff.; 1 Pet. 4:7, 17; 1 John 2:18.

97. E.g., Rom. 13:2ff.; Eph. 6:10ff.; Phil. 3:18ff.; 1 Thess. 5:1ff.; Titus 3:1ff. See further L. J. Kreitzer ("Eschatology," in *DPL,* pp. 265-66) on Pauline eschatology and ethics.

98. Rom. 13:1ff.

99. Rom. 16:17ff.; 1 Cor. 5:1-2; Phil. 3:18ff.; 2 Thess. 2:9ff.

100. Rom. 2:1ff. See F. F. Bruce, *Romans: An Introduction and Commentary* (London: Inter-Varsity, 1974), p. 86; E. F. Harrison, "Romans," *EBC,* 10.30ff. For a discussion of this passage as a true, classical diatribe, see Zeisler, *Paul's Letter to the Romans* (London: SCM, 1990), p. 7.

101. Rom. 2:14ff.; e.g., Persius (*Satires* 3.52-53; 5.104-5) applauds the Stoics' moral influence upon the young. See T. Engberg-Pedersen, *Paul and the Stoics: An Essay in Interpretation* (Edinburgh: T. & T. Clark, 2000), who finds close similarities between the socioethical teaching of Paul and that of the Stoics.

102. Rom. 1:18ff.

103. Rom. 2:17ff.; 3:9ff. In 2:21, Paul apparently refers to a particularly notorious cause célèbre which involved the misappropriation of funds destined for the Jerusalem temple (Josephus, *Antiquities* 10.8.81-82).

104. Rom. 3:9; 5:12ff.; cf. Gal. 3:1ff., 22; 1 John 1:8ff.

105. Rom. 8:3ff.; cf. 2 Cor. 5:21; Eph. 1:19; 2:10; Col. 1:4; Heb. 4:15; 1 Pet. 2:22; 1 John 3:5. Homiletically, the presentation of the death of Jesus in sacrificial terms is very powerful since atoning sacrifice lies at the heart of virtually all contemporary religious systems.

106. Rom. 5:1ff.; Gal. 3:9. More than half the New Testament's references to πίστις occur in Paul's epistles, where it forms a central theme of his preaching.

107. Rom. 6:4ff.; 7:6; cf. 1 Pet. 2:2; Rom. 13:12.

108. Rom. 8:6; 9:8. Cf. 2 Pet. 2:18; 1 John 2:16.

109. Rom. 6:12ff.; cf. 1 Cor. 5:1; Eph. 4:31; Col. 3:5ff.; James 2:6-7. Demas deserts Paul because he "loves the good things of this world" (2 Tim. 4:10).

110. Rom. 13:14.

111. Rom. 1:24-32.

112. Rom. 1:22ff.; cf. 1 Cor. 5:11; 6:9; Gal. 5:20. The imperial cult is concerned solely with respect for the emperor and the safety of the state. Popular religion normally is more concerned with correct ritual than with ethical concerns. Persius (*Satires* 2.71ff.) untypically urges his readers to "offer to the gods a heart rightly-tuned," but Paul uses the unusual word θεοστυγής (God-haters) to describe pagan society (Rom. 1:30).

113. Rom. 1:29. This destructive attitude is summed up in a group of associated words (ἐπιθυμία, ἡδονή, πλεονεξία) variously translated as "lust," "covetousness," and "desire."

114. Rom. 1:24ff.; cf. 2 Pet. 2:18; 1 John 2:16-17. In popular parlance *libido* and *cupiditas* mean simply "eager desire" or "passionate longing," and *ad libidinem* signifies little more than "according to inclination." For the neutral use of ἐπιθυμία in LXX, see H. Schönweiss, "Desire, Lust, Pleasure," in *DNTT,* 1:456.

115. Rom. 1:29-30; e.g., Juvenal (*Satires* 6.46ff.; 2.93-94) exposes the heedless extravagance of the rich women. The noblest emperors are noted for their "love of money" and the unscrupulous ones finance their extravagances by stealing from the people (Suetonius, *Vespasian* 16; Juvenal 14.174ff.). The rich ruin themselves in order to provide ever more lavish feasts, and all are gripped by gambling fever (Juvenal 8.178ff.; 1.89-90; Tacitus, *Annals* 1.3.54; Suetonius, *Vitellius* 13.1-2). In their search for new thrills, Nero and Gallus haunt the slums of Rome at night and Tiberias retires to Capri to indulge ever more bizarre sexual depravities (Tacitus 13.25; 15.36; Ammianus Marcellinus, *Rer. gest.* 14.1.9).

116. Agrippina poisons her husband Claudius and is, in turn, murdered by her son Nero, who kicks to death his pregnant wife.

117. In 1:29 Paul specifically refers to the all-pervading love of malicious "gossip" which is also mentioned by Martial (*Epigrams* 9.102-3).

118. Rom. 1:30; cf. Ammianus Marcellinus, *Rer. gest.* 14.6.9.

119. Rom. 1:31; e.g., Aurelian has slaves killed in his presence "through sheer love of cruelty" (Flavius Vopiscus, *Aurelian* 49.3; cf. Julius Capitolinus, *Opellius Macrinus*

12.1ff.). Tacitus (*Annals* 16.14) speaks of a "torrent of wasted bloodshed" in Roman society.

120. Audiences are obscenely excited by the horrors of the contests in the arena (Martial, *On the Spectacles* 12ff.; Ammianus Marcellinus, *Rer. gest.* 14.7.3). "One of the most far-reaching changes introduced by Christianity into the conduct of life was the idea that human life as such was sacred, an idea distinctly opposed to the actual practice of pagans, if not quite novel to them" (J. B. Bury, *A History of the Later Roman Empire: From Arcadius to Irene (395 AD to 800 AD)*, 2 vols. [London: Macmillan, 1889], 1:21).

121. E.g., Galba decimates a rebellious company of soldiers. Aurelian is praised for killing forty-eight men in a single day, and Domitian kills "gratuitously for the most trivial reasons" (Suetonius, *Galba* 12.2; Flavius Vopiscus, *Aurelian* 6.4; 7.4; Suetonius, *Domitian* 10.1ff.).

122. Rom. 3:23; 5:12.

123. Rom. 8:11, 13; cf. 1 Cor. 3:16; Gal. 5:16; Phil. 1:27; cf. James 4:5.

124. Rom. 15:13; cf. Eph. 1:17ff.; 2 Tim. 1:7.

125. Rom. 12:11-12; cf. 1 Thess. 5:17; 1 Tim. 2:1. The preachers exhort their congregations to pray both individually (1 Cor. 7:5; James 5:13) and corporately (2 Thess. 3:1; Heb. 13:18).

126. G. N. Stanton, *Jesus of Nazareth in New Testament Preaching*, SNTSMS 27 (New York: Cambridge University Press, 1974), p. 187.

127. L. Hurtado, *Mark* (Carlisle: Paternoster Press, 1995), p. 5.

128. See Lane, p. 10; Marshall, "Jesus in the Gospels," 1:519.

129. Mark 1:14.

130. Eph. 2:17.

131. 1 Pet. 3:19-20; 4:6. See further, D. Horrell, *The Epistles of Peter and Jude* (Peterborough: Epworth Press, 1998), pp. 77ff.; J. N. D. Kelly, *A Commentary on the Pastoral Epistles* (New York: Harper and Row, 1983), pp. 152ff.; S. K. Kistemaker, *Exposition of the Epistles of Peter and the Epistle of Jude* (Welwyn, England: Evangelical Press, 1987), pp. 141ff.; I. H. Marshall, *I Peter* (Leicester: Inter-Varsity, 1991), pp. 122ff.

132. M. D. Atkins, *Preaching in a Cultural Context* (Peterborough: Foundery Press, 2001), p. 4.

133. Luke 4:14ff.; 7:22; Mark 1:15; Matt. 4:17; 11:5.

134. Jesus distinguishes his ministry from the prophetic ministry of the Baptist (Luke 4:24; 24:19; Matt. 11:19), but his sayings and actions strongly suggest that he regards himself as prophet (Mark 6:4; Luke 4:24; John 4:44). His ministry displays a prophetic amalgam of words and deeds (Matt. 4:23; 9:35; 11:23; Mark 6:1ff.; Luke 4:17ff.; 6:17ff.), and his miracles are of a piece with his preaching ministry. E. P. Sanders (*Jesus and Judaism* [London: SCM Press, 1985], p. 158) insists that there is "an interrelationship among preaching, healing and the crowds." How far Jesus sees himself as *the* eschatological prophetic preacher is unclear. See further, Fuller, pp. 125ff.; G. N. Stanton,

The Gospels and Jesus (Oxford: Oxford University Press, 1989), pp. 191, 178; Pannenberg, pp. 217ff.

135. Luke 4:18.

136. Mark 12:37; Matt. 21:26; Mark 11:32; Luke 3:15; 4:42; 8:40; John 6:24; Acts 5:13; 8:6. The term *'am hā'āreṣ* may distinguish the masses from the aristocracy or rural peasants from city dwellers. (See R. de Vaux, *Ancient Israel: Its Life and Institutions* [London: Darton, Longman and Todd, 1998], pp. 70ff.; Sanders, pp. 174ff.) For the constituents of Jesus' congregations, see G. Theissen and A. Merz, *The Historical Jesus: A Comprehensive Guide*, trans. J. Bowden (Minneapolis: Fortress, 1998), pp. 217ff. For an analysis of the society from which the congregations are drawn, based on Gerhard Lenski's sociological model of advanced rural societies, see R. L. Rohrbaugh, "The Jesus Tradition: The Gospel Writers' Strategies of Persuasion," in *ECW*, 1:198.

137. E.g., Matt. 8:5ff.; Luke 7:1ff.; Matt. 18:2-3; Mark 10:13ff.; Luke 9:4; 18:16-17; Matt. 14:21; 15:28; Mark 5:24ff.; Luke 17:35; 7:37ff.; Matt. 8:2ff.; Mark 1:40ff.; Luke 17:11ff.; cf. Acts 5:13; 8:6. For the social limitations placed upon women, see J. Jeremias, *Jerusalem in the Time of Jesus: An Investigation into Economic and Social Conditions during the New Testament Period*, trans. F. H. Cave and C. H. Cave (London: SCM Press, 1996), pp. 359ff.; Theissen and Merz, pp. 219ff. Jesus seems to have a special relationship with the τελῶναι (Luke 7:29; 15:1), although they are regarded as no better than murderers and robbers (*Bekhoroth* 30b; *Baba Kamma* 113a).

138. Mark 6:2; Luke 4:16f., 44; John 6:59. The tradition of expository sermons as part of synagogue worship develops after the exile (P. H. Davids, "Homily, Ancient," in *DNTB*, p. 517), and although most surviving Jewish sermons are from the Amoraic period (200-500 C.E.), there are some from the Tannaitic period (70-200 C.E.), which probably represent the kind of synagogue preaching Jesus himself hears. His own synagogue sermons are unlike those normally delivered (Mark 1:21ff.). The early Christian preachers also preach in synagogues (e.g., Acts 13:5; 14:1ff.; 18:7), and Schnackenburg (*The Church in the New Testament*, trans. W. J. O'Hara [London: Burns and Oates, 1981], p. 38) suggests that they are greatly influenced by the synagogue sermons. For Jewish preaching see R. V. Friedenberg, "Jewish Preaching," in *CEP*, pp. 281ff.

139. E.g., Mark 2; cf. Acts 5:42; 20:20, for apostles also preaching in houses. R. N. North ("How Loud Was Jesus' Voice? Mark 4:1," *ET* 112, no. 4 [January 2001]: 117ff.) suggests that vast open-air meetings are a literary device on the part of the Evangelists, but Josephus (*Antiquities* 1.8.64) confirms Luke's claim that Jesus draws great crowds (Luke 5:19).

140. When Jesus speaks, he *preaches* (κηρύσσω) and he also *teaches* (διδάσκω) what God has given him to *proclaim* (εὐαγγελίζω) (Matt. 8:19; 11:5; 22:33; Mark 12:14; Luke 4:18; 20:1; John 8:4).

141. Marshall, "Jesus in the Gospels," 1:519.

142. Eugene Lowry, an exponent of preaching as a narrative art form, urges preachers "to upset the equilibrium of the listeners in such a way as to engage them in

the sermon theme" (*The Homiletical Plot: The Sermon as Narrative Art Forms* [London: Westminster John Knox, 2001], p. 28). The parables of Jesus achieve this brilliantly. See further J. Jeremias, *The Parables of Jesus*, trans. S. H. Hooke (London: SCM Press, 1955), pp. 9ff.; C. H. Dodd, *The Parables of the Kingdom* (New York: Scribner, 1936), pp. 11ff.; D. O. Via, "The Parables of Jesus," in *CEP*, pp. 358ff.

143. H. Palmer, "Seeking Verdicts for Parables," *ET* 111, no. 8 (May 2000): 262ff.

144. Matt. 5–7; Luke 6:17ff. W. D. Davies (*The Setting of the Sermon on the Mount* [London: Cambridge University Press, 1964], pp. 1, 5) takes a skeptical view of the sermon's authenticity, regarding it as "a collection of unrelated sayings of diverse origins, a patchwork" in which it is impossible to discern "an interrelated totality derived from the actual teaching of Jesus." Stott (*The Message of the Sermon on the Mount* [Leicester: Inter-Varsity, 2000], pp. 23-24) represents a more conservative view of the sermon and adopts A. B. Bruce's suggestion that it is a summary of the teaching given by Jesus during a retreat. See further in situ references in standard commentaries and R. H. Mounce, "Sermon on the Mount," in *NDB*, pp. 1078ff., for a useful basic bibliography. It is unclear how much of the "sermon" is addressed privately to Jesus' disciples, since the term is used somewhat elastically: οἱ μαθηταί is not automatically the equivalent of οἱ δώδεκα. In Luke 6:17 "a great crowd of his disciples" hears "the sermon plain" (ὄχλος πολὺς μαθητῶν αὐτοῦ). The "seventy-two" referred to in Luke 10:1 are clearly counted as disciples. Whatever the exact constitution of Jesus' audience, the sermon's material provides useful clues to the content of Jesus' preaching because subjects clarified in private teaching sessions seem often also to be themes of public sermons (e.g., Matt. 13:10-11; Luke 8:9-10; 10:23).

145. Luke 8:9ff. For references to the kingdom see Stanton, *The Gospels and Jesus*, pp. 189ff.

146. The Galileans are noted for their bellicose nature, and some revolutionaries may even have joined the followers of Jesus. See D. Dunn-Wilson, "The Portrayal and Significance of Judas Iscariot in Christianity" (M.Phil. thesis, University of Sussex, 1983), pp. 13ff.; E. W. Stegemann and W. Stegemann, *The Jesus Movement: A Social History of Its First Century* (Edinburgh: T. & T. Clark, 1999), pp. 170ff.

147. M. D. Hooker-Stacey, "Jesus and Christology," *ET* 112, no. 9 (June 2001): 299.

148. Luke 10:9; 17:21; 6:20ff.

149. The church and the kingdom are not identical. Ridderbos ("Kingdom of God," in *NBD*, p. 649) helpfully likens their relationship to two concentric circles, the outer being "the whole of God's redeeming activity in Christ" and the inner, "the assembly of those who have accepted the gospel of the Kingdom."

150. Matt. 22:36ff.; Mark 12:28-29; Luke 10:25-26; cf. Rom. 13:8ff.; 1 Cor. 6:13; Gal. 5:22; Eph. 5:32.

151. Matt. 8:11ff.; 13:43; Mark 13:27; Luke 12:32; John 6.35ff.; cf. 1 Cor. 15:51ff.; Col. 1:12ff.; 1 Pet. 1:4-5.

152. Matt. 23:7ff.; Luke 4:28ff.; John 6:66.

153. E. Dargan, *A History of Preaching* (London: Hodder and Stoughton and G. H. Doran, 1905), 1:23.

154. Matt. 10:1ff.; Mark 6:7ff.; Luke 9:1ff.; 10:1ff.; Matt. 28:19-20; Mark 16:19; Luke 24:47ff.; Acts 1:8ff.

155. Matt. 10:20, 40; Mark 16:16-17; Luke 24:47ff.; cf. 1 Cor. 10:8; Titus 2:15; 1 Pet. 5:1.

156. Rom. 1:1; 9:1; 1 Cor. 1:17; 15:12; 2 Cor. 2:17; 5:20; Gal. 2:20; 2 Tim. 4:17.

Chapter 3 — "'After the Apostles': The Early Fathers"

1. E. Dargan, *A History of Preaching* (London: Hodder and Stoughton and G. H. Doran, 1905), 1:43.

2. It is claimed that *The Epistle to Diognetus* was written by "a disciple of the apostles" (*Diog.* 11.1), that Papias was "a hearer of John," and so utters "the living and abiding voice" of the apostles (Jerome, *De vir. illus.* 1.11.18; Irenaeus, *Adv. haer.* 5.33.4; Eusebius, *HE* 3.39.frag.). *The Epistle of Barnabas* is attributed to Paul's fellow preacher, and the *Didache* enshrines the apostles' teaching.

3. *Mart. Pol.* 16.2; *1 Clem.* 48.

4. Ignatius, *Phld.* 7.1.

5. *1 Clem.* 7.6; Ignatius, *Phld.* 5; *1 Clem.* 42.1 and 5.1 (in which he refers to the apostles as "those champions who lived nearest our time"); *Did.* 11.

6. Ignatius, *Eph.* 3.2; *Trall.* 6.1.

7. E.g., Ignatius, Rom. 1.

8. Ignatius, *Rom.* 4.1; *Trall.* 12.3; *Pol.* 8.1; Polycarp, *Phil.* 13; *Herm. Vis.* 5.5ff.; e.g., *The Martyrdom of Polycarp* is originally sent to the church in Philomelium before being passed on to be read in other congregations.

9. J. B. Lightfoot, ed., *The Apostolic Fathers* (London: Macmillan, 1893), introduction, p. 41; cf. O. Heick (*A History of Christian Thought*, 2 vols. [Philadelphia: Fortress, 1965], 1:46), who calls it "the most ancient homily that has been preserved."

10. Lightfoot comments (p. 41): "as a literary production it has no value." The two epistles of Clement are included in the approved list of books in the *Apostolic Constitutions* (Ecclesiastical Canons 85). Eusebius (*HE* 3.38) doubts whether it was universally accepted as canonical.

11. Polycarp, *Phil.* 13.

12. Eusebius, *HE* 3.16.

13. *Herm. Vis.* 5.7.

14. Churches and individual Christians begin to create libraries. See H. Y. Gamble's full treatment of this subject in *Books and Readers in the Early Church* (New Haven: Yale University Press, 1995).

15. Eusebius, *HE* 1.37; *The Passion of the Scillitan Martyrs* describes how Africa's proto-martyrs carry Paul's epistles with them to their death.

16. Christians regard with horror the *traditores* who surrender sacred books to be burned during the Diocletian persecution (ca. 303).

17. Public reading needs skill because the words in codices are not divided. Eventually lectors become a minor order of ministry with strict regulations for their appointment and conduct (*Apost. Constit.* 8.2.10).

18. *Apost. Constit.* 6.3.16. To avoid any misunderstanding, a list of acceptable books is appended (Ecclesiastical Canons 85). For the emendation of texts see B. D. Ehrman, *The Orthodox Corruption of Scripture: The Effects of Early Christological Controversies on the Text of the New Testament* (New York: Oxford University Press, 1993), p. xii.

19. B. H. Streeter (*The Primitive Church: Studied with Special Reference to the Origins of the Christian Ministry* [New York: Macmillan, 1929], pp. 225-26) refers to an instruction which requires that lectors must be "capable of clear expounding" because they "assume the position of the Evangelist."

20. Listening to public readings becomes increasingly debased, and by the third century, even the worst examples of oratorical incompetence are sycophantically applauded.

21. *Did.* 4.13.

22. Tertullian, *Apol.* 39.

23. One of the most popular collections is *The Preaching of Peter,* a late-second-century work which purported to be a collection of the apostle's sermons. It is mentioned by Eusebius (*HE* 3.3), is quoted by Clement of Alexandria (*Strom.* 6.5), and is widely used by preachers, including Origen. Such sermons are taken so seriously that it is said (*Epistle of Peter to James* 4.1) that Peter himself insists that "the books of his preaching" are to be shared only with those who are "good and religious."

24. Ignatius, *Eph.* 4.1; *Trall.* 6.2.

25. Ignatius, *Eph.* 9.1.

26. *Herm. Sim.* 2; *1 Clem.* 38.2; *Did.* 4.6ff.

27. Polycarp, *Phil.* 4.2ff.; *1 Clem.* 38.2-3; *Did.* 4.10; *Herm. Vis.* 1.1; Ignatius, *Pol.* 4. The care accorded widows in the churches is especially impressive (Ignatius, *Pol.* 4.1; Polycarp, *Phil.* 4.3).

28. Husbands are to love their wives and to forgive them if they are unfaithful but repentant (*1 Clem.* 1.3; Ignatius, *Pol.* 5.1; *Herm. Man.* 4). Young men and women are to be modest and pure, and children are to be "partakers of instruction" (*1 Clem.* 21.5ff.; Polycarp, *Phil.* 4.2; *Did.* 4.9). Slaves are to be well treated (Ignatius, *Pol.* 4.3).

29. Ignatius, *Eph.* 9.1; *Trall.* 6.2; *1 Clem.* 1.1; *Herm. Man.* 11.

30. *1 Clem.* 1.1.

31. Ignatius, *Eph.* 10; *Herm. Vis.* 4.1.1.

32. Cf. Acts 12:3; 20:3, 19; etc. According to Gibbon (31) even after the accession of Constantine paganism is "still revered by numerous people."

33. Ignatius, *Magn.* 10.3; *Phld.* 6.1; *The Epistle of Barnabas* (2.6) seeks to show how the Jewish faith is "annulled by the new law of Christ."

34. E.g., *Herm. Man.* 8.4-5.

35. *2 Clem.* 14.1. Hermas (*Vis.* 3.5, 8) depicts the church as a magnificent tower built by angels and surrounded by the Virtues.

36. *Herm. Vis.* 3.5, 8; *Sim.* 3; 9.9; *Vis.* 3.10; 5.2.

37. *2 Clem.* 6.

38. Ignatius, *Eph.* 5.3; 13.1; *Phld.* 6.2; *Diog.* 12.9; *Did.* 9.4; cf. Ignatius, *Eph.* 20; *Magn.* 7.2; *Pol.* 4.2.

39. *Barn.* 4.10; *Herm. Sim.* 8.3.2; *Diog.* 12.9.

40. E.g., Tacitus, *Annals* 4.60ff.; Julius Capitolinus, *Antoninus Pius* 10.

41. Romans' lives are dominated by astrology and superstition, from emperors like Hadrian and Augustus (Aelius Spartianus, *Hadrian* 16.7; Suetonius, *Augustus* 91-92) to the poorest women haunting the fortune-tellers' booths at the races (Juvenal, *Satires* 6.582ff.).

42. Persius, *Satires* 2.31ff.

43. Many Christians do not resist the temptation, and by the fourth century Saturninus (Flavius Vopiscus, *Firmius Saturninus* 8.2ff.) reports that in the Egyptian churches there is scarcely a presbyter who is "not an astrologer, soothsayer or anointer."

44. Ignatius, *Eph.* 19.3; Tatian, *Orat. ad Graec.* 7.

45. Tatian, *Orat. ad Graec.* 12, 14-19; *Herm. Man.* 11.

46. Eventually candidates are anointed with oil to drive out evil spirits and receive milk and honey for protection. Similar rites are used in the mystery religion. See F. C. Grant, *Hellenistic Religions: The Age of Syncretism* (New York: Liberal Arts, 1953), p. 59.

47. Hermas (*Man.* 4.3) commends regular postbaptismal repentance. For exorcism, see B. Newns, "Exorcism," in *DLW*, pp. 174ff.; A. Harrison, "Exorcism," in *DCS*, pp. 140-41.

48. Ignatius, *Eph.* 11.1; *Did.* 16; *Barn.* 4.3. The fragments of Papias's *Expositions of the Oracles of Our Lord* suggest that he draws heavily on Jewish apocalyptic ideas. It is quoted by Andreas of Caesarea and Irenaeus. For eschatology see *DECB*, pp. 236ff. Heick (1:55) suggests that it is the conviction that the parousia is near "which holds the congregations together."

49. *Herm. Sim.* 5.5.3.

50. Ignatius, *Rom.* 5.2-3.

51. *Mart. Pol.* 20, 18. The anonymous *Passion of the Holy Martyrs*, which tells of the death of Justin, is another of the many *martyria* written for the encouragement of Christians.

52. Later this leads to the creation of the catacombs as focal points for veneration. See A. Gowans, "Catacomb," in *EB* (1970), 5:57ff.; P. Toon, "Catacomb," in *NIDCC*, p. 199, for basic bibliography.

53. Heick, 1:46.

54. In his first letter Clement quotes several New Testament books, e.g., the Synoptic Gospels (*1 Clem.* 13; 24; 46), Hebrews (43), and 1 Peter (49).

55. *Barn.* 1.7.

56. E.g., *1 Clem.* 56.16; Ignatius, *Magn.* 6.1; *Eph.* 18.2; *Trall.* 9; *Herm. Sim.* 5.6; *2 Clem.* 9.5.

57. E.g., *1 Clem.* 58.2; *Herm. Sim.* 5.6 (a rather confused statement of trinitarian doctrine); Ignatius, *Eph.* 9.1.

58. Polycarp, *Phil.* 7.2.

59. The problem is illustrated in the fourth-century *Clementine Recognitions* (8-9) where, when Barnabas presents "a simple discourse, those who thought themselves learned or philosophic began to laugh at him," so that he has to be rescued by Clement.

60. *2 Clem.* 1.5ff.

61. E.g., Plato, *Philebus* 1a; *Phaedrus* 274c; Aristotle, *Metaphysics* 1074b.

62. Tatian, *Orat. ad Graec.* 31. He taunts the philosophers, saying, "What noble thing have you produced by your pursuit of philosophy?" (2).

63. E.g., *1 Clem.* 7.4; *Barn.* 5.1.

64. Heick, 1:46.

65. Vivid images are used to describe the choice between rival "ages," "coinages," "paths," and "angels" (*2 Clem.* 6; Ignatius, *Magn.* 5.1-2; *Did.* 1; *Barn.* 16; *Herm. Man.* 6.2).

66. Ignatius, *Eph.* 12.

67. *Herm. Man.* 8.3. These special areas of danger are confirmed by similar lists in Paul's epistles (e.g., 2 Cor. 12:20; Gal. 5:19ff.) and by Clement (*1 Clem.* 3).

68. E.g., Juvenal (*Satires* 6.11ff.) mockingly observes that chastity has disappeared since "the days of Jupiter when the world was young."

69. Ignatius, *Phld.* 4 (the longer version).

70. *Herm. Man.* 4.1.

71. *Diog.* 5.6; Ignatius, *Phld.* 4 (the longer version).

72. Ignatius, *Phld.* 4 (the longer version).

73. Ignatius *Phld.* 4 (the longer version); cf. Polycarp, *Phil.* 4.3.

74. E.g., *Herm. Sim.* 9.13, where "righteous men" are beguiled by "beautiful women clothed in black, with dishevelled hair" tempting them to surrender the strength given them by the virginal "powers of the Son of God" (9.2).

75. Tatian (*Orat. ad Graec.* 33) derides the pagan, lesbian heroine Sappho as "a lewd, love-sick female (who) sang her own wantonness."

76. The popular view of sex is symbolized by the pornographic tales of Petronius's *Satyricon*, although Tacitus and other traditionalists condemn the sexual perversions which invade Rome (Tacitus, *Annals* 14.20); cf. Juvenal's hypocritical protests against "foreign strumpets" (*Satires* 3.65-66).

77. *Did.* 2.2, where prohibition of child abuse is added to the more familiar Ten Commandments. Cf. Augustine's condemnation of "boy-stealers" within the church (*Tract. ep. Jo.* 3.9).

78. E.g., Tacitus, *Annals* 5.6; Suetonius, *Nero* 28; Juvenal (*Satires* 6.602ff.) says there are particular pools where unwanted babies are exposed to die or to be taken as fodder

for adult sexual perversions. Child prostitution is rife, and Martial, who himself owns a young boy, declares that "the cradle has become the pimps' property" (*Epigrams* 1.58; 9.7, 59).

79. *1 Clem.* 30.1; cf. Plato, *Symposium* 180-81, 192. Paul's epistles suggest that such views have long been present *within* the churches (1 Cor. 5:1ff.; cf. Rom. 1:26ff.; Eph. 4:19).

80. *Herm. Man.* 12.1.1; 2.1.

81. E.g., Juvenal, *Satires* 11.1ff.; 5.30ff.; 6.352ff.; 7.178ff. The lifestyle of the emperors is the most extravagant of all (e.g., Suetonius, *Tiberius* 43.1; *Vitellius* 7.13; *Titus* 7.1; *Domitian* 4).

82. *1 Clem.* 2.1.

83. Polycarp, *Phil.* 11.2. *Avaritia* is regarded as a cardinal sin, ranked with "withcrafts and magic" as part of the "way of the Black One" (*Barn.* 20.1; *2 Clem.* 4.3; 6.4).

84. *Herm. Sim.* 2; *Did.* 4.5ff.; *2 Clem* 4.3.

85. *2 Clem.* 6.3; 4.3.

86. *1 Clem.* 4.

87. E.g., Juvenal, *Satires* 8.142ff.; 9.102ff. Suetonius's *Lives of the Caesars* and Tacitus's *Annals* reveal the atmosphere of intrigue surrounding the imperial courts.

88. *1 Clem.* 1.1.

89. *1 Clem.* 16.1.

90. *Barn.* 1.7.

Chapter 4 — "*Fidei Defensores*': The Apologists"

1. E. R. Dodds, *Pagans and Christians in an Age of Anxiety: Some Aspects of Religious Experience from Marcus Aurelius to Constantine* (Cambridge: Cambridge University Press, 1965), p. 3. See further for the economic condition of the empire, F. Oertel, "The Economic Life of the Empire," in *CAH,* 12:232ff.

2. Aelius Spartianus, *Hadrian* 24.8.

3. Athenagoras, *Legatio pro Christianis* 11. He admires their bravery and purity. Minucius Felix (*Octavius* 16) says the presence of such people in the congregations is the church's glory.

4. Dodds, *passim*. See further A. D. Nock's discussion of the popular quest for personal religion ("The Development of Paganism in the Roman Empire," in *CAH,* 12:503ff.).

5. Dodds's thesis does not depend, as critics suggest, upon "the notion that paganism was discredited or somehow in decline, and that Christianity rose to fill the resultant gap" (A. Cameron, *The Later Roman Empire* [London: Harper Collins, 1993], p. 11).

Dodds takes the pagan revival very seriously. Colin Wells (*The Roman Empire* [London: Harper Collins, 1992], p. 245) is much more ready to accept Dodds's proposals.

6. W. H. C. Frend, "The Winning of the Countryside," *JEH* 18, no. 1 (April 1967): 3. For the development of paganism see A. D. Nock, in *CAH*, 12:409ff.; S. Dill, *Roman Society in the Last Century of the Western Empire* (London: Macmillan, 1898), pp. 23ff.

7. Nero is said to "despise all cults" and Hadrian commands "scrupulous observance of Roman" ones (Suetonius, *Nero* 56; Aelius Spartianus, *Hadrian* 22.9-10).

8. The cult of the Mother Goddess is especially embraced. Reputedly brought to Rome in the first century B.C.E., it is given new impetus by the Antonines. The statement (Aelius Spartianus, *Septimus Severus* 17.1) that Septimus Severus "forbade conversion to Judaism under heavy penalties" and "enacted a similar law in regard to Christians" is probably false.

9. Aelius Lampridius, *Severus Alexander* 22.4; 29.2; cf. 45.7; 49; 43.6-7. He even uses the maxim "What you do not wish that a man should do to you, do not do to him" (51.7).

10. Aelius Lampradius, *Antoninus Elagabalus* 3.5.

11. Eusebius, *HE* 7.18; Sozomer, *HE* 5.21.

12. Carpocrates teaches his form of syncretistic Christianity in Alexandria ca. 135 (Irenaeus, *Cont. Haer.* 1.35.6).

13. Perhaps the Colossian heresy (Col. 2:8ff.) is an early experiment in syncretism which seeks to reconcile Christianity with unusual forms of Judaism and with pagan systems.

14. Hatred of the Jews climaxes with their rebellion in the time of Hadrian (Aelius Spartianus, *Hadrian* 14.2), and Christians are regarded as part of the "Jewish" problem (e.g., Sulpicius Severus, *Claudius* 2.3.1; Suetonius, *Claudius* 25; *Domitian* 12).

15. Minucius Felix, *Octavius* 10. Celsus (Origen, *Cont. Cels.* 7.2) condemns them for "walling themselves off from the rest of mankind," and their exclusiveness gives credibility to the rumors that they practice unspeakable rites (Minucius Felix 9).

16. Tertullian, *Apol.* 1.

17. Tertullian, *Ad nat.* 1.3; Justin Martyr, *Apol. II* 1.

18. Porphyry, *Adversus Christianos* 80.

19. Tertullian, *Ad nat.* 1.9.

20. Justin Martyr, *Apol. II* 7; cf. Arnobius (*Ad. nat.* 1), who also refutes the charge that Christians are responsible for the evils of the time.

21. E.g., rescripts by Hadrian and Antoninus (Eusebius, *HE* 4.9.13).

22. E.g., Tertullian, *Ad nat.* 1.2.

23. Origen, *Cont. Cels.* 3.52. This appears to be an interesting reference to "open air" preaching.

24. Tertullian, *De praesc. haer.* 21.

25. C. L. Rice (*ER,* 11:295) observes that "During the first few centuries of the church's life, the preacher was teacher, spiritual leader and apologist."

26. Ben Witherington III (*The Acts of the Apostles: A Socio-Rhetorical Commentary* [Carlisle: Paternoster Press, 1998], p. 41) rightly points out that even "ancient historical writings were meant to be *heard* primarily and read only secondarily."

27. Irenaeus, *The Apostolic Preaching,* pref. (ed. J. Behr, p. 39).

28. Justin Martyr, *Apol. II* 14.

29. E. Dargan, *A History of Preaching* (London: Hodder and Stoughton and G. H. Doran, 1905), 1:47.

30. O. Bardenhewer, *Patrology: The Lives and Works of the Fathers of the Church,* trans. T. J. Shahan (Freiburg: B. Herder, 1908), p. 180. Among the lost sermons are *On Evil Speaking, On Fasting,* and *To the Newly-Baptized.*

31. *Who Is the Rich Man Who Will Be Saved?* and his expository *Hypostasis of the Catholic Epistles.*

32. Bardenhewer, p. 176.

33. Jerome (*De vir. illus.* 24) refers to Melito's "fine oratorical genius." Before the discovery of this sermon, Melito's works were known largely from the fragments preserved by Eusebius (*HE* 4.26). After 2 *Clement,* it is possibly the oldest extant sermon and displays the refinements of contemporary rhetorical style, interwoven with effective references to the poetical books of LXX.

34. Bardenhewer, p. 218. Some fragments of his homilies remain (ANF, 5:489ff.). For a recent reexamination of the vexed question of the identity of Hippolytus, see J. Cerrado, *Hippolytus between East and West,* Oxford Theological Monograph (Oxford: Oxford University Press, 2002).

35. Eusebius, *HE* 6.22, records the extant sermons of Hippolytus, and Jerome says that he preaches a memorable sermon, *De laude Domini Salvatoris,* to a Roman congregation which includes Origen. There are also his *Homily on Talents (Matt. 25:14ff.),* preserved by Theodoret, and the homily *In quatriduanum Lazarum II* (Bardenhewer, p. 217).

36. Lactantius, *Divine Institutes* 5.1, says that Cyprian is "glorious in the art of oratory" with "a ready, copious and pleasant faculty, and that clearness which is the greatest excellence in a discourse, so that it would be difficult to say whether he was more ornate in stating or ready in illustrating or powerful in persuading" (cf. 5.4).

37. Origen, *De princ.* Pref. 3. For Origen as a preacher see further M. Simonetti, *Biblical Interpretation in the Early Church: An Historical Introduction to Patristic Exegesis,* trans. J. A. Hughes (Edinburgh: T. & T. Clark, 2001), p. 40.

38. R. P. Beaver, "Augustine: Servus Servorum Christi," *CH* 3 (1934): 191-92.

39. H. Chadwick, "The Early Christian Community," in *OIHC,* p. 53. For a useful treatment of the Alexandrian form of exegesis, see Simonetti, pp. 34ff.

40. Gregory Thaumaturgus, *Oration to Origen* 15. Origen influences a group of significant preachers. Besides Gregory Thaumaturgus, there are three important Alexandrians — Dionysius, an able expositor, the eloquent Anatolus, and Pierius, a noted preacher and catechetical teacher. (See ANF 6.4.)

41. See A. Menzies' introduction to Origen's *Comm. in Ev. Jn.* (ANF 10).

42. R. M. Grant, *Greek Apologists of the Second Century* (Philadelphia: Westminster, 1988), p. 40.

43. With the notable exceptions of Tatian's *Address to the Greeks* and the *Epistle to Diognetus.*

44. For a useful summary of the relationship between these preachers and Greek philosophy, see L. Mattei, *Philosophy and Early Christianity* (Nairobi: Consolata Press, 1995), pp. 91ff.

45. For the effect of this on hermeneutics, see Simonetti, pp. 19ff.

46. The third century sees a number of brilliant Christian scholars such as Julius Africanus, the imperial librarian in Rome for Severus, and the eloquent mathematician Anatolius of Alexandria.

47. Tertullian, *De praesc. haer. 7.*

48. Cyprian, *Ad Don.* 1.2; cf. Jerome, *Ep.* 12.29-30.

49. E.g., Eusebius (*HE* 7.20-21) commends Dionysius of Alexandria for his evangelistic zeal and for his pastoral letters which sustain his people during times of persecution and famine.

50. Origen, *Cont. Cels.* 3.29.

51. Gregory Thaumaturgus, *Hom. ann. Virg.* 2.

52. Justin Martyr, *Apol. I* 67. For the developing liturgy, see *Did.* 8-9.

53. Tertullian, *De coron.* 3; *De spec.* 4.

54. E.g., Justin Martyr, *Trypho* 39, 137; Hippolytus, *Treatise against the Jews;* Melito, *Paschal Homily;* Cyprian's three *Books of Testimonies against the Jews.*

55. *Apost. Constit.* 2.61; Commodianus, *Instruct.* 38, 34.

56. Irenaeus (*Cont. haer.* 4.9.3) writes, "the New Testament was known and foretold by the prophets and he who was to order it according to the Father's will was predicted."

57. Clement of Alexandria, *Strom.* 5.4; cf. Justin Martyr, *Trypho* 113.

58. Irenaeus, *Cont. haer.* 4.33.

59. E.g., the words "from the tree" are added to Ps. 95:10 to clarify the link with the crucifixion (Justin Martyr, *Trypho* 83ff.). In his *Homily on Psalms I and II,* Hippolytus gives mystical meanings to each psalm.

60. Clement of Alexandria, *Strom.* 6.18; Irenaeus, *Cont. haer.* 4.33.15.

61. Justin Martyr, *Trypho* 100; 113; 137.

62. See M. Wiles, "Eastern Christendom," in *CUHB,* 1:454ff.; R. P. C. Hanson, "Alexandrian Theology," in *DCT,* pp. 4-5.

63. Origen, *De princ.* 1. pref.8; 4.11.

64. Tertullian observes (*De praesc. haer.* 9) that Christians no longer thirst for clever philosophical ideas ("nobis curiositate opus non est post Christum Iesum"); cf. *Ad nat.* 2.2; 1.4.

65. Justin Martyr, *Apol. II* 10; *Apol. I* 12; 60; *Hort. ad Graec.* 32.

66. Clement of Alexandria, *Strom.* 5.1; 6.7-8.

67. Although preachers like Gregory Thaumaturgus, Cyprian, and Dionysius the Great are sent into safety, eventually they join Justin and Victorinus as martyrs. Both Origen and Tertullian write major works on martyrdom (Origen, *Exhortatio ad martyrium;* Tertullian, *Ad martyres*), and Clement devotes the fourth book of his *Stromateis* to the subject.

68. Gregory Thaumaturgus, *Can. ep.* 7. Cyprian, in particular, writes at length on the subject in *De lapsis* and *De unitate ecclesiae.* It is interesting that the punishment of defectors includes being denied access to preaching. Gregory Thaumaturgus (*Can. ep.* 7.7ff.) decrees that the worst offenders are to be "debarred even from being auditors in the public congregations," while less serious offenders are allowed "to hear the Scripture and doctrine . . . and then to be put forth and reckoned unfit for the privilege of prayer."

69. Clement of Alexandria, *Strom.* 4.17.

70. Tertullian, *De bapt.* 17; *Scorp.* 6; Eusebius, *HE* 5.2; e.g., the story of Potomoena who prays for her torturer and Magistranus who is martyred for rescuing a Christian virgin from a Corinthian brothel (Hippolytus, *De virgine Corinthica*); cf. Eusebius's account of the martyrdom of Apollonius in Rome (5.21).

71. Clement of Alexandria, *Strom.* 4.9, 14.

72. Tertullian, *De fuga in persecutione* 4; 12; Justin Martyr, *Apol. II* 4; Clement of Alexandria, *Strom.* 4.9-10.

73. E.g., Cyprian's *To the People of Thibaris, Exhorting to Martyrdom* (*Ep.* 55) and *Exhortation to Martyrdom Addressed to Fortunatus* (*Treatise* 11).

74. Clement of Alexandria, *Strom.* 4.7; Gregory Thaumaturgus (attrib.), *Hom. Omn. Sanct.* Satirically, Lucian (*De morte Peregrini* 12) describes how, when imprisoned, his antihero Peregrinus has "every form of attention shown him" by duped Christian visitors.

75. Tertullian, *Scorp.* 6; Justin Martyr believes persecution is the result of diabolical attacks upon Christians (*Apol. I* 57). Origen cheers Ambrose by reminding him that after his death, his prayers will achieve much for those left behind (Origen, *Exhort. mart.* 38). Many worshipers believe that martyrs also have power to forgive sins.

76. Clement of Alexandria, *Strom.* 4.8; cf. Justin Martyr's declaration (*Apol. II* 12) that "Christians are fearless of death."

77. Cf. Clement of Alexandria, *Paed.* 3.4.

78. Origen, *Hom. Gen.* 10.1. Hippolytus also has a reputation as a strict disciplinarian. From the earliest days, preachers play a significant part in the development of discipline (e.g., 1 Cor. 5:3ff.; 2 Cor. 13:10; 1 Tim. 1:20). Tertullian (*Apol.* 39) refers to the church's "unity of discipline" and describes the penitential regulations (*De poen.* 9; cf. *Apost. Constit.* 2.16). See Bethune-Baker's useful summary of the development of the penitential system (*An Introduction to the Early History of Christian Doctrine* [London: Methuen, 1951], pp. 372-73).

79. Clement of Alexandria, *Paed.* 1.10; Cyprian, *Patient.* 19; 12.

80. Justin Martyr, *Apol. I* 14; cf. Athenagoras, *Legat. Christ.* 26.

81. Tertullian, *De poen.* 11; *Apost. Constit.* 1.2; Commodianus, *Instruct.* 59.

82. Cyprian, *De laps.* 6. The clergy are involved in money lending, although usury is condemned (Tertullian, *Adversus Marcionem* 4.17; Cyprian, *Test.* 3.48). Paul of Samosata, bishop of Antioch (260-72), is typical of such worldly prelates. It is even necessary to forbid bishops to accept bribes (*Apost. Constit.* 2.3).

83. Tertullian, *On Fasting* 13; 3ff.; 7; 15.

84. Gregory Thaumaturgus, *Can. ep.* 1.

85. Origen, *De princ.* pref. 5. Duschesne (*The Early History of the Christian Church,* 3 vols. [London: John Murray, 1950], 1:248) observes, "It would not be his fault if orthodox Christians were outdone in asceticism by the sternest philosophers, or by these Gnostics and Montanists who had most cruelly macerated the flesh."

86. Clement of Alexandria, *Quis div. salv.* 1.3.

87. Clement asserts that "a poor and destitute man may be found intoxicated with lusts; and a man rich in worldly goods, temperate and trustworthy, intelligent and pure" (*Quis div. salv.* 18).

88. Clement of Alexandria, *Quis div. salv.* 11.

89. Clement of Alexandria, *Quis div. salv.* 30.

90. Rom. 15:26; 2 Cor. 9:7; Gal. 2:10; James 2:16-17; cf. Cyprian, *To the Clergy concerning the Care of the Poor and Strangers* (*Ep.* 35).

91. Clement of Alexandria, *Paed.* 3.6. He also generally condemns extravagant lifestyles (2.1-3, 11-13).

92. A. J. Malherbe (*Social Aspects of Early Christianity* [Baton Rouge: Louisiana State University Press, 1977], p. 63) attributes this, in part, to the fact that in cities "there was a greater . . . willingness to give a hearing to preachers of new religions."

93. Tertullian, *Ad mart.* 2; *De spec.* 18. The services of prostitutes are advertised openly in the theaters, and common inns also serve as bordellos.

94. E.g., Clement of Alexandria, *Paed.* 3.9.5; *Apost. Constit.* 1.9.

95. Juvenal, *Satires* 6.447. The great Baths of Gargilus in Carthage are used for a conference of bishops in 411.

96. Tertullian, *Ad mart.* 1.

97. "Bathing, drinking, love-making corrupt our bodies; / But they make life worthwhile — bathing, drinking, love-making." See further Martial, *Epigrams* 1.96. Elagabalus creates public baths in his palace so that he can bathe with women and choose his male sexual partners (Aelius Lampridius, *Antoninus Elagabalus* 31.7; 8.6); cf. the activities of Licinius Gallienus (Trebellius Pollio, *The Two Gallieni* 17.9); *Apost. Constit.* 6.

98. Hippolytus, *Sanct. theoph.* 10.

99. Tertullian, *Apol.* 43; Gregory Thaumaturgus, *Can. ep.* 1.

100. Tertullian, *Ad uxor.* 2.6; *Apol.* 1.9.

101. Tertullian, *De poen.* 3.

102. Tertullian, *Ad uxor.* 2.6; *De coron.* 13.

103. Clement of Alexandria, *Strom.* 4.19. He even speaks of God in feminine terms (*Paed.* 3.1) and declares that for love of humanity, God "became feminine" (*Quis div. salv.* 37). For his approach to women, see S. Heine, *Women and Early Christianity: Are the Feminist Scholars Right?* trans. J. Bowden (London: SCM Press, 1987), pp. 33-34. Cyprian highly regards the women in his congregations and addresses a pastoral letter specifically to them (*De habitu virginum* 3).

104. Tertullian, *Ad mart.* 1; Methodius, *Symposium* 3.8.

105. Tertullian, *De pat.* 15.

106. In the homilies on the annunciation attributed to Gregory, it is said that Mary "forms the new Adam in her womb" (1) and thus is made "the mother of God" (2), an unusually early use of *theotokos;* cf. Ambrose, *Exhort. virg.* 10.

107. Clement of Alexandria, *Strom.* 4.20.

108. Tertullian, *Ad uxor.* 1.3. Heine (pp. 27ff.) insists that Tertullian's view of women is more sympathetic than is usually acknowledged. Some Christian women apparently claim to remain virgins although cohabiting with men. Cf. Cyprian, *To Pomponius concerning Some Virgins* (*Ep.* 61).

109. Congregations are taught to applaud the shining example of martyrs like Lucretia, who stabbed herself so that "she might have the glory of her chastity" (Tertullian, *Ad mart.* 4).

110. *Herm. Vis.* 4.2.4.

111. Tertullian, *De oratione* 22; cf. Ambrose, *De virgin.* 1.12.

112. *Clement. Hom.* 13.16. The exaltation of chastity is treated in 13.13-21; cf. the picture of the virtuous woman in *Apost. Constit.* 1.8. See further M. T. Malone, *Women and Christianity,* vol. 1, *First Thousand Years* (Dublin: Columba Press, 2000).

113. E. A. Judge, "The Early Christians as a Scholastic Community," *JRH* 1 (1960-61): 125. Floyd Filson ("The Significance of the Early House Churches," *JBL* 58 [1939]: 109ff.) emphasizes the educative element of congregational life, asserting that the early house churches are "schools" for those who have to lead the church after it loses apostolic guidance.

114. J. Daniélou, *Gospel Message and Hellenistic Culture: A History Of Early Christian Doctrine before the Council of Nicea,* trans. J. A. Baker, 2 vols. (London: Darton, Longman and Todd, 1973), p. 9.

115. E.g., Justin Martyr, *Apol. I* 1.9; Athenagoras, *Legat. Christ.* 13; 15; Theophilus, *Autol.* 1.2.

116. Eusebius, *HE* 6.45.

117. E.g., Dionysius of Rome, *The Books against Sabellius;* Archelaus, *Disputation with Manes;* Alexander of Alexandria, *The Epistles on the Arian Heresy.* Until the discovery of the Nag Hammadi treatises in the mid-1940s, most information about Gnostic writings came from the sermons and writings of the apologist-preachers.

118. E.g., Acts, 8; *Herm. Sim.* 9.22. See further R. M. Grant, *Gnosticism* (New York: Harper, 1961) and *Gnosticism in Early Christianity* (New York: Harper and Row, 1966).

119. E.g., Florinus is an eminent Roman clergyman (Eusebius, *HE* 5.15). Marcion, the son of a bishop, comes to Rome specifically to take control of the church there (4.14). Valentinus almost succeeds in becoming bishop of Rome (4.10). Saturninus sets up a Gnostic school in Syria, and Basilides creates a similar academy in Alexandria (4.7).

120. Carpocrates and Marcion create their own churches. The claim that Gnostic Gospels contain new sayings of Jesus makes them, homiletically, very attractive. The *Gospel of Thomas* is attributed to Valentinus. A letter from Serapion of Antioch shows how the reading of the *Gospel of Peter* leads the congregation at Rhossus into heresy (Eusebius, *HE* 6.12).

121. R. Roukema, *Gnosis and Faith in Early Christianity,* trans. J. Bowden (London: SCM Press, 1999), p. 157.

122. Tertullian, *De praesc. haer.* 21.4. Irenaeus (*Cont. haer.* 1.1.20) refers to the "traditions of truth" and may be the first of the preachers to use the expression. Athenagoras (*Res. mort.* 1) writes of "true doctrine." Hippolytus (*Refut. omn. haer.* 9.12) defends the "doctrine of truth." Clement of Alexandria (*Strom.* 7.7) uses "canon" to signify a "rule of faith." For a general survey of material see Hanson, pp. 341ff.; Bethune-Baker, pp. 55ff.

123. E.g., Athenagoras, *Suppl.* 1.4; 7; 10; Theophilus, *Autol.* 1.5; 2.3, 9; Justin Martyr, *Apol. I* 10; 13.1, 25.

124. Theophilus (*Autol.* 2.15) may be the first preacher to use *trias* of God.

125. Irenaeus, *Cont. haer.* 3.18.1.

126. E.g., Irenaeus, *Cont. haer.* 5.1.1. The metaphor will appeal, especially, to congregations who have to ransom friends from barbarian marauders.

127. Origen, *Comm. Matt.* 12.25; Clement of Alexandria, *Quis div. salv.* 37.

128. Justin Martyr, *Apol. I* 12; cf. *Apol. II* 9; Theophilus, *Autol.* 1.14; 2.38; Justin claims (*Apol. I* 20) that the prophets and philosophers confirm the preachers' warning.

129. Clement of Alexandria, *Paed.* 2.10; Theophilus, *Autol.* 1.8; Athenagoras, *Legat. Christ.* 36; Justin Martyr, *Apol. I* 1.19; Clement of Alexandria, *Paed.* 1.6.

130. Clement of Alexandria, *Strom.* 6.6, who stresses that the deliverance has included Jews and pagans.

131. E.g., Justin Martyr, *Apol. I* 14.

132. Daniélou, p. 9.

133. Justin Martyr (attrib.), *Cohort. ad Graec.* 1; *Apol. I* 55.8; *Apol. II* 14; Aristides, *Apol.* 16.5; 16.3-4.

134. Aristides, *Apol.* 16.5; 17.8.

135. Justin Martyr, *Cohortatio ad Graecos* 1; *Apol. I* 53; 57; Theophilus, *Autol.* 1.14.

136. See P. Tillich, *A History of Christian Thought from Its Judaic and Hellenistic Origins to Existentialism,* ed. C. E. Braaten (New York: Simon and Schuster, 1968), p. 26.

137. See Daniélou, p. 11.

138. Justin Martyr, *Apol. I* 68.

139. E.g., Theophilus, *Autol.* 2.37; Clement of Alexandria, *Strom.* 5.2.

140. Justin Martyr, *Protrep.* 12.1.18; 6.89.1; 1.41.3. See further, A. Wessels, *Europe: Was It Ever Really Christian?* (London: SCM Press, 1994), pp. 31ff. Origen (*De princ.* 1.7.3) accepts the current view that the heavenly bodies are rational creatures with free will. Theophilus frequently quotes the Sybils (e.g., *Autol.* 2.3, 9, 36) and, in *Apost. Constit.* 5.7, the sybils are used with the Stoics and the mythical phoenix to prove the reality of the resurrection. The last "proof" is especially cogent because it is widely believed that the phoenix exists and has appeared in Egypt (Tacitus, *Annals* 6.27).

141. Hippolytus, *Refutatio omnium haeresium* 7.1.

142. Theophilus, *Autol.* 2.38; cf. Athenagoras, *Legat. Christ.* 6.

143. Tatian, *Orat. ad Graec.* 5.

144. Justin Martyr, *Apol. I* 7; 48.

145. Tatian, *Orat. ad Graec.* 7; Athenagoras, *Legat. Christ.* 36.

146. Daniélou (p. 22) identifies a belief in judgment as "the distinctive character of the Kerygma in the Greek environment." Theophilus (*Autol.* 2.38) argues that ultimate judgment is firmly attested by "sybils, prophets, poets and philosophers."

147. Tatian, *Orat. ad Graec.* 6; cf. Athenagoras (*Legat. Christ.* 36), who argues that logically "the incorporeal is prior to the corporeal." Theophilus, *De resurrectione.*

Chapter 5 — "'Immensity of Holiness': The Ascetics and Mystics"

1. 1 Thess. 4:11; cf. Polycarp's instruction (*Phil.* 5) to "please God in this present world and abstain from evil things."

2. Plato, *Rep.* 3.403e; 4.430, etc.; *Phaedrus* 256b; *Theat.* 1.76; Aristotle, *Mag. mor.* 2.6, 1203b.13ff. H. Baltensweiler ("Discipline," in *DNTT*, 1:494ff.) finds few examples of *enkrateia-askesis* vocabulary in the New Testament. It is arguable that Paul advocates "self-control" rather than strict asceticism (Gal. 5:23; cf. 2 Pet. 1:6), and Athanasius (*De incarnat.* 51.2.1) sees it as his duty to "preach . . . about virtue and self-control."

3. Plato, *Theat.* 1.76; cf. *Rep.* 7.517.

4. E.g., Num. 6:1ff.; Ezek. 1:3. The Essenes arise in the middle of the second century B.C.E. (Josephus, *Wars* 8); cf. Philo, *De migrat. Abr.* 35. See further, E. Underhill, *The Mystic Way: A Psychological Study in Christian Origins* (London: Dent, 1913), pp. 73ff.; S. Fanning, *The Mystics of the Christian Tradition* (London: Routledge, 2001), pp. 14ff.; W. R. Inge, *Christian Mysticism: Considered in Eight Lectures Delivered before the University of Oxford* (London: Methuen, 1899), pp. 39ff.; A. Louth, "Mysticism," in *DCS*, pp. 272ff.; G. Finkenrath, "Secret, Mystery," in *DNTT*, 3:501ff.

5. Luke 9:23. Christians who interpret it more radically can claim the authority of

the ascetic element in homiletic material provided in Matthew and Luke; e.g., Matt. 5:3ff.; Luke 6:20ff.; 12:33.

6. E.g., 1 Cor. 7:29; 13:2; 2 Cor. 12:2; cf. Polycarp's instructions for celibate women (*Phil.* 4-5).

7. Theophilus, *Autol.* 2.34-35; 3.15; cf. Athenagoras, *Legat. Christ.* 32ff.

8. Tertullian, *De poen.* 3.

9. Tertullian, *Apol.* 40.

10. Tertullian, *De cult. fem.* 2.8.

11. Tertullian, *De virg. vel.* 17. He commends those who, though married, have become "voluntary eunuchs for the sake of their desire for the celestial kingdom" (*Ad uxor.* 6). Cf. Athanasius, who, while admiring ascetics, insists that the church is "adorned" equally by its celibates and by those who are "honourably married" (*Epp. heor.* 1.3; 10.4).

12. Tertullian, *De Modestia* 1; cf. Commodianus (*Instruc.* 57), who also complains about "liberal" leaders who mislead congregations.

13. Clement of Alexandria, *Strom.* 4.3.

14. Clement of Alexandria, *Strom.* 6.9; 7.11; 4.21; 2.9.

15. Clement of Alexandria, *Strom.* 7.10, 55; 6.9.

16. Clement of Alexandria, *Strom.* 7.9; 6.9.

17. Origen, *De princ.* 1.1.5. In this process of liberation, humans are hindered by demons but assisted by angels (1.8).

18. Origen, *Comm. Matt.* 19.12.

19. Origen, *Comm. Matt.* 3.60. The teaching is developed in Origen's treatise *De oratione.*

20. Tertullian, *Ad mart.* 3; Origen, *Exhort. mart.* 2; cf. *The Martyrdom of Perpetua and Felicitas* 1.3 (*ANF* 1.1260ff.), attributed to Tertullian.

21. E.g., during her visit to Jerusalem, the empress Helena gathers a congregation of "women who have vowed perpetual chastity" (Theodoret, *HE* 1.17).

22. The desert is part of the Jewish eschatological hope (e.g., Isa. 40:3; Ezek. 34:25) and, for the Greeks, a place of divine intervention (e.g., Euripides, *Bacchae* 874ff.); cf. 1 Cor. 10:1ff.; Heb. 11:38; Mark 6:31; Acts 8:26; Rev. 17:3; 12:6.

23. In the first century, Christian ascetics are living in the deserts. Eusebius (*HE* 2.17) equates them with the Therapeutae. When Antony, generally regarded as the founder of Christian monasticism, goes into the wilderness in 269, he finds recluses already living there. Cf. Sozomen, *HE* 1.13-14, in which he tells the story of Ammon the ascetic.

24. For general introductions see P. Gardner-Smith, *The Expansion of the Christian Church* (Cambridge: Cambridge University Press, 1934), pp. 79ff.; K. S. Latourette, *A History of Christianity,* 1 vol. edition (London: Eyre and Spottiswood, 1955), pp. 221ff.; H. Chadwick, *The Early Church* (London: Penguin Books, 1978), pp. 174-75; H. Leitzmann, *The Era of the Early Church Fathers,* trans. B. L. Woolf (London:

Lutterworth, 1958), pp. 124ff.; B. Ward, "Monastic Spirituality, Monasticism," in *DCS* pp. 267ff.

25. E.g., the Alexandrians, Cyrus the physician and Didymus the blind mathematician.

26. Macarius the Egyptian is "distinguished for his miracles" (Gennadius, *De vir. illus.* 10); Antony and his pupil Paul the Simple are "great in expelling demons" (Sozomen, *HE* 1.13). Pachomius has "grace in performing miracles" (Gennadius 7).

27. Apollonius is supposed to have gathered fifteen thousand disciples at Thebias. Pachomius assembles a huge congregation at Bau to celebrate the Passover (Gennadius, *De vir. illus.* 7). Pagan writers confirm the numbers of Christian ascetics in the deserts (e.g., Ammianus Marcellinus, *Rer. gest.* 18.10.4).

28. Sozomen (*HE* 1.13) comments, "Whether the Egyptians or others are to be regarded as the founders of this philosophy, it is universally admitted that Antony, the great monk, developed this course of life."

29. Athanasius, *Vit. Ant.* 16-44, purports to be a sermon preached to a congregation of monks — "Antony's brethren" — and although attributed to Athanasius, may not be by his hand.

30. Sozomen, *HE* 1.13-14.

31. Sozomen, *HE* 1.13. Although Antony's readiness to debate and his opposition to the Meletians and Arians suggest that he is not totally unconcerned about doctrinal matters.

32. E.g., Isa. 53:5; Rom. 8:15-18, 32; Phil. 2:6-11. He is reputed to have forsaken all worldly goods after hearing a reading from Matthew, presumably 19:21; 6:34 (Sozomen, *HE* 1.13).

33. Sozomen, *HE* 3.14; Gennadius, *De vir. illus.* 7.

34. The *Rule* exists only in Jerome's Latin version. See D. F. Wright, "Pachomius," in *NIDCC*, p. 741; G. Grutzmacher, "Pachomius," in *NSHE*, 8:297.

35. Palladius's *Historia Lausiaca* is a record of the miraculous feats of the desert mystics, written by a Galatian monk ca. 420. Sozomen, *HE* 3.14, includes a list of other minor desert mystics. Medieval pictures show Macarius exposing himself naked to the bites of insects when he lives in a swamp for six months as a penance for killing a mosquito.

36. Since the sixteenth century, the *Fifty Homilies* have been ascribed to his pen, plus seven more sermons added at the end of the First World War. The *Letters*, mentioned by Gennadius (*De vir. illus.* 10), are homilies preached to his followers.

37. Medieval mystical theology is greatly influenced by the dualistic teaching about "darkness" and "light" which is attributed to Macarius.

38. Sozomen, *HE* 3.14; Gennadius, *De vir. illus.* 10.58. He is reputed to be able to transport himself to heaven for five days at a time.

39. See S. Fanning, *Mystics of the Christian Tradition* (London: Routledge, 2001), pp. 29-30.

40. Gennadius, *De vir. illus.* 11. Evagrius is a disciple of Macarius the Great, and among his more distinguished followers are Palladius and Rufinus.

41. Gennadius, *De vir. illus.* 82; Sozomen, *HE* 3.15.

42. Theodoret, *To the Presbyter Basilius* (*Ep.* 19).

43. He is supposed to have written his life of Antony as an expression of his gratitude to the monks (Gardner-Smith, p. 82).

44. See A. Robertson, introduction to "Athanasius," in NPNF, 2nd ser., 4:xlvii-xlviii; Theodoret, *HE* 1.25.

45. Cf. his famous comment (*De incarn.* 54.3): "He became man, that we might be deified."

46. Athanasius, *Cont. gent.* 2.34.3.

47. Athanasius, *De incarn.* 47.5.

48. Athanasius, *Epp. heor.* 1.3.

49. Athanasius, *Epp. heor.* 1.7.

50. Athanasius, *Epp. heor.* 1.3; *De incarn.* 48.2; 51.1.

51. Gennadius, *De vir. illus.* 9; 82; 10.

52. *The Great Letter* is attributed to Macarius the Great but is probably not his work.

53. Jerome, *De vir. illus.* 109. See P. Toon, *NIDCC*, p. 346.

54. A. Hastings, *The Church in Africa, 1450-1950* (Oxford: Oxford University Press, 1996), p. 7.

55. Theodoret's address *To the Soldiers* (*Ep.* 144) reminds us that Antioch is a garrison town and that the military members of the Christian congregation require guidance for their conduct. The church has many wealthy members who support a considerable program of charity. It numbers among its leaders intellectual converts like Malchion the Sophist and leading Christian thinkers such as Theophilus, Diodore, and Theodoret.

56. It is unclear whether the first congregation is formed from pagan Greeks (ἕλλην) or Grecian Jews (ἑλληνιστής); see J. M. Houston, "Antioch (Syrian)," in *NIDCC*, p. 49; F. F. Bruce, *The Acts of the Apostles: The Greek Text with Introduction and Commentary* (London: Tyndale Press, 1952), pp. 235-36. Latourette, p. 73, believes that almost from its inception, "the young Christian community in Antioch was drawing largely from non-Jews." Perhaps the name *Christian* symbolizes the break from Judaism (E. J. Bickerman, "The Name of Christian," *HTR* 42 [1949]: 109ff.).

57. Acts 13:1ff.; 14:23ff.; 11:27. The ruins of about twenty churches have been unearthed, dating from the fourth century.

58. See H. D. McDonald's useful brief survey ("Antiochene Theology," in *NIDCC*, p. 49).

59. The speeches in Acts may be derived from Antiochene material (G. W. H. Lampe, "Acts," in *PC*, pp. 882, 885; S. E. Johnson, *The Gospel according to St. Mark* [London: A. & C. Black, 1960], p. 7), and Matthew may be "the result of a 'school of exege-

sis'" located in Antioch (C. F. D. Moule, *The Birth of the New Testament* [London: A. & C. Black, 1973], p. 74) designed to satisfy the homiletical and catechetical needs of the church there (K. Stendahl, "Matthew," in *PC*, p. 769; cf. A. M. Hunter, *Introducing the New Testament* [London: SCM Press, 1972], p. 56). It is suggested that the consequent lively debates are reflected in Jude (G. H. Boobyer, "Jude," in *PC*, p. 1041; cf. Hunter, p. 184; E. A. Blum, "Jude," in *EBC*, 12:383-84). Johnson (p. 7) says Antiochene evangelists are equipped with tracts, modeled on "the missionary propaganda of the diaspora synagogue." Matthew itself may have been a missionary tract to be used for the conversion of Jews (Moule, p. 88).

60. With the possible exceptions of Serapion and Babylas.

61. Latourette (p. 228) maintains that Antiochene Christianity includes a strong ascetic element long before the arrival of monasticism.

62. John "Chrysostom," the greatest pupil of Diodore and epitome of Antiochene preachers, receives much fuller treatment later.

63. After seven years in the Convent of St. Euprepius, he says how he "loves the quiet of those who wish to administer the churches in a monastic state" (*To the Consul Nomus* [*Ep.* 81]).

64. He is a historian, theologian, and controversialist who masters Greek, Syriac, and Hebrew.

65. Theodoret provides funds to carry on public works in Cyrrhus and to supply medical help for the people. He writes wonderful pastoral letters to rich and poor, expressing condolence to the bereaved and pleading clemency for the condemned; e.g., *Epp.* 7; 8; 32.

66. Theodoret, *To John, Bishop of Germanicus* (*Ep.* 147).

67. Theodoret, *To the Clergy at Beraea* (*Ep.* 75).

68. Theodoret, *To Leo, Bishop of Rome* (*Ep.* 113).

69. Theodoret, *A Festal Letter* (*Ep.* 56).

70. Theodoret, *Festal Letters* (*Epp.* 6; 25; 26).

71. Theodoret, *A Festal Letter* (*Ep.* 38).

72. He asks plaintively (*To Bishop Irenaeus* [*Ep.* 16]), "What does it matter whether we style the holy Virgin at the same time mother of man and mother of God?"

73. Theodoret, *To the Presbyter Renatus* (*Ep.* 116); *To John, Bishop of Germanicus* (*Ep.* 147).

74. Theodoret, *To Dioscorus, Archbishop of Alexandria* (*Ep.* 83).

75. Socrates Scholasticus, *HE* 7.29.

76. Socrates, *HE* 7.29.

77. Anastasius preaches a sermon declaring that the virgin Mary is "but a woman" (Socrates, *HE* 7.32).

78. Socrates, *HE* 7.29, 32. It must be remembered that Socrates is not always completely unbiased in his judgments.

79. Socrates, *HE* 7.34.

80. Among the most outstanding of the Nestorian preachers is Narsai, who founds a Nestorian school at Nisibis and has 360 homilies credited to his name, mostly written in poetic couplets. See J. A. Robinson, ed., *The Liturgical Homilies of Narsai* (London: Cambridge University Press, 1909).

81. Perhaps the most famous is Daniel the Stylite, who counts emperors and patriarchs among his hearers.

82. We use the term "Mesopotamian church" of the congregations which grow up around Edessa and Nisibis. The two expansionist emperors, Trajan and Septimus Severus, both create provinces of Mesopotamia carved from the Parthian empire (Trajan in 116 and Severus in 197, establishing Nisibis as the provincial capital), but the eastern frontier of the empire is notoriously ill defined.

83. Eusebius, *HE* 5.23. For translations of the most relevant texts, see ANF 8. The account of the coming of Christianity is recorded in *The Story concerning the Kings of Edessa*, but Duschesne (*The Early History of the Christian Church*, 3 vols. [London: John Murray, 1950], 1:328) rightly says that the tradition that the Mespotamian church is founded by the apostle Thaddaeus abounds in "historical and chronological difficulties," and it is more likely that the area is converted during the reign of Abgar IX. Duschesne provides a useful account of the history of the church in Mesopotamia (1:326ff.).

84. *The Teaching of Addaeus the Apostle.*

85. Aphrahat, *Demonst. 10, On Pastors* 8.

86. *Instruct. Apostol.* 20.

87. The *Diatessaron* is commended in the Syriac *Teaching of Addaeus the Apostle*. It is often circulated in a corpus with the Acts of Peter, John, Andrew, and Paul. See J. N. Birdsall, "The Acts of Thomas," in *NIDCC*, p. 971. Thomas is especially revered because it is believed that he sent Thaddaeus to evangelize Edessa, where pilgrims flock to the basilica built over his tomb.

88. Tatian, *Address to the Greeks* 22.

89. Aphrahat, *Demonst. 1, On Faith* 4; Ephrem, *Of Admonition* 13-14.

90. *Martyrdom of Barsamaya of Nisibis* and Mar Jacob, *Homily on Habib the Martyr*, a metrical sermon. He preaches similar homilies on the popular martyrs Guria and Shamuna.

91. Aphrahat, *Demonst. 1, On Faith* 3.

92. Aphrahat, *Demonst. 5, On Monks* 19.

93. Sozomen, *HE* 3.16. Ephrem, born in Nisibis, moves to Edessa.

94. Ephrem, *Homily on the Lord* 25. See Birdsall, in *NIDCC*, p. 345.

95. Sozomen, *HE* 3.16. The *Liber Graduum* is a collection of thirty homilies on the spiritual life.

96. E.g., his graphic account of the sinful woman's remorse in imaginary conversations between herself, the seller of perfume and Satan (*Homily on the Sinful Woman* 1.2ff.; 5.6-7).

97. For Ephrem's skill as a hymn writer, see K. E. McVey, "Ephrem the Syrian," in *ECW,* 2:1228ff. Gennadius (*De vir. illus.* 75) also refers to Peter of Edessa, another "famous preacher" and hymn writer.

98. E.g., Ephrem pleads with the "Son of the carpenter" to "lay his cross as a bridge over death, that souls may pass over it from the dwellings of the dead to the dwelling of life" (*Homily on Our Lord* 4).

99. E.g., "Speak not overmuch; not even words that are wise" (*Homily on Admonition* 11).

100. Ephrem, *Homily on Admonition* 1.

101. He writes works against Marcion and Mani, and in his later years he composes commentaries on many biblical texts. Brian Daley (*On the Dormition of Mary: Early Patristic Homilies* [Crestwood, N.Y.: St. Vladimir's Seminary Press, 1998], p. 2) describes the "celebratory, poetic character" of the sermons inspired by "the rich theological rhetoric of St. Ephrem's Syriac hymns and verse homilies on Mary."

102. Ephrem, *Homily on Admonition* 5.

103. Ephrem, *Homily on Admonition* 17; 7. He allows that marriage is not wrong in itself, providing the couple "preserve purity in their marriage" (8).

104. E.g., "Set not over the flock, leaders who are foolish and stupid, covetous and lovers of possessions" (*Demonst. 10, On Pastors* 6), a written response to a request for guidance, indicating the respect in which Aphrahat is held.

105. Aphrahat, *Demonst. 1, On Faith* 6, an epistolary sermon, intended to be "heard."

106. C. H. Kraft, *Communication Theory for Christian Witness* (New York: Orbis, 1991), pp. 27-28.

107. Aphrahat, *Demonst. 1, On Faith* 1.

108. Aphrahat, *Demonst.* 1; *On Faith* 2. Ten *Demonstrations* deal with spiritual growth, others warn against heresy, and Aphrahat dedicates no fewer than eight of them to anti-Jewish themes.

109. Aphrahat, *Demonst. 22, On Death and the Latter Times* 7.

110. E.g., Aphrahat warns his hearers to beware of "divinations and sorcerers and Chaldean arts and magic" (*Demonst. 1, On Faith* 19).

111. Aphrahat, *Demonst. 6, On Monks* 6; 3. Aphrahat's appeal to reject "fornication and adultery" (*Demonst. 1, On Faith* 19) may well suggest that these are present in his congregations.

112. Aphrahat, *Demonst. 1, On Faith* 6; 4.

113. Aphrahat, *Demonst. 21, On Persecution* 21. The threats may arise from fierce internecine struggles within the churches, from incursions by the Persians, or from continuing sporadic attacks by pagans.

114. Aphrahat, *Demonst. 21, On Persecution* 23; *Demonst. 6, On Monks* 1.

115. Aphrahat, *Demonst. 6, On Monks* 1, 18; cf. 33.

116. Duschesne, 1:328; see further pp. 328ff.

117. He makes a considerable contribution to the collection of 150 hymns used by the Bardasenes.

118. There is much to commend the idea that he is Simeon of Mesopotamia. See G. A. Maloney, ed., *Intoxicated with God: The Fifty Spiritual Homilies and the Great Letter* (New York: Paulist, 1992), pp. 6ff. For his considerable influence see pp. 20ff.

119. For the suggestion that *The Great Letter* is written by Gregory of Nyssa or is a paraphrase of *De institutio,* see Maloney, pp. 249-50; cf. S. Brock, "Macarius the Egyptian," in *DCS,* pp. 255-56.

120. E.g., *Hom.* 26; 40.1.

121. E.g., "Therefore, each of *us* must examine himself" (*Hom.* 50, italics mine). "Listen! Examine yourself. . . . Do you believe that your soul is receiving healing from Christ?" (49.4; 48.3). "How lovely it is when a spiritual person consecrates himself totally to the Lord and clings to him alone!" (9.12).

122. Kallistos Ware (in *Intoxicated with God,* p. xiv) speaks of his use of "the language of feeling and conscious awareness, employing as his key-words, *plerophoria* (assurance), *aethesis* (feeling), *peira* (experience), *energeia* (energy) and *dynamis* (power)."

123. Maloney, pp. 3-4; J. Wesley, Letter to Dr. Conyers Middleton, *Letters,* 2:387.

124. *Hom.* 5.1-2.

125. *Hom.* 19; 44.4; 17.13.

126. *Hom.* 1.9, 12; 2.3; 6.1; 15.11; 17.22; 13.7. He often uses the homiletic device of "the opening illustration" in his sermons and prefaces illustrations with the words, "Let us take an example. . . ." Some sermons are largely compilations of illustrations; e.g., *Hom.* 43, a short sermon containing references to lamps, burning sticks, trading merchants, pregnant women, beautiful gardens, the wonders of the eye, and the power of strong winds.

127. *Detachment (The Great Letter).* Pseudo-Macarius interprets the Scriptures allegorically in order to apply them to the needs of his congregations but his theology is orthodox, and attempts to associate him with the Messalian heresy are unconvincing. See Maloney, pp. 8ff.

128. *Hom.* 15.14; 15.8; 3.2. John Wesley (*Sermons,* 2:45) admiringly comments, "How exactly did Macarius . . . describe the present experience of the children of God!"

129. *Suffering Persecution (The Great Letter); Hom.* 46.3; 27.1; 4.16; 15.25.

130. *Hom.* 8.4.

131. *Hom.* 12.1; 20.5; 2.1, 3; 4.10; 30.2.

132. *Hom.* 44.4; 20.3.

133. *Hom.* 15.17; 30.2; 11.3; *The Indwelling Spirit (The Great Letter).*

134. *Hom.* 29.1-2; 17.6; 8.4; *The Danger of Pride (The Great Letter).*

135. *Hom.* 5.6; 15.44; 16.1; 15.49; 45.1.

136. *Detachment (The Great Letter).*

137. *Hom.* 15.4; 3.2; *Simplicity and Concord (The Great Letter).*

138. *The Role of the Superior (The Great Letter); Hom.* 38.1; *Love Begets Fraternal Love (The Great Letter).*

139. *Hom.* 30.1.

140. *Hom.* 4.3, 7.

141. *Hom.* 5.6; *The Passions (The Great Letter); Hom.* 10; 9.2.

142. *Hom.* 31.5; 15.2; 30.1.

143. *Hom.* 40.1; *Unceasing Prayer (The Great Letter); Hom.* 8.1; 40.2.

144. *Hom.* 15.2; cf. *Mystical Union (The Great Letter).*

145. Maloney, pp. 9ff.

Chapter 6 — "'Choirs of Angels': The Liturgists"

1. There are four main families of ancient liturgy: the Jerusalem liturgies generally adopted throughout the East; the Alexandrian liturgy, used in Egypt; the western Roman and Gallic liturgies; and the Persian and Edessa liturgies. To these may be added the Clementine liturgy encompassed in *Apost. Constit.* 8. See further *Early Liturgies,* ANF, 7.

2. Eusebius, *HE* 8. For house churches see F. V. Filson, "The Significance of the Early House Churches," *JBL* 58 (1939): 109ff. The most famous house church is that at Dura-Europa, dated about 232. The church at Nicomedia is destroyed by fire (Lactantius, *De mort. persec.* 12).

3. *Apost. Constit.* 2.57.

4. Normally basilicas consist of two or four aisles, with pillars supporting horizontal architraves. Above these is the clerestory, pierced with windows. The building is approached through a narrow narthex and is completed by an apse at its east end, everything being covered by an almost flat roof. Constantine also restored many ruined churches to their former grandeur (Theodoret, *HE* 14).

5. *Apost. Constit.* 8.5.

6. Gregory Thaumaturgus, *Hom. ann. virg. (Hom.* 1).

7. It is not certain whether antiphonal singing begins in Antioch in the second century or is the product of a fifth-century experiment with two choirs. Christians are urged to sing hymns (Chrysostom, *Hom. Col.* 1.10; Gregory Thaumaturgus, *Hom.* 1; 2).

8. See K. S. Latourette, *A History of Christianity,* 1 vol. edition (London: Eyre and Spottiswood, 1955), p. 207. For examples from preacher–hymn writers, see, e.g., Clement of Alexandria's *Hymn to Christ the Saviour (Paed.* 3.12) and Ephrem's Syriac hymns. Bardaeus is a hymn writer, and the missionary-preacher Niceta of Dacea is reputed to be the author of the *Te Deum.* See G. A. Catherall, "Niceta," in *NIDCC,* pp. 707-8. In the West, Hilary of Poitiers (see E. W. Watson, "Introduction to the Works of Hilary," in NPNF, 2nd ser., 9:xlviiff.) and Ambrose (*Ep.* 40.34; cf. Augustine, *Conf.* 9.7.15) are great hymn writers. Amongst Ambrose's most famous hymns are *Aeterne rerum Conditor,*

Deus Creator Omnium, Veni Redemptor Gentium (for Christmas Eve), and *O Lux Beata Trinitas*. Ambrose has to defend his hymns against the charge of being newfangled (*Contra Auxentius* 34.19-20; cf. Augustine, *Conf.* 9.7).

9. Tertullian, *On Prayer* 17; 23; Serapion of Thumis (d. ca. 362), a friend of Antony, possibly provides the earliest collection of written prayers in his sacramentary, *The Euchologion*. See J. G. G. Norman, "Serapion of Thumis," in *NIDCC*, p. 897.

10. Prudentius, *Cont. Symmach.* 1.551. See R. MacMullen, *Christianizing the Roman Empire: AD 100-400* (New Haven: Yale University Press, 1984), p. 86.

11. See MacMullen, p. 86; W. H. C. Frend, "Town and Countryside in Early Christianity," *SCH* 16 (1979): 25ff.; R. Fletcher, *The Conversion of Europe from Paganism to Christianity, 371-1386 A.D.* (London: Harper Collins, 1997), pp. 34ff.

12. Flavius Vopiscus (*Saturninus* 8.2-3) records the rumor that in Egypt even "those who call themselves bishops of Christ are, in fact, devotees of Serapis."

13. Oratory is much admired. Caligula has so "great a concern" for it that he arranges public contests in which the losers "are ordered to erase their writings with their tongues" (Suetonius, *Caligula* 53.1; 20). The pagan rhetor Libanius is active in Antioch at the same time as Chrysostom and commands a large following.

14. Chrysostom, *Hom. Eph.* 3; *Hom. Acts* 24; 29.

15. Pelagius (*De virgin.* 6.1) urges his hearers to impress pagan neighbors "not simply by abominating evil deeds but also by performing good works." It is often forgotten that Pelagius also is an eloquent and popular preacher.

16. Instructions for these arrangements are found in *Apost. Constit.* 2.67.

17. Justin Martyr, *Apol. I* 66; cf. Ignatius, *Rom.* 7. In his *Homily on the Baptism of Christ*, Gregory of Nyssa asserts that "the bread becomes the Body of Christ . . . and so with the wine."

18. Chrysostom, *Hom. 1 Tim.* 10.

19. Chrysostom welcomes one such group in one of his sermons (*Hom. Statues* 19).

20. Chrysostom, *Hom. Stat.* 20.1; the forty days of the Lenten fast are particularly appropriate for systematic teaching.

21. *Apost. Constit.* 2.67. At least it is not required that *all* the presbyters present must participate. In the West, it seems that presbyters are not encouraged to preach when the bishop is present (Socrates, *HE* 5.22; Sozomen, *HE* 7.12).

22. *The Pilgrimage of Etheria* in B. J. Kidd, *DIHC*, 2:116.

23. Gregory Thaumaturgus, *Hom. omn. sanct.* (*Hom.* 4); *Hom. annun. Virg.* (*Hom.* 1); Gregory of Nyssa, *Sermon on the Baptism of Christ*. The liturgical calendar now embraces additional feasts besides Easter, Pentecost, and Epiphany; e.g., in the fourth century the Jerusalem church celebrates the Feast of Christ's Presentation or the Purification of the Virgin Mary and the Festival of the Holy Cross, celebrating the supposed discovery of the true cross.

24. Gregory Thaumaturgus, *Hom. ann. Virg.;* Leo the Great, *For Whitsuntide I*

(*Hom.* 75.2); Gregory Thaumaturgus, *Hom. omn. sanct.*; Leo the Great, *For the Ascension I* (*Hom.* 73.4).

25. E.g., about the middle of the fourth century, the Roman festival of Christ's nativity becomes confused with the worship of the rising sun (Leo the Great, *Hom.* 27.4; 7). The Christian festival has to be separated from pagan practices. See Leo the Great's *Sermons on the Nativity* (*Hom.* 27.4) and Chrysostom, *Hom. Matt.* 37.1.

26. Chrysostom, *Hom. Matt.* 37.9.

27. E.g., Virgil, *Aeneid* 5.42-103.

28. E.g., Paulinus of Nola builds a church in honor of the martyred Felix and equips it with paraphernalia similar to that used for the veneration of a pagan deity. For the cult of the martyrs, see further D. Dunn-Wilson, "The Biblical Background of Martys and Its Derivatives, with Special Reference to the New Testament" (M.A. thesis, University of Birmingham, 1958), pp. 246ff.

29. Prudentius writes his *Peristephanon Liber* to celebrate the faith of the martyrs and encourage their veneration. It is not clear whether it ever forms part of the liturgy.

30. Chrysostom (*Hom. 1 Cor.* 4) describes how the martyrs' "bones are forced apart by levers" and they are "placed in frying-pans and hurled into cauldrons." Leo the Great (*Hom.* 85.2-3) also gives a vivid account of the betrayal and torments of Saint Lawrence.

31. It is said that for their part in the passion, the Jews "deserve the hatred of mankind," but by contrast Gentiles play a noble part in the person of Simon of Cyrene (Leo the Great, *Hom.* 54.4; 59.4). Cyprian writes *Three Books of Testimonies against the Jews* (*Treatises* 12). Chrysostom denounces Jews as "senseless and unrepentant, unbelieving and disputatious, boastful and arrogant" (*Hom. Matt.* 10.2-3). Synagogues have to be protected from the attacks of outraged Christian congregations (*Codex Theodosianus* 16.8-9; 16.82).

32. Possibly many of these observances originate in the Jerusalem church but are carried by Christian travelers throughout the empire. See the account of Good Friday events in Jerusalem in the late-fourth-century *Pilgrimage of Etheria*.

33. The other main season for baptisms is Pentecost. The sixth-century *Canons of Hyppolitus* 9 instruct that, for baptism, three years of training is required, followed by careful examination. At the beginning of the third century, in Rome and Carthage, *The Discipline of the Secret* emphasizes the mysteries associated with Christian initiation; e.g., Cyril of Jerusalem, *Catechesis;* Chrysostom, *Two Instructions to Candidates for Baptism;* Augustine, *De symbolo ad catecumenos et sermones tres de eodem.*

34. Prudentius writes the *Inventor Rutili* to be sung at the Paschal Vigil, and a deacon sings the *Praeconium* or *Exultet.*

35. Cyril, *Catech.* 3.20.

36. Leo the Great, *Hom.* 72.1.

37. Perhaps Tertullian's prohibition of kneeling for prayers "on the Day of Resurrection" (*De Oratione* 23) has as much to do with safety as with theology.

38. In the second century, Justin Martyr speaks of the president at the sacramental meal expounding the Scripture (*Apol. I 67*).

39. See further, G. S. Sloyan, "Liturgical Preaching," in *CEP*, pp. 311ff.

Chapter 7 — "'The Doctrine of the Lord': The Theologians"

1. *Ep.* 173. The *Basilead* is an ecclesiastical complex containing a church, clergy house, poorhouse, and hospital. In 368, when famine strikes Caesarea, Basil ministers to the needs of the hungry out of his own pocket.

2. *Ep.* 194. Most of the 365 extant letters attributed to Basil are probably authentic. He is a careful correspondent and rebukes careless penmanship on the part of others (*Ep.* 324).

3. *Epp.* 42.4; 44.1; 46.1.

4. *Epp.* 44.2; cf. 199.8.

5. *Ep.* 8.1.

6. *Epp.* 221; 220.

7. *Hom.* 8.8; cf. *Epp.* 92.2; 240.1.

8. *Hom.* 5. Basil's own faith is greatly influenced by his grandmother, mother, and sister, and he insists that "women no less than men are made after the image of God" (*Hom.* 5).

9. E.g., *Hom.* 6.1; *Epp.* 6.1; 105.1.

10. *Epp.* 217.53; 199.49. Basil instructs that such desperate women are to be pardoned. Christian parents are urged to adopt orphans and bring them up in the faith (*Apost. Constit.* 2.7; 4.1; cf. 4.13).

11. Basil knows that soldiers can be away from home for such a long time that their wives remarry, believing their husbands to be dead, and he decrees that such situations are treated with sympathy (*Ep.* 199.36).

12. *Ep.* 289.1.

13. *Hom.* 6; 7; *Ep.* 194.

14. *Hex.* 3.1; *Ep.* 106. The much-admired martyr Gordius is a demoted captain (*Hom.* 18). Basil gives an eloquent sermon to celebrate the forty martyred soldiers of Sebaste (*Hom.* 19).

15. *Hex.* 3.1.

16. *Hom.* 12; cf. *Ep.* 92.2. For the seating of the elderly see *Apost. Constit.* 2.57.

17. Despite Julian's edict of 362, intended to prevent the conversion of students by effectively banning Christian teachers, many young people continue to enter the churches.

18. *Hom.* 12; *Epp.* 260; 90.2.

19. *Hom.* 22; 7; *Hex.* 9.4.

20. *Hom.* 18. Basil refers especially to their absence from special intercessory services held during the disastrous famine of 368 (*Hom.* 6).

21. *Hom.* 14. Basil specifically forbids Christians to sing obscene songs (*Hom.* 7).

22. *De Spirit.* 30.77-78.

23. *De Spirit.* 30.77; cf. *Ep.* 229. A woman complains that her reputation is ruined by a fellow believer who "affixes libellous placards to the church door" (*Ep.* 289). Vocations are supposed to reflect favorably upon the girls' families and so Basil has to control potential abuses (199.18). He instructs monks to calm down and "do Christ's work quietly" (226.3).

24. *Hom.* 12.

25. *Epp.* 199.21; 22.1; *Hom.* 14.7.

26. *Hex.* 8.8.

27. *Ep.* 188.1. There are three "canonical letters" addressed to Amphiliocus, bishop of Iconium, whose legal training probably explains his eagerness to have Basil's detailed comments on the regulations.

28. *Ep.* 53-54, which is written to the *choriepiscopoi* who are involved in the scandal. The cause célèbre is the self-styled patriarch Deacon Glycerius, who neglects his duties and "absconds at night with a group of virgins" (*Ep.* 169). Basil makes provision for unfrocking such unworthy clergy (188.3).

29. *Epp.* 90.2; 209.2; 217.69; 188.3; *De Spirit.* 30.78; cf. *Ep.* 22.3.

30. E.g., *Hex.* 6.11; *Ep.* 8.7.

31. Some of Basil's dissertations, such as *De Spiritu Sancto,* are more formal than seemingly extempore pieces like the *Hexaemeron.* The sermon *On the Festival of St. Eupsychius* is preached in the presence of many of Basil's detractors.

32. *Hex.* 8.2, 7; *Ep.* 8.2.

33. E.g., "How did you like the fare of my morning's discourse? . . . It is for you to judge . . ." (*Hex.* 9.1).

34. *Ep.* 8.2; *Hex.* 8.2; 2.1.

35. *Hex.* 7.6; 9.6; 8.8.

36. *Hex.* 6.1-2; cf. 1.1; *Hom.* 24.

37. E.g. — "reverence the hoary head of fasting," "anger is the intoxication of the soul," "in all things, try to avoid bigness" (*Hom.* 12; 1; 20).

38. *Hex.* 9.6; 8.1, 6; cf. 7.3, "I will not pass in silence the cunning and trickery of the squid."

39. *Hom.* 3.

40. *Ep.* 2.3; *De Spirit.* 27.65-66.

41. At least thirteen are recognized as authentic.

42. *Ep.* 22.2; *Hom.* 12; cf. *De Spirit.* 30.78.

43. *De Spirit.* 12.28; 10.26; *Ep.* 8.4.

44. Basil observes (*Hom.* 1) that "smoke drives away bees and debauch drives away the gifts of the Spirit."

45. *Hex.* 8.4; *Hom.* 11. Basil's sermon against drunkenness *(Hom.* 14, *Against Drunkards)* is worthy of any nineteenth-century temperance reformer. He asks the self-indulgent, "What will you answer the Judge?" (7).

46. *Ep.* 22.2; *Hom.* 20.

47. *Ep.* 23. Basil's *On the Perfection of Solitaries* (*Ep.* 22), although primarily addressed to monks, is equally concerned with the conduct of "ordinary" Christians. Basil's *Sermo Asceticus* and *Sermo de Ascetica* advocate moderate asceticism; see further W. K. L. Clarke, *St. Basil the Great: A Study in Monasticism* (London: Cambridge University Press, 1913), pp. 63ff.

48. *Ep.* 284.

49. *Epp.* 42.1; 199.18-19; *Regul. brev.* 137. Basil produces two monastic Rules *(Regulae brevius tractatae* and *Regulae fusius tractatae)* which are basically homiletic dialogues, comprised of questions and answers. Through their influence upon the *Rule of Benedict* they have considerable impact upon medieval ideas about the religious life. See NPNF, 2nd ser., 8.

50. *Reg. fus.* 2.

51. Basil's admiration for the martyrs is shown in his panegyric sermons: *Hom.* 5; 17; 18; 19; 23.

52. *Hom. in Psalm.* 32.1.

53. *Hom.* 1, *First Homily on Faith.*

54. E. Underhill, *The Mystic Way: A Psychological Study in Christian Origins* (London: Dent, 1913), p. 294.

55. *Ep.* 236.6. He likens the Trinity to different forms of light (38.4-5).

56. *Hom.* 24; *Ep.* 159.2.

57. *Hex.* 2.5; *Hom.* 9; *Hom. in Psalm.* 48.3.

58. *Ep.* 261.3; *Hom. in Psalm.* 43.3.

59. *Reg. brev.* 267; cf. *Hom.* 6; *Hom. in Psalm.* 48.2.

60. *Hom. in Psalm.* 33.

61. J. A. Broadus, *Lectures on the History of Preaching* (New York: Sheldon, 1886), p. 61.

62. *Ep.* 3.

63. *De baptismo Christi; Ep.* 13.

64. *Ep.* 13 (a good example of Gregory's epistolary homilies); *De virgin.* 4.

65. *Ep.* 13; *De baptismo Christi.* The "separateness" of the clergy is declared by the fact that their hands alone are permitted to touch the Holy Table.

66. *Ep.* 17, in which Basil asserts that to "fight against" the preacher is to resist Christ himself.

67. *De baptismo Christi.*

68. *De infantibus qui praemature abripiuntur.*

69. *Ep.* 17; R. Gregoire ("Homily," in *EEC,* 1:394ff.) points out the difficulty of es-

tablishing clear boundaries between the different genres of patristic homiletic material. *Tractatus, homilia, sermo,* and *colloquium* often overlap and intertwine.

70. E.g., he preaches at the funerals of Princess Pulcheria and the empress Flacilla.

71. E.g., he urges his hearers to "scrape off the rust that grows on the soul like a sort of evil mould." "It seems to me, that it would be an excellent idea to discuss this matter briefly" (*De beat. orat.* 10.6; 6), Gregory says. "It is better to make our argument clear by illustration, to explain by means of earthly and lowly matters, those matters which are greater and invisible to the senses" (*Ep.* 3).

72. Gregory draws his most lyrical illustrations from the natural world. He calls it "all-contriving nature" (*De hom. opific.* 30.30) and draws widely upon it, from "the chants of the song birds" to the "scaly hide of the crocodile" (1.5; 7:3) and from the composition of wheat to the wonders of human anatomy (29:3; 30).

73. He produces five *Homilies on the Lord's Prayer,* eight *Sermons on the Beatitudes,* eight *Sermons on Ecclesiastes,* and *Sermons on Genesis 1:26,* in homage to his brother's *Hexaemeron.*

74. *De hom. opific.* 25.2; *Titles of the Psalms* 2. Gregory's *Song of Songs* and *Titles of the Psalms* are strongly allegorical, but in *The Life of Moses* he utilizes both the literalist and the allegorical approaches. See further M. Simonetti, *Biblical Interpretation in the Early Church: An Historical Introduction to Patristic Exegesis,* trans. J. A. Hughes (Edinburgh: T. & T. Clark, 1994), pp. 65ff.

75. Although Gregory does suggest, somewhat gauchely, that God ends young lives prematurely in order to save children from committing future sins.

76. *De virgin.* 23.

77. *De peregrinis.*

78. See further, S. R. F. Price, *Rituals of Power: The Roman Imperial Cult in Asia Minor* (London: Oxford University Press, 1984), pp. 133ff.

79. One sermon for Epiphany, several for Easter, Ascension, and Pentecost, although the authenticity of the one remaining Christmas sermon is questioned. See T. K. Carroll and T. Halton, *Liturgical Practice of the Fathers* (Wilmington: Michael Glazier, 1988), pp. 114ff. (Easter), pp. 179ff. (Epiphany), pp. 194ff. (Ascension), pp. 307-8 (Pentecost).

80. A. C. McGiffert (*A History of Christian Thought,* 2 vols. [London: Scribner, 1932], 1:291) describes Gregory as "the leading theologian of the Cappadocian group." He augments his doctrinal treatises with the *Catechetical Oration,* a compendium of theology widely used by the Eastern church for the instruction of congregations.

81. S. Dill, *Roman Society in the Last Century of the Western Empire* (London: Macmillan, 1898), p. 27; cf. *Oratio catechetica magna* introduction, *Ep.* 2, for Gregory's own similar diagnosis.

82. For useful summaries of Gregory's teaching, see F. Bethune-Baker, *An Introduction to the Early History of Christian Doctrine* (London: Methuen, 1951), pp. 220ff., 251ff., 411ff.; J. Gribomant, "Gregory of Nyssa," in *EEC,* 1:364-65, and for his continuing

theological significance, see J. Milbank, "Gregory of Nyssa: The Force of Identity," in *Christian Origins, Theology, Rhetoric, and Community*, ed. L. Ayres and G. Jones (London: Routledge, 1988), pp. 94ff.

83. *Orat. cat. mag.* 5-6; 22; *De baptismo Christi.*

84. *Orat. cat. mag.* 31, a sermon probably preached on the day after the Feast of Epiphany.

85. *De baptismo Christi.*

86. *De baptismo Christi.*

87. *De infantibus qui praemature abripiuntur.*

88. *De baptismo Christi; De beat. orat.* 6.

89. Basil says (*De virg.* 4) the ascetic is "in every way free and at peace."

90. *De virg.* 21.

91. He writes of "the bright eyes beneath the lids, the arching eyebrows, the cheek with its sweet, dimpling smile, the natural red that blooms the lips, the gold-bound hair, shining in many twisted masses on the head" (*De virg.* 3).

92. *De virg.* 9; 13.

93. *De virg.* 8; 3.

94. *De virg.* 11; 4. For Gregory's "progressive asceticism," see H. von Campenhausen, *The Fathers of the Greek Church*, trans. M. Hoffmann (London: A. & C. Black, 1963), pp. 123-24. Gregory proposes a threefold *scala: apatheia* (freedom from passion), *gnosis* (knowledge of the unseen world), and *theoria* (the highest stage of contemplation) (*Song of Songs* 1.24; cf. *The Life of Moses* and *Ecclesiastes*). For a useful discussion of the homilies on the Song of Songs, see A. Meredith in *The Cappadocians* (Crestwood, N.Y.: St. Vladimir's Seminary Press, 1995), pp. 78ff.

95. *De virg.* 11.

96. *De anima et resurrectione.*

97. *De infantibus qui praemature abripiuntur; De anima et resurrectione.* For the origins of a purgatorial state, see V. C. Pilcher, *The Hereafter in Jewish and Christian Thought: With Special Reference to the Doctrine of Resurrection* (London: SPCK, 1940), pp. 83ff.; D. C. Steinmetz, "Purgatory," in *NIDCC*, p. 814; C. O'Donnell, *Ecclesia* (Collegeville: Liturgical, 1996), pp. 392ff. For a useful list of other patristic references (especially Tertullian), see *EDB*, pp. 191ff. For the development of the doctrine, see H. Bietenhard, "Fire," in *DNTT*, 1:653ff.; A. Hamman, "Purgatory," in *EEC*, 2:725.

98. *De hom. opific.* 27.2-3.

99. *De anima et resurrectione.*

100. Gregory of Nazianzus, *Orat.* 18.16; *Ep.* 189.

101. *Orat.* 3.1. After his enforced ordination, he flees in panic to Pontus and returns reluctantly to Nazianzus. After his first petulant sermon, he writes a long apology explaining his flight (*Orat.* 2). It becomes the influential *Treatise on the Priesthood.*

102. *Orat.* 3.5.

103. *Ep.* 152; *Orat.* 2.4.

104. *Orat.* 2.43, 49.

105. *Orat.* 2.41.

106. *Orat.* 2.42, 49.

107. *Orat.* 2.40.

108. *Orat.* 3.6.

109. *Orat.* 1.1.

110. *Orat.* 16.18-19.

111. *Ep.* 144.

112. *Orat.* 8.8; 10. Gregory sets before his congregations the example of certain godly women: his mother Nonna (18.9-10), his sister Gorgonia (*Orat.* 8.9-10), and Theosobia, whom he calls "truly a consort of a priest" and who may have been his wife (*Ep.* 197).

113. *Orat.* 8.8; 7.23.

114. *Orat. theol.* 4.1; *Ep.* 76, in which Gregory pleads with Bishop Theodore of Tyana not to take legal action against the Arians, despite their attacks upon catholic congregations.

115. *Orat. theol.* 1.1; 2.2, in which Gregory seems to be aware of spies and hecklers in his congregation.

116. R. H. Hardy, ed., *Christology of the Later Fathers*, LCC 3 (London: SCM Press, 1954), p. 117.

117. *Orat. theol.* 1.2.

118. *Orat. theol.* 1.5; 7.1.

119. Five orations are on catholic doctrine.

120. *Orat.* 16.4; 2.76; 12.1.

121. *Orat. theol.* 2.4; *Orat.* 2.25, 29.

122. He admits that he can be "too discursive" (*Orat.* 41.2), and that sometimes his sermons can be too "minute for most people to listen to" (*Orat. theol.* 2.11).

123. E.g., *Orat.* 3 is unduly self-indulgent and Gregory himself admits it is a "toilsome consideration" (3.112).

124. He loves complicated sentences with multiple subsidiary clauses (e.g., *Orat.* 2) and elegant descriptions. E.g., "Look also at the fishy tribe, gliding through the waters and, as it were, flying through the liquid element and breathing its own air but in danger when in contact with ours" (*Orat. theol.* 2.24).

125. *Orat.* 40.1.

126. He insists (*Ep.* 51) that "useful" letters must "avoid the oratorical style and are sparing in their use of figures of speech," and he is capable of similar simplicity in the pulpit; e.g., when the crew of an Egyptian grain ship joins his congregation, he preaches a simple sermon to welcome them (*Orat.* 24). Yet he is master of the memorable phrase, e.g., "Let us become like Christ, since Christ became like us" (1.5). He declares that wrangles in the church are as "out of place as geometry in mourning and tears at a carousal" (*Orat. theol.* 1.5).

127. E.g., *Orat.* 7.6.

128. *Orat.* 2.34. He regards his father as a fine example of a "good shepherd" (*Orat.* 18).

129. *Orat.* 40.16. Gregory himself is not baptized until 358-59, and his brother, Caesarius, is not baptized until just before his death in 369.

130. *Orat.* 40.11; 39.10-11.

131. *Orat.* 42.8.

132. E.g., *Orat.* 38.12, expounding law and free will, and 41.5, dealing with "the mysteries of Christ."

133. *Orat.* 17-31, preached in the *Anastasia* Chapel in the summer or autumn of 380. They blend theology with devotion and praise. Hardy (p. 123) claims that "no series of doctrinal sermons have ever been so successful in simultaneously meeting the current intellectual problems of the age and making a permanent contribution to the formulation of Christian thought."

134. *Orat. theol.* 2.4, 24ff.

135. *Orat. theol.* 3. Gregory may have drawn the material from a Eunomanian manual of instruction.

136. *Orat. theol.* 5.24. Gregory also considers the doctrine of the Spirit in his Pentecost Oration (41).

137. *Orat. theol.* 38.1, 17.

138. *Orat. theol.* 42.2, 6, 22, 17.

139. *Orat. theol.* 45. It is an Easter sermon, and it may be a sign of Gregory's weariness that two passages are taken verbatim from one of his earlier Christmas orations (12.4).

140. Great translator and commentator though Jerome is, perhaps the cantankerous genius which exercises such Rasputin-like power over pious ladies is not the stuff of which truly great preachers are made.

141. *Tract. Pss.* 53.10.

142. See further F. J. Foakes-Jackson, *History of the Christian Church to 460* AD (Cambridge: J. Hall, 1905), pp. 325ff., 356ff.

143. *Tract. Pss.* 53.13.

144. *Tract. Pss.* 53.10; 1.8.

145. *Tract. Pss.* 1.9, italics mine.

146. *De Trin.* 1.1-2.

147. *Tract. Pss.* 52.13.

148. *Tract. Pss.* 135.4.

149. *Tract. Pss.* 53.5; 135.4.

150. In order to improve congregational singing, Hilary sets some of his hymns to march time.

151. E.g., long passages in *De Trinitate* are couched in sonorous rhetoric befitting the work's awesome theme.

152. Some of his sermons are very brief (e.g., *Hom. Pss.* 130), but others, too lengthy to have been preached in their present form, probably survive as shorthand notes and are later edited and extended into treatises.

153. *De. Trin.* 1.3.

154. He seems much more at home among fields, harvests, trees, fruit, and streams. E.g., *Tract. Pss.* 1.3, 13-14; 130.2.

155. *De Trin.* 1.5.

156. *Tract. Pss.* 120.4; *De Trin.* 1.20.

157. *De Trin.* 1.21; *Tract. Pss.* 14, "The Psalm which has been read," whereas the normal practice is probably that it is sung by the lector as part of the liturgy.

158. *Tract. Pss.* 31.1.

159. For a comparison of the exegetical methods of Hilary and Origen, see E. W. Watson, "Introduction to the Works of Hilary," in NPNF, 2nd ser., 9:xliiiff.

160. *Tract. Pss.* 53.1. E.g., Hilary sees the "trees by the water" in Ps. 1 as pointing to "Christ the Tree of Life" (1.3, 14) and declares that David's sufferings "prophetically foretold" the passion of Christ (53.1).

161. *Tract. Pss.* 118.5ff.

162. *De Trin.* 1.8, 13.

163. *Tract. Pss.* 1.9. In 1.6 Hilary lists the five enemies of human happiness.

164. *Tract. Pss.* 53.130; 1.14.

165. *Tract. Pss.* 130.1; *De Trin.* 9.14; 11.48-49; 12.6. For Hilary's Christology, see Bethune-Baker, pp. 297ff. and 425-26.

166. Leo, *Serm.* 1.1; 3; 62.2.

167. *Serm.* 3.4.

168. E.g., *Serm.* 21.1; 22.1. He celebrates his birthdays and anniversaries of his ordination and consecration (*Serm.* 1; 2; 3), but the tone of these sermons does not suggest that Leo sees these occasions as opportunities for self-aggrandizement.

169. *Serm.* 84.1; 88.4.

170. *Serm.* 34.5.

171. *Ep.* 9.3; *Serm.* 2.2. Some sermons, such as 28, appear to be longer. Leo is a master of memorable phrases; e.g., in the incarnation, God "being invisible in His own nature, became visible in ours," and "coming down Himself to us, to Whom we could not ascend" (32.2; 33.3).

172. *Serm.* 34.1. The particular occasion is a sparsely attended service of thanksgiving to commemorate Rome's liberation after fourteen days of pillage by Geneseric in 455 — an event in which Leo himself takes a prominent part.

173. E.g., *Serm.* 46.1.

174. *Serm.* 46.1. The reference is to Manichaean and Pelagian heresies.

175. *Epp.* 17; 12.9-10; 1.42; 10.6. Bishops vie with each other to entice favorite clergy into their dioceses (12.10).

176 *Ep.* 4.2. Leo, who is at ease with the crème of imperial society (e.g., *Epp.* 24; 21;

37), inherits its class consciousness. He attacks Hilary of Arles for "ordaining men who are quite unknown" (15.6).

177. *Ep.* 12.5. Leo does not condemn marriage per se (e.g., 15.8).

178. Deacons do not preach (Ambrosiaster, *Comm. Eph.* 1.11) and presbyters do not preach in the presence of bishops (Jerome, *Ep.* 52.7). Sozomen's enigmatic comment (*HE* 7.19) that in Rome "the people are not taught by the bishop in the church" has been interpreted to mean that Roman bishops seldom preach in public.

179. *Serm.* 62.1.

180. *Serm.* 32.1; 23.1; 63.1; 51.8.

181. *Serm.* 77.1-2; 51.1; 67.1.

182. *Serm.* 26.3; 22.3; 24.2; 49.3.

183. *Serm.* 16.3; cf. 36.2; 42.3.

184. *Serm.* 27.3; 36.3; 42.3. Leo has to explain that the Feast of the Nativity has no connection with the pagan sun festival.

185. *Serm.* 23.5.

186. *Ep.* 16.7; *Serm.* 63.6; 88.3; 82.6.

187. *Serm.* 83.3; 78.4; *Ep.* 10.1. Leo even asserts that God creates the Roman Empire in order that Peter's "preaching of the Word might quickly reach all people" (*Serm.* 82.2).

188. *Serm.* 67.1; cf. 51.1; 67.1. He tells his people that "A sermon is still required of us, that the priest's exhortation may be added to the solemn reading of Holy Writ" (72.1).

189. *Serm.* 24.1. E.g., Christmas (*Serm.* 21-27), Epiphany (31; 32; 34; 36), Transfiguration (51), Passiontide (54; 55; 58; 59; 62; 63; 67; 68), Easter (71; 72), Ascensiontide (73; 74), Whitsuntide (75; 77; 78).

190. *Serm.* 2.2; 31.1; 28.1; 21.1; 22.1. Not even Lenten discipline is to destroy the joy of worship with "gloomy self-restraint" (73.4; 42.2).

191. *Serm.* 71.5, Incarnation (91.3), the Passion (54.1), Resurrection (71.3-4), Ascension (74.4-5), Pentecost (78.3).

192. *Serm.* 88.2. Some of Leo's most effective sermons are preached on the theme of the ecclesiastical fasts; e.g., *On the Fast of the Seventh Month* (88; 90; 91), *On the Fast of the Tenth Month* (12; 16; 17; 19), *On Lent* (39; 40; 42; 46; 49).

193. *Serm.* 10.3-4; 17.1; 88.1.

194. *Serm.* 42.3-5; 40.2.

195. *Serm.* 19.1; 10.4.

196. *Serm.* 17.1; 12.4.

197. *Serm.* 19.2; 9.1; 42.2; 39.5; 10.1.

198. *Serm.* 17.3; *Ep.* 4.4-5; *Serm.* 39.5; 40.

199. *Serm.* 95.1ff., 8ff.; 49.6.

200. *Serm.* 27.1.

201. *Serm.* 36.2; cf. 69.3; 59.2-3; 68.3; 54.3, 6; 62.4; 67.4.

202. *Ep.* 7.1.

203. *Serm.* 9.4. He explains that it is "naught but piety to disclose the hiding-place of the wicked and, in them, to overthrow the devil whom they serve."

204. *Serm.* 95.4. He urges his congregations to pray for the "ruined souls" among them (34.5; 24.5) and commends that, when truly repentant, sinners be restored to the fellowship (*Epp.* 38; 18).

205. *Ep.* 28.

206. Leo says (*Serm.* 67.2) the three persons are involved "in such a way that the Father should be propitiated, the Son should propitiate and the Holy Ghost enkindle."

207. In the Eucharist (*Serm.* 91.3), nativity (28.1), Lent (40.3), transfiguration (51.8), passion (63.6), resurrection (72.2), and ascension (74.5).

208. *Serm.* 24.2.

209. *Serm.* 75.1; 78.3; 40.1.

210. *Serm.* 95.9.

Chapter 8 — "'Delightful Persuaders': The Homileticians"

1. F. H. Dudden, *The Life and Times of St. Ambrose*, 2 vols. (Oxford: Clarendon, 1935), 2:11.

2. I. H. Marshall, "In Honesty of Preaching: An Assessment," *ET* 112, no. 2 (November 2000): 41.

3. See P. J. Els, *"leqah"* in *DOTTE*, 2:812ff.; O. Becker, "Faith, Persuade," in *DNTT*, 1:587ff.; R. MacMullen, "Modes of Persuasion before 312," in *Christianizing the Roman Empire: AD 100-400* (New Haven: Yale University Press, 1984), pp. 25ff.

4. Quintilian (*Orat.* 5.1.5–2.31) teaches his pupils to present "a persuasive exposition" of their material. Schools teaching grammar and rhetoric appear in Rome about the second century B.C.E.

5. Cassiodorus (*Institutiones divinarum* 20) commends Ambrose for being "most sweet in his power of gentle persuasion." Augustine (*De doct. Chr.* 4.3.4) tells his pupils they must "learn how to speak persuasively" and make persuasion their chief aim.

6. Aristotle, *Rhet.* 1.3.

7. Quintilian, *Orat.* 2.15.34. He considers several other definitions before selecting this one. Like Augustine, he complains that boys are not introduced early enough to the discipline (2.1.1; Augustine, *De doct. Chr.* 4.3.4-5).

8. The lasting connection is illustrated by works like Christlieb's *Homiletics: Lectures on Preaching*, trans. C. H. Irwin (Edinburgh: T. & T. Clark, 1897), a ponderous, Teutonic work, immensely influential at the end of the nineteenth century. The link between rhetoric and "the science of preaching" is carefully traced (p. 25), and the fourth chapter is entitled "The Rhetorical Form and Delivery of the Sermon" (pp. 312ff.).

9. E.g., Jerome, *Comm. in Gal.* 3.praef. Yet he does not seem opposed to eloquence

itself (*Epp.* 52.9; 53.3; 58.11). Augustine teaches rhetoric and admires Ambrose for his eloquence (*Conf.* 5.8.14; 12.22). Chrysostom studies rhetoric in Antioch under the renowned Libanius. Many other preachers must have been nurtured under Quintilian's *Training of an Orator*, which remains a classic textbook long after the death of its author in 100 C.E.

10. The basic meaning of "hermeneutics" is "to speak aloud" or "to explain." For brief introductions to the concept see A. Richardson, "Hermeneutics," in *DCT*, pp. 154ff.; A. Thiselton, in *NDCT*, pp. 293ff.; J. A. Sanders, "Hermeneutics," in *CEP*, pp. 175ff., for its homiletic use.

11. Augustine, *De doct. Chr.* 4.12.27. The "offices" function as follows: *invention* analyzes the topic of the oration, *disposition* arranges the material for the oration, *elocution* adapts the oration for its speaker and audience, *memory* lodges the subject of the oration in the mind.

12. For Ambrose's influence upon emperors and empresses, see E. Gibbon, *The Decline and Fall of the Roman Empire,* ed. C. A. Robinson, abridged ed. (London: Penguin Books, 1980), XII; Ambrose, *Epp.* 17; 20; 41; 51; 57. He preaches funeral orations for emperors (*De obitu Theodosii oratio* and *De obitu Valentiani consolatio*).

13. *De. virginib.* 3.1.1, quoting Liberius. Cf. *De Poenitentia* 2.83ff. Some of his largest congregations are to be found at funerals; e.g., *De Exc. Sat.* 1.5; *Ep.* 22.3.

14. Ambrose observes (*Ep.* 22.7) that the Milanese congregation has not been tested to the point of martyrdom.

15. E.g., the discomforted Theodosius admits, "You have been preaching about me!" (*Ep.* 41.27).

16. Such *pagano-Christians* are encouraged by the fact that not even so-called Christian emperors wholeheartedly condemn paganism. See A. Cameron, *The Later Roman Empire* (London: Harper Collins, 1993), pp. 73ff. Ambrose himself writes (*Ep.* 18.10): "Let the voice of our Emperor utter the name of Christ alone and speak of Him only." Some distinguished intellectuals, like Symmachus, Pretextatus, and Nichomachus Flavius, honestly oppose the church and fight for the return of the old Roman religions.

17. Paulinus (*Vita S. Ambrosii* 12) says Ambrose's "antiphons, hymns and vigils" have spread "throughout almost all the provinces of the West." Ambrose denies that "the strains of his hymns" "lead astray" the people and exacerbate the problems of the church (*Serm. cont. Aux.* 34). See "The Services of Ambrose to Church Music" (Dudden, 1:293ff.).

18. *De virginib.* 1.6.29; cf. *Ep.* 63.112.

19. *Comm. Cant.* 1.19; *De Nab.* 56; 3; *Hex.* 6.52.

20. *De Tob.* 19; cf. *De Elia* 24; 32; *Hex.* 5.27.

21. *Hex.* 3.30; *De Tob.* 17.

22. *De Elia* 67; *Comm. Cant.* 1.14; *In Pss.* 37; *De Elia* 54; *De offic.* 1.20.86; *De Elia* 63.

23. *De Nab.* 20; *De Tob.* 38; *De offic.* 3.6.37; 9.58.

24. *Ep.* 63.92.

25. *De offic.* 2.16.76; *De Nab.* 21; 30; *De Tob.* 39; *De Nab.* 1; 25.

26. *De Nab.* 40; 56.

27. *De Nab.* 56; 54; 44; 45; 4; 35; *De Abr.* 1.12; *In Pss.* 98.167; *De offic.* 2.41; *De Cain* 1.14.

28. *De virginib.* 3.3.13.

29. O. C. Edwards, "History of Preaching," in *CEP,* p. 191; G. L. Carey, "Ambrose," in *NIDCC,* p. 32; cf. "a star performer" (Cameron, p. 72), "one of the most famous of . . . preachers" (K. S. Latourette, *A History of Christianity,* 1 vol. edition [London: Eyre and Spottiswood, 1955], p. 98), "a truly great man . . . above all his eloquence . . . [is] suffi-cient proof" (F. J. Foakes-Jackson, *History of the Christian Church to 460 AD* [Cam-bridge: J. Hall, 1905], p. 427). Simonetti (*Biblical Interpretation in the Early Church: An Historical Introduction to Patristic Exegesis,* trans. J. A. Hughes [Edinburgh: T. & T. Clark, 1994], p. 53) says Ambrose and Chrysostom originate a distinctive style of hom-ily. In itself, the production of such a major work as Dudden's indicates the importance of Ambrose as a preacher; cf. the adulatory opinions of earlier writers. Cassiodorus, *Institutiones divinarum* 20; Augustine, *Conf.* 5.13.23.

30. *De virginib.* 1.1.1.

31. Augustine, *Conf.* 6.3.3; e.g., Ambrose, *De virginib.* 1.2.5; *In Pss.* 118.20, 44 (Sebastian); 6.16 (SS Gervasius and Protasius).

32. He calls his addresses *sermons* and *tractates* (e.g, *Serm. cont. Aux.* 26; *In Eph.* 63.10; *Epp.* 20.4; cf. 2.8; 63.10), and he adopts the verb *tractare* to signify "preaching" (*Epp.* 11.15, 23, 37; 1.41, 27; etc.).

33. E.g., *De Exc. Sat.* 2.42. Dudden (2:455 n. 2) lists nearly thirty addresses which are expanded into treatises or commentaries.

34. Augustine, *Conf.* 5.13.23; 5.13.3; Ambrose, *De offic.* 1.23.104.

35. E.g., the sermons of Maximus of Turin (ca. 380–ca. 469) bear many similarities to those of Ambrose.

36. E.g., *De Exc. Sat.* 1.63-64; *In Pss.* 118.20ff.; *De obit. Val.* 52-55; *Hex.* 1.38; 3.22; 6.76.

37. Augustine, *Conf.* 5.14.24; cf. Cassiodorus (*Institutiones divinarum* 20), who finds Ambrose's arguments "weighty, yet acute."

38. *De Exc. Sat.* 2.114.

39. *Serm. cont. Aux.* 21.13; read to a congregation disturbed by the rumor that he has abandoned them "for his own safety."

40. *Ep.* 22.3; *De Exc. Sat.* 2.60.

41. *De offic.* 1.23.102-3; e.g., *De Elia* 14-15, where he lampoons the frenetic prepara-tions for a lavish feast.

42. *In Pss.* 118.14.37.

43. For Ambrose's love of nature see Dudden, 2:474ff.

44. E.g., the *Quo Vadis* legend of Peter in *Serm. cont. Aux.* 12ff.; St. Lawrence (*De*

offic. 1.41.214), St. Agnes (*De virginib.* 1.2.5ff.), Thecla and Pelagia (*De virginib.* 2.3.19ff.; 4.22ff.).

45. E.g., *De virginib.* 1.4.17; *In Pss.* 118.16, 11, 41.

46. E.g., *De Nabuthe Jezralita; De Tobia.* Ambrose appears to have little knowledge of Hebrew and depends heavily on Philo's commentaries.

47. The emphasis Ambrose gives to these elements varies considerably; e.g., in *De Cain et Abel* the mystical element predominates whereas the literal and allegorical are more prominent in works like *De Noe et arca.*

48. Dudden, 2:59. See his full treatment of Ambrose's allegorical preaching (2:457ff.).

49. Simonetti, p. 89. It is noteworthy that the homilies on the Song of Songs (*Tractatus de Epithalamio*) by Ambrose's contemporary, Gregory of Elvira (d. ca. 392), are much less moderate in their treatment of the biblical text.

50. *De poen.* 1.6.29; *Epp.* 41.20; 51.11. See further on the penitential system, NPNF, 2nd ser., 10:715ff. *De poen.* 1.16.90; 2.1.2. Ambrose urges his clergy to display the gentleness of Christ but insists that those who have "grievously fallen" must not be allowed to corrupt the churches (1.1.1, 15.78-79).

51. *De poen.* 1.3.10; 2.11.98; cf. *In Luc.* 7.76.

52. *De fide* 1.6.46; *De Sp. Sanc.* 1.16.183.

53. E.g., *De fide* 1.1.6, 3.30; 2.15.130; *Epp.* 21.13; 40.10; 20.14.5.

54. *De fide* 2.7.53, 16.142.

55. *De Sp. Sanc.* 1.6.79; cf. 2.7.64; *De myst.* 3.8-9; 4.19; *De Sp. Sanc.* 1.6.79; *De myst.* 9.55.

56. *De poen.* 1.15.80; *De offic.* 1.33.70.

57. *De myst.* 3.14; *De fide* 3.1.6.

58. *De offic.* 1.24.105, 20.85.

59. See further S. Wibbing, "σωφροσύνη," in *DNTT*, 1:501ff.; *De offic.* 1.18.67ff.; 2.16.76; 1.22.99.

60. *De offic.* 2.22.112; *De virginib.* 3.3.9; *De poen.* 1.14.69.

61. *De offic.* 1.28.130; 29.142; 30.145.

62. *De offic.* 1.31.158; 2.15.73; cf. *De vid.* 5.28; *De offic.* 1.30.48; 32.165; 2.15.69. Ambrose refers (*Ep.* 20.6) to the custom of marking Lent by "loosing the bonds of debtors."

63. *De offic.* 2.15.69; *De Exc. Sat.* 1.1; *De offic.* 2.15.70-71. Ambrose himself sells church plate to redeem such victims (*De offic.* 2.28).

64. *Ep.* 63.8. The specific references are to Sermatio and Barbantianus, who are disturbing the church at Vercellae (*De Sp. Sanc.* 1.16.183).

65. *De virginib.* 1.6.24; cf. 7.34; *De vid.* 11.68. Sermons on this theme are developed into major treatises. *De virginibus* is three books addressed to Marcellina, revised from an address originally delivered on the Feast of Saint Agnes. *De virginitate* and *De institutione virginis* are treatises on the virtue and guidance of virgins. *Exhortatio*

virginitatis is a sermon preached at the consecration of a church in Florence. Ambrose adds *De viduis,* a treatise on the importance of celibate widowhood.

66. *De vid.* 13.81; *De virginib.* 1.6.27ff., 25.

67. *De virginib.* 1.6.30; 10.56. The contemporary view of marriage as advantageous alliances between families lends some justification to Ambrose's censure. Some mothers apparently forbade their daughters to attend his services lest they were led to embrace celibacy and so ruin their family's fortunes.

68. *De virginib.* 2.3.19. Ambrose does not hide the fact that women who follow his advice risk the fate of Thecla, who is "condemned through her husband's rage."

69. *De virginib.* 3.4.18-19; 2.5; 5.25; *De vid.* 7.40.

70. *De virginib.* 2.2.9; 3.3.9, 11.

71. *De vid.* 10.45; *De offic.* 1.1.258.

72. Edwards, p. 191. Little is known of Zeno, bishop of Verona (ca. 362-75), who is probably African by birth and owes much to Tertullian in his sermons.

73. *De offic.* 1.10.35.

74. *De offic.* 2.24.123, 119; 1.20.86ff.

75. *De offic.* 1.19.84.

76. *De offic.* 1.23.102ff.; *In Luc.* 8.70.

77. *De offic.* 1.22.100-101.

78. *De offic.* 1.22.100-101; *In Luc.* 7.218; 8.13.

79. *De offic.* 1.22.101. Ambrose, following his own advice in *De mysteriis,* daily addresses candidates for baptism during Lent.

80. Foakes-Jackson, p. 411.

81. R. Payne, *The Fathers of the Western Church* (London: Heinemann, 1952), p. 136.

82. Nero maintains a whole corps of claqueurs to applaud his speeches (Suetonius, *Nero* 20.3).

83. *Ep.* 29.3, 9. Augustine speaks of the "perverse multitudes that fill the churches . . . drunkards, misers, tricksters, gamblers, adulterers, fornicators, people wearing amulets, assiduous clients of sorcerers, astrologers," and he observes that "the same crowds that press into churches on Christian festivals also fill the theatres on pagan holidays" (*De cat. rud.* 7.11).

84. Severian, an eloquent preacher, is bishop of Gabala and an opponent of Chrysostom.

85. F. Van der Meer, *Augustine the Bishop: Church and Society at the Dawn of the Middle Ages,* trans. B. Battershaw and G. R. Lamb (New York: Harper and Row, 1961), p. 418.

86. E.g., the *exordium* and *propositio* of his sermons are often so brief as to be almost nonexistent. He seems to be following Aristotle's advice (*Rhet.* 3.14.427), "give the key-note and then attack the main subject."

87. *De doct. Chris.* 4.12.27. Augustine wants his congregations to "listen with plea-

sure" (*Tract. Jn. ev.* 96.4) and is an "entertainer" in the classical sense of one who "holds the attention" of his hearers.

88. *Hom.* 40.5, on Matt. 22:2; *Tract. Jn. ev.* 45.13; 2.86. His sermons are often applauded and cheered (e.g., *Hom.* 52.9, on Luke 10:2), but he keeps applause under careful control (88.14, on John 10).

89. *Enn. Pss.* 51.1; *Hom.* 49.4, on Luke 7:37.

90. Pellegrino (*The True Priest* [New York: Philosophical Library, 1968], p. 43) says Augustine preaches "every Sunday, on the feast days of the martyrs, Saturday and on the vigils of all feast days."

91. E.g., *Hom.* 38.17, on Matt. 20:30; *Hom.* 87.14, on John 10; *Ep.* 29.2.

92. E.g. *Tract. Jn. ev.* 4.1.

93. *Hom.* 51.4, on Luke 10:2; *Tract. Jn. ev.* 3.1.

94. E.g., *Hom.* 55.10-13, on Luke 11:5.

95. *In ep. Jn.* 1.5.

96. Possidius, *Vit. Aug.* 31.244.

97. E.g., *Hom.* 1.6; *Enn. Pss.* 51.1; *Hom.* 43.1, on Matt. 25:1.

98. *Hom.* 49.4, on Luke 7:37; *Tract. Jn. ev.* 19.1.

99. *In ep. Jn.* 5.1-2.

100. *Hom.* 7.11, on Matt. 6; cf. *Hom.* 49.4, on Luke 7:37; *Enn. Pss.* 51.1.

101. *Enn. Pss.* 84.8; *In ep. Jn.* 8.11.

102. Members of Augustine's congregations write down his sermons with varying degrees of accuracy, but he also has a large establishment of personal *notarii* (e.g., *Epp.* 139.3; 158.1; 169.13).

103. *Hom.* 49.4, on Luke 7:37.

104. *Hom.* 38.17, on Matt. 20:30.

105. *Hom.* 55.7, on Luke 11:5; *Hom.* 12.7, on Matt. 8:8; *Hom.* 59.1, on Luke 12:56, 58.

106. T. Rowe, *St. Augustine Pastoral Theologian* (London: Epworth Press, 1974), p. 38 (J. H. S. Burleigh, *Theology,* September 1952, p. 342).

107. *Hom.* 24.3, on Matt. 13:52; *Hom.* 7.11, on Matt. 6; *Hom.* 6.9, on Matt. 6:9.

108. *Hom.* 30.2-3, on Matt. 17:19; *Hom.* 33.8, on Matt. 17:21; *Hom.* 11.10, on Matt. 7:7; *Hom.* 12.18, on Matt. 8:8.

109. *Hom.* 84.3, on John 8:31; *Hom.* 67.2, on John 1:1.

110. Quintilian (*Orat.* 6.3.20-21) compares the humorless Demosthenes with witty Cicero and considers the complexity of the subject of humor (6.8.35-36).

111. E.g., *Hom.* 10.4, on Matt. 6:19 (the stupidity of acquiring riches only to be robbed of them); *Hom.* 20.2, on Matt. 11:28 (the discomfort endured by hunters to catch inedible game). Rowe refers to Augustine's "humorous illustrations" (p. 38).

112. *Hom.* 75.1, on 1 John 5:2. See further M. M. Deems, "Augustine's Use of Scripture," *CH* 14 (1945): 188ff.; D. S. Schaff, "Augustine as an Exegete," in NPNF, 1st ser., 7:viiff.

113. *In ep. Jn.* prologue; *Hom.* 74.1, on John 5:2; e.g. *De gest. Pelag.* 35; *De grat. Chr.* 1.6.

114. *Ep.* 29.4.

115. *Conf.* 6.4.6; *De doct. Chr.* 3.5.9.

116. Simonetti, pp. 103ff.; J. Goldinghay, *Models for Interpretation of Scripture* (Carlisle: Paternoster Press, 1995), p. 154.

117. *Enn. Pss.* 138.7. Augustine asserts (106.32) that "by searching in the prophets" his hearers will discover "the Old Testament revealed in the New: the New veiled in the Old."

118. Augustine's introduction to Ps. 138 (*Enn. Pss.* 138.1) may be an instruction to sing. *De civ. Dei* 17.20. For a useful approach to the patristic use of the Song of Songs, see G. S. Wakefield, "Song of Songs," in *DCS,* pp. 355ff.

119. *Hom.* 12.18, on Matt. 8:8; *Hom.* 24.3, on Matt. 13:52; *Hom.* 1.11; *Enn. Pss.* 7.15.

120. Rowe, p. 24.

121. Most notable is Augustine's clash with Pelagianism. See J. F. Bethune-Baker, *An Introduction to the Early History of Christian Doctrine* (London: Methuen, 1951), pp. 308ff.

122. *Enn. Pss.* 99.4; *In ep. Jn.* 1.2. See Bethune-Baker, pp. 368ff., for a summary of Augustine's doctrine of the church.

123. *Hom.* 31.9, on Matt. 18:7; *Hom.* 12.8, on Matt. 8:8.

124. *Hom.* 79.3, on John 5:39; *Hom.* 21.4ff., on Matt. 12:32.

125. Cameron, p. 76.

126. *Hom.* 12.17, on Matt. 8:8; *Hom.* 6.8, on Matt. 17. He urges Christians to pray for their enemies (6.8, on Matt. 6:9).

127. *Ep.* 22.3ff. Writers such as Eunapius (349–ca. 404) and Libanius (314-93) express the anger felt by many pagans at attacks by Christians.

128. *Hom.* 6.11, on Matt. 6:9; *In ep. Jn.* 3.6.

129. *Hom.* 3.16, on Matt. 5:3, 8. For a summary of Augustine's doctrine of the atonement, see Bethune-Baker, pp. 349ff.

130. *Hom.* 27.3, on Matt. 15:21; cf. *Hom.* 33.8, on Matt. 17:21.

131. *Conf.* 10.27.38.

132. *Hom.* 82.1, on John 6:55.

133. *Hom.* 73.3, on John 2:2.

134. *Ench.* 53.

135. *Tract. Jn. ev.* 124.5.

136. *Ench.* 29; cf. *De civ. Dei* 11.12. Bonner ("Augustine of Hippo, St.," in *DCS,* p. 35) says Augustine believes that Christians attain the glorious prize of "deification . . . by adoption."

137. *De moribus ecclesiae catholicae et de moribus Manichaeorum* 10.17. Absolution is effective, says Augustine, even if conferred by "reprobate and hypocritical clergymen." *Hom.* 21.37, on Matt. 12:32.

138. *Duas ep. Pelag.* 4.19.

139. *De praed. sanct.* 10-11.

140. *In ep. Jn.* 3.5.

141. Augustine's doctrine is set out especially in *De praedestinatione sanctorum*. For useful bibliographies see the brief articles by Dirk Jellema, "Predestination," in *NIDCC*, pp. 797ff., and T. H. L. Parker, "Predestination," in *DCT*, pp. 264ff. For the New Testament background of the doctrine, see the articles by Jacobs and Krienke, "Foreknowledge, Providence, Predestination," in *DNTT*, 1:692ff.

142. *Tract. Jn. ev.* 45.12.

143. *Hom.* 38.25, on Matt. 20:30; *Hom.* 12.8-15, on Matt. 8:8; 1 Cor. 8:10.

144. *Hom.* 6.8, on Matt. 6:9; *De civ. Dei* 2.19.

145. *Hom.* 40.6, on Matt. 22:2; *Hom.* 6.12, on Matt. 6:9; *Hom.* 38.17, on Matt. 20:30; cf. *Hom.* 11.12, on Matt. 7:7.

146. *Hom.* 11.10, on Matt. 7:7.

147. *Hom.* 36.2, on Matt. 19:21; *In ep. Jn.* prol.2.13.

148. *Hom.* 31.9, on Matt. 18:7; *In ep. Jn.* 6.2.

149. *Hom.* 8.10, on Matt. 6.

150. *Hom.* 1.25, *Of the Agreement of the Evangelists Matthew and Luke in the Generations of the Lord*. As Hordern explains ("Man, Doctrine of," in *DCT*, p. 204), Augustine sees "original sin as being biologically transmitted to later generations through the sexual procreation of the human race." Perhaps he never really shakes off his former Manichaean attitudes toward sexuality.

151. *Hom.* 82.3, on John 6:55.

152. *Hom.* 1.25, on Matt. 18:7. Infidelity within marriage seems to have invaded the churches (*Hom.* 32.12, on Matt. 18:15; *Hom.* 31.4, on Matt. 18.7; *Hom.* 1.9; 82.2, on John 6:55).

153. *Hom.* 82.3, on John 6:55.

154. *Hom.* 12.8, on Matt. 8:8. Clearly such exhortation is necessary in a society where child abuse is rife. Augustine identifies "boy-stealers" even in Christian congregations (*In ep. Jn.* 3.9).

155. *Hom.* 36.11, on Matt. 19:21. Augustine writes movingly, "you have lost a child; not that you have indeed lost him, but have sent him on before you . . . surely you too will go thither."

156. G. Lawless, "Augustine of Hippo," in *CEP*, p. 19.

157. *Conf.* 1.1.1 (the reference is to Ambrose); *De serm. Dom.* 2.16.54.

158. *Hom.* 78.7, on John 5:31; *Hom.* 9.6, on Matt. 6; cf. *Enn. Pss.* 51.1.

159. *Ep.* 41.1; *Hom.* 44.1, on Matt. 25:24.

160. *Hom.* 6.11, on Matt. 6:9; *Hom.* 64.4, on Luke 17:3; *Hom.* 41.5, on Matt. 22:42.

161. *En. Pss.* 104.18; *Tract. Jn. ev.* 57.3. See Van der Meer, p. 430, for Augustine's awareness of his own weakness for applause.

162. *Hom.* 96.1, on John 21:16; *Hom.* 88.7, on John 5:31; *Hom.* 75.1, on John 5:2.

163. *Enn. Pss.* 103.1; *De serm. Dom.* 2.16.64. Augustine maintains that "Those who preach the Gospel should live the Gospel."

164. As part of his attempt to encourage good preaching, Augustine asks his clergy to send him copies of good sermons so that he can read them (*Ep.* 41.2).

165. J. I. H. McDonald, *Kerygma and Didache: The Articulation and Structure of the Earliest Christian Message*, SNTSMS 37 (Cambridge: Cambridge University Press, 1989), p. 39; cf. E. C. Dargan, *A History of Preaching*, vol. 1, AD 70-1572 (London: Hodder and Stoughton and G. H. Doran, 1905), p. 35.

166. *De doct. Chr.* 4.30.63; cf. 4.15.32 (the fourth book was added in 426); Rowe, p. 45.

167. See also Augustine's letter to Deogratius (*Ep.* 102).

168. *De cat. rud.* 15.23; 13.18.

169. *De cat. rud.* 2.3; 13.18; 11.16.

170. Aristotle (*Rhet.* 1.3.33) says every speech is composed of three parts, "the speaker, the subject of which he treats and the person to whom it is addressed." In his second book he examines carefully the mind-sets of various component parts of an audience. Augustine, *De cat. rud.* 15.23; 12.17.

171. *De doct. Chr.* 4.15.32; 4.30.63; 4.10.25.

172. *De doct. Chr.* 4.12.28; 4.13.29; *Hom.* 9.6, on Matt. 6.

173. *De doct. Chr.* 2.18.28; 2.29.63; 2.27-40.

174. *De doct. Chr.* 2.9.14; 4.5.8; 4.11.16. To avoid misunderstanding, Augustine lists the books he considers to be acceptable (2.8.12-13). The injunction to memorize is necessary because access to the entire Bible is not always assured and its *codices* are not easily portable.

175. Simonetti, p. 107.

176. *De doct. Chr.* 3.10.14–15.23.

177. *De doct. Chr.* 3.5.9; 2.9.14; 3.26.37.

178. *De doct. Chr.* 2.31.48.

179. *De doct. Chr.* 2.31.48; 4.8.22.

180. See Cicero, *De oratore*; *De doct. Chr.* 4.7.11. Augustine examines the words of Paul and Amos to illustrate his point (4.8.22; 4.10.24).

181. For rhetoric's part in the process see C. A. Loscalzo, "Rhetoric," in *CEP,* pp. 409ff.

182. Aristotle, *Rhet.* 1-3; Quintilian, *Institutio oratoria.*

183. Lucian, *De morte Peregrini*; Augustine, *Hom.* 87.7, on John 10.

184. *De doct. Chr.* 4.27.59; 4.5.7. For a study of *ethos* in rhetoric see A. Resner, Jr., *Preacher and Cross: Person and Message in Theology and Rhetoric* (Cambridge: Eerdmans, 1999), and for Augustine's use of the term in particular, pp. 45ff. Augustine reflects the views of Aristotle (*Rhet.* 1.2.4; 17), Cicero (*De orat.* 3.14, 51), and Quintilian, (*Orat.* 4.2.18). R. Brown ("Preaching and Spirituality," in *DCS,* p. 319) quotes Fulgen-

tius, the sixth-century bishop of Ruspe, who avers that a preacher does "better by the piety of his prayers than by the fluency of his speech."

185. *De doct. Chr.* 4.13.29.

186. *De doct. Chr.* 4.4.6. Augustine draws on classical rhetoric, which categorizes figures of speech and teaches their effective use. The categories are εἰκών (the image), ὁμοίωσις (the comparison), παραβολή (the parable), παράδειγμα (the illustrative story), and ἀλληγορία (the allegory).

187. *De doct. Chr.* 4.13.29.

188. Quintilian, *Orat.* 2.1.4.

189. *De doct. Chr.* 2.5.6. Augustine (*Ep.* 84.2) laments the lack of preachers who can speak Punic and eventually this problem is addressed. The inability of catholic preachers to speak Berber consigns huge areas of North Africa to the Donatists. See S. Neill, *A History of Christian Missions* (London: Penguin Books, 1986), p. 38.

190. *De doct. Chr.* 4.10.24. Augustine (*Ep.* 172.2) complains about the lack of Latin secretaries and strongly criticizes Jerome's Latin version of the Bible for its lack of sophistication (*Ep.* 71.2.3). In his *In Heptateuchum locutiones,* he proposes ways of improving the quality of Latin used in churches.

191. E.g., the extended wordplay on the name Adam (*Tract. Jn. ev.* 10.12). See further, Van der Meer, p. 425.

192. *De doct. Chr.* 2.1.1; 2.3.4. For a more recent consideration of words as "signs," see D. Buttrick, *Homiletic: Moves and Structures* (London: SCM Press, 1987), pp. 175ff.

193. *De doct. Chr.* 2.4.5.

194. *De doct. Chr.* 3.2.2ff.; 3.3.6ff. In practical terms, this instruction is necessary because contemporary texts have no clear punctuation and often little space between words.

195. M. E. Lyons, "Style," in *CEP,* p. 457.

196. *De doct. Chr.* 4.22.51; cf. 4.19.38.

197. *De doct. Chr.* 4.17.34. Augustine points preachers to the examples afforded by Paul, Cyprian, and Ambrose (4.20.39; 4.21.45ff.).

198. *De doct. Chr.* 4.25.55; 4.20.40.

199. *De doct. Chr.* 4.19.38; 4.20.42.

200. *De doct. Chr.* 4.22.51.

201. Rowe, p. 45.

202. See Cameron, pp. 170ff., for a comparison of the two cities. Compared with Constantinople's population of half a million by the sixth century, estimates for Antioch vary from 200,000 (Chrysostom, *Ignatius of Antioch* 4) to 800,000 by the time of Chrysostom's death (J. M. Houston, "Antioch (Syrian)," in *NIDCC,* p. 49).

203. Chrysostom appears to claim 100,000 Christians for both cities (*Hom. Matt.* 75.4; *Hom. Acts* 11). Half of Antioch's population is reputed to be pagan. For a comparison of the two congregations, see further W. Mayer, "John Chrysostom and His Audiences: Distinguishing Different Congregations at Antioch and Constantinople," *Studia*

Patristica, 31:70ff. Gibbon (*Decline and Fall,* 8, ed. Saunders, p. 303) observes that "many considerable estates were bestowed on the opulent churches of . . . Antioch . . . and the other great cities."

204. *Hom. 1 Cor.* 7.18; *Hom. Matt.* 17.6; 89.3; *Hom. 1 Tim.* 8; *Hom. Col.* 10; *Hom. Eph.* 13.

205. *Hom. Acts* 41.

206. MacMullen, "The Preacher's Audience (AD 350-400)," *JTS,* n.s., 40 (1989): 503ff.; *Hom. Matt.* 57.5. Chrysostom reminds the posturers that their ancestors were "cooks, drivers of asses and shopkeepers."

207. *Hom. 2 Cor.* 17; *Hom. Matt.* 58.5; 59.4; *Hom. 1 Cor.* 20.11.

208. E.g., *Hom. 2 Cor.* 17. Chrysostom, whose father was a career officer, insists that Gothic mercenaries must have worship in the vernacular and preaches to them himself through an interpreter (Theodoret, *HE* 5.30).

209. *Hom. Acts* 54; *Hom. 1 Cor.* 7.18. For children see *Hom. Matt.* 54.7; *Hom. Acts* 26; *Hom. Eph.* 21; *Hom. Those Not Attending the Assembly* 3.

210. *Hom. Statues* 19.2. They are attending an Ascensiontide festival, but they share the common anxiety aroused by the smashing of the imperial statues. The "foreign language" to which Chrysostom refers is probably Syriac.

211. Gibbon (8, ed. Saunders, p. 311) asserts that 3,000 poor people are supported by the church in Antioch. See *Hom. Col.* 7; *Hom. Gen.* 5; *Hom. 1 Thess.* 11.

212. Chrysostom often addresses them specifically, suggesting that he has a significant following of women of all classes, e.g., *Hom. John* 61.4; *Hom. 2 Cor.* 4.6-7; *Hom. Heb.* 20.

213. *Hom. 1 Cor.* 9.9; *Hom. 1 Tim.* 9; cf. "To be abusive is womanly" (*Hom. Acts* 11). J. N. D. Kelly, *Golden Mouth: The Story of John Chrysostom, Ascetic, Preacher, Bishop* (London: Duckworth, 1995), pp. 50-51.

214. *Hom. Eph.* 20. Chrysostom insists that women are to be treated "with great thoughtfulness, affection and kindness."

215. He describes a woman "in the very flower of her age" with her "eye tender and soft . . . ringed with dark lashes . . . a cheek shaded to exact redness" (*Hom. Col.* 12).

216. *Hom. Matt.* 17.3; *Hom. Rom.* 12.

217. *Hom. 1 Tim.* 8.

218. *Hom. Eph.* 13.

219. *Hom. 1 Tim.* 4.

220. *Hom. Matt.* 30.6.

221. *Hom. 1 Cor.* 26.8; *Hom. 2 Cor.* 13.4; cf. *Hom. Phil.* 15; *Hom. Eph.* 15; *Hom. Rom.* 13.

222. *Hom. 1 Thess.* 6.

223. *Hom. 1 Tim.* 9.

224. E.g., *Hom. Heb.* 20.4; *Hom. John* 64.4.

225. *Hom. Matt.* 48.4; cf. Commodianus, *Instruct.* 60.

226. *Hom. John* 31-35; 32.3; 34.1.

227. *Hom. Rom.* 30, in which he sets forth the example of "noble women"; cf. *Hom. John* 61.4. Chrysostom apparently has no difficulty in accepting women holding official positions in the church and commends those who "hold the rank of deaconess" (*Hom. 1 Tim.* 11).

228. *Hom. Eph.* 13.

229. *Hom. 2 Cor.* 4.5-6.

230. *Hom. Matt.* 59.4; cf. *Hom. 1 Cor.* 20.11.

231. *Hom. 2 Cor.* 17.

232. Either the scandals in Constantinople are greater or Chrysostom is simply forced to take his episcopal responsibility for discipline with increased seriousness.

233. Chrysostom insists that he does not depend upon gossip. *Hom. Frat. pecc.* 10; *Hom. Rom.* 8; *Hom. Heb.* 15.8; *Hom. Acts* 24.

234. *Hom. Statues* 4.1; *Hom. Those Not Attending* 2.

235. *Hom. Heb.* 30.5-6.

236. The most likely annual attendance will be at Easter, but Chrysostom adds that "some never approach to communicate at all" (*Hom. Eph.* 11).

237. *Hom. Those Not Attending* 1-2; cf. *Hom. Acts* 3.

238. *Hom. Eph.* 22; *Hom. Those Not Attending* 3.

239. *Hom. John* 83.3; *Hom. 2 Cor.* 30; *Hom. Acts* 29.

240. *Hom. Matt.* 19.4; *Hom. Frat. pecc.* 10.

241. *Hom. Matt.* 20.1; *Hom. Acts* 29.

242. *Hom. John* 73.3; *Hom. Matt.* 19.4; *Hom. Eph.* 3.

243. *Hom. John* 3.1; *Hom. 1 Cor.* 36.8; *Hom. Matt.* 32.10; *Hom. 1 Cor.* 36.9; *Hom. Heb.* 15.3.

244. *Hom. Eph.* 3; *Hom. 1 Tim.* 9; 8; *Hom. 1 Cor.* 24.7.

245. *Hom. Heb.* 15.8-9; *Hom. Acts* 24. Chrysostom allows that even in church, children may sometimes laugh simply because they find "the mysteries" strange and unfamiliar (*Hom. Matt.* 54.7).

246. *Hom. Frat. pecc.* 10; *Hom. Matt.* 17.6.

247. *Hom. Heb.* 17.8.

248. *Hom. Acts* 30; *Hom. Matt.* 1.17.

249. *Hom. Rom.* 11; 30; *Hom. 1 Tim.* 8.

250. *Hom. Col.* 10; *Hom. Matt.* 89.3.

251. *Hom. 2 Thess.* 3; *Hom. Rom.* 11.

252. *Hom. Matt.* 73.3; cf. *Hom. Col.* 10.

253. See further W. Mayer and P. Allen, *John Chrysostom* (London: Routledge, 2000), pp. 17ff., 23ff.

254. It is likely that the sermons on Matthew, Timothy, Titus, Philemon, and Corinthians are preached at Antioch. Of the Constantinople sermons, we have those on Acts (although their original form is not always easy to reconstruct) and the "Pauline"

sermons (Romans, Ephesians, Philippians, Colossians), of which those on Romans are most rhetorically correct. The sermons on Hebrews are recorded by Constantius, a presbyter of Antioch, and published after Chrysostom's death. How far he controlled the editing of his sermons is unclear. See Kelly, pp. 93ff.

255. Socrates, *HE* 6.5. Sometimes his congregations insist that he preach ex cathedra (6.16).

256. *Hom. 1 Cor.* 36.9.

257. J. Milton, *Areopagitica*. Kelly, p. 22. It is this weakness that the astute, unscrupulous Serapion is able to exploit, urging Chrysostom to exercise his episcopal authority "with a single rod" (Socrates, *HE* 6.4).

258. His outspokenness transforms the empress Eudoxia from his greatest supporter to his most fanatical enemy, when he condemns her aspiration to share the divinity accorded the Caesars.

259. *Hom. Acts* 8.

260. *Hom. Acts* 3 (a sermon which deals at length with the frustrations of being a bishop); *Hom. 1 Cor.* 12.11; *Hom. Matt.* 30.6.

261. *Hom. Matt.* 15.15; *Hom. Acts* 29; 6.

262. *Hom. John* 12.1.

263. *Hom. 2 Cor.* 10.5.

264. *Hom. Acts* 29; cf. *Hom. 1 Cor.* 40.6; 36.9; 43.3.

265. *Hom. Acts* 30.

266. E.g., *Hom. Acts* 14; cf. *Hom. Statues* 2.12; 5.21; *Hom. Acts* 30; *Hom. 1 Cor.* 13.5.

267. *Hom. 1 Cor.* 8.8.

268. *Hom. John* 2.11. Chrysostom commends this method (14.3), which he believes is also that of the Baptist and John the Apostle.

269. *Hom. 1 Cor.* 4.5. He observes, "If oratory were taken away, our life would be nothing the worse" (*Hom. Matt.* 52.5).

270. Mayer and Allen, p. 27.

271. E.g., his description of a glutton who can "scarce step forward and scarce see and scarce speak and scarce do anything" (*Hom. 1 Cor.* 39.18).

272. E.g., "Did I not seem yesterday to you to have spoken some great and exorbitant things?" (*Hom. Matt.* 9.3).

273. *Hom. Matt.* 9.3.

274. *Hom. 2 Cor.* 13.4.

275. *Hom. 1 Cor.* 39.18.

276. E.g., his verbal cartoon of the ridiculous rich man who "throws his whole house into confusion" because he sees "a little drop" of rain but callously ignores the plight of the poor man shivering at his gate (*Hom. 1 Cor.* 11.10).

277. E.g., "The whole of life of men in ancient times was one of action and contention; ours, on the contrary, is a life of indolence" (*Hom. Titus* 2).

278. E.g., "As natural oil (ἔλαιον) contains light, so then doth mercy (ἔλεος) grant a great and marvellous light" (*Hom. 1 Cor.* 39.18).

279. Some of his illustrations are quite lengthy; e.g., his description of the two tables — one for the rich, the other for the poor — constitutes almost an entire sermon (*Hom. Col.* 1).

280. P. Schaff, *Prolegomena* 12, in NPNF, lst ser., 9:17.

281. *Hom. Rom.* 14.

282. *Hom. Acts* 3; *Hom. Statues* 14.4; *Hom. Rom.* 4; *Hom. 1 Thess.* 11.

283. *Hom. Statues* 19.13; *Hom. Acts* 29; *Hom. Statues* 13.6; *Hom. Matt.* 77.6; 15.14.

284. *Hom. Eph.* 2; *Hom. Phil.* 7; *Hom. Eph.* 10; *Hom. Heb.* 15.7; *Hom. 1 Cor.* 12.11; *Hom. Matt.* 58.7; *Hom. Eutropius* 1.1-2.

285. *Hom. Acts* 18; *Hom. Evil Comes of Sloth* 5. Like all civilized people, Chrysostom believes that baths "have their appointed times" (*Hom. John* 17.4). Some large houses have their own baths but most people attend the palatial public baths. When Theodosius wants to punish the rebellious people of Antioch in 387, he closes their baths (*Hom. Statues* 18.13).

286. *Hom. Rom.* 12.

287. *Hom. Matt.* 83.4; *Hom. 2 Cor.* 15.4; *Hom. Matt.* 49.5; 44.6.

288. *Hom. Matt.* 48.9; *Hom. 1 Tim.* 3. Parasites (*para* — "beside"; *sitos* — "food") originally meant dinner companions, but they become toadies and flatterers who feed off the patronage of the rich.

289. *Hom. Matt.* 2.9; 37.7.

290. *Hom. Rom.* 13; 29; *Hom. Matt.* 69.3; 80.2.

291. *Hom. Matt.* 71.5.

292. *Hom. Acts* 38. As a child, Chrysostom throws a book of magic into a river just in time to avoid discovery and punishment.

293. *Hom. Matt.* 28.3; 37.8.

294. *Hom. Matt.* 35.5. The festivities of the Saturnalia begin on January 13 and coincide with the Christian festival of Epiphany.

295. *Hom. Eph.* 12, in which he lists many popular superstitions.

296. *Hom. Eph.* 15; cf. *Hom. Matt.* 68.4; *Hom. Acts* 34. It is likely that Chrysostom's family has sufficient status to own both a town house in Antioch and a country estate.

297. *Hom. 1 Cor.* 9.9; *Hom. Matt.* 48.5; *Hom. 2 Cor.* 6; *Hom. Phil.* 7, in which Chrysostom links the characteristics of animals from lions to ants.

298. *Hom. Matt.* 61.3; 56.7.

299. *Hom. Statues* 3.7; *Hom. Evil Comes of Sloth* 5; *Hom. 1 Cor.* 12.9; *Hom. Heb.* 22.7.

300. *Hom. Acts* 7; *Hom. Matt.* 13.4. Cf. *Hom. Those Not Attending* 5; *Hom. Statues* 1.18; *Hom. Matt.* 71.

301. *De sac.* 5.1; *Hom. Statues* 13.6.2.

302. *Hom. 2 Cor.* 10.6; *Hom. Statues* 7.7; cf. *Hom. Matt.* 13.8; *Hom. Rom.* 11; 31.

Chrysostom often mentions the crime of grave robbing, which is profitable because of the custom of burying riches in tombs.

303. *Hom. Matt.* 56; *Hom. Frat. pecc.* 5; *Hom. 1 Thess.* 8; *Hom. Statues* 13.3; *Dem. non gub.* 5.

304. *Hom. Frat. pecc.* 1.

305. *Hom. Acts* 52; 39; *Hom. Matt.* 18.6.

306. *Hom. Matt.* 26.8; *Hom. Frat. pecc.* 4; *Hom. 2 Thess.* 3; *Hom. Matt.* 35.1; *Contra Marcion* 1.

307. *Hom. Heb.* 15.6; *Hom. Matt.* 27.7.

308. *Hom. Statues* 6.19; *Hom. 1 Cor.* 3.9.

309. *Hom. Acts* 1.

310. *Hom. Acts* 4; *Hom. Matt.* 1.10; 33.5.

311. *Hom. John* 21.1; 11.1; *Hom. Matt.* 5.1.

312. P. Schaff, *Prolegomena,* in NPNF, 1st ser., 9:5. Chrysostom's limited coverage of the Old Testament may be due to his lack of Hebrew. His commentaries cover the New Testament except for Mark, Luke, the Catholic Epistles, and Revelation. See further M. B. Riddle, "St. Chrysostom as an Exegete," in NPNF, 1st ser., 10:xviiff.

313. E.g., his account of the sun standing still: "Why was this? The name of Joshua (JESUS) was a type. For this reason, because of the very name, the creation reverenced him" (*Hom. Heb.* 27.6).

314. Sequences survive on Genesis, Matthew, John, Acts, and portions of Isaiah, Psalms, and the Pauline epistles, for which he has a special passion (*Hom. Rom.* Argument). The great nineteenth-century preacher and homiletician J. A. Broadus wrote, "John of the Golden Mouth is, upon the whole, our very best example . . . in respect of expository preaching" ("St. Chrysostom as a Homilist," in NPNF, 1st ser., 13:5).

315. The sermons on 1 Corinthians are especially catechetical in tone and are later circulated with Cyril's *Catechesis* and Cyprian's *Epistolae* for the guidance of teachers and catechumens.

316. *Hom. Statues* 6.1; cf. 14.1; *Dem. non gub.* 5; *Hom. 2 Cor.* 27. In *Hom. Statues* 1.14, Chrysostom expands the theme by setting out eight reasons why God permits the saints to suffer.

317. *Hom. John* 78.1; *Hom. 1 Cor.* 15.6; *Hom. John* 84.1.

318. *Hom. Matt.* 40.5; *Hom. Acts* 3; *Hom. Rom.* 14; *Hom. 2 Tim.* 2.

319. *Hom. 1 Tim.* 11; cf. *Hom. Phil.* 1; *Hom. Acts* 3; *Hom. Statues* 3.1; *Hom. Col.* 3; *Hom. 1 Tim.* 10. As a terrible warning, Chrysostom cites the fate of Julian the Apostate and his prefect Felix, who assaulted Bishop Eliozus in Antioch (*Hom. Matt.* 4.2; cf. Theodoret, *HE* 3.8).

320. *Hom. John* 42.3; cf. *Hom. Phil.* 6.

321. *Hom. Matt.* 23.8; *Hom. 1 Tim.* 7; *Hom. Matt.* 46.1.

322. See further W. H. Willimon, "Anti-Jewish Preaching," in *CEP,* pp. 11ff.; *Hom.*

Matt. 87; Theodoret, *HE* 8.29, 31. While still a lector, Chrysostom writes *Against the Jews* (Socrates, *HE* 6.3).

323. Cameron, p. 77.

324. E.g., *Hom. John* 55.1; 53.1; 83.3; *Hom. Phil.* 10; *Hom. Rom.* 18; 19; *Hom. Matt.* 6.4-5. In *Hom. John* 66.1, Chrysostom at least allows that, in the Gospels, "the multitude of the Jews is sound and their leaders corrupt."

325. *Hom. Matt.* 26.7; *Hom. John* 25.2. Chrysostom's emphasis is reflected in the work of other great preachers. For a comparison of his sermon *On the Baptism of Christ* with Basil of Caesarea's *Exhortation to Baptism,* Gregory of Nazianzus's *Oration* 40, and Gregory of Nyssa's *Against Those Who Delay,* see E. Ferguson, "Preaching at Epiphany: Gregory of Nyssa and John Chrysostom on Baptism and the Church," *CH* 66, no. 1 (March 1997): 2ff.

326. *Hom. Acts* 24; *Hom. 2 Cor.* 30; 24.7.

327. *Hom. Statues* 10.1, in which Chrysostom also assures that they are welcome at the Table even without fasting. He warns them against participating unworthily as Judas did (*Hom. Matt.* 82.6).

328. *Hom. Matt.* 37.9.

329. E.g. *Hom. 1 Cor.* 4.7, Saint Ignatius of Antioch. Ignatius's relics are supposed to reside in a chapel at Antioch. Chrysostom is especially fond of the "miracles relating to the martyr Babylas" (*Hom. Acts* 41), a former bishop of Antioch martyred in the Decian persecution. See *Hom. The Holy Martyr Babylas* 3.

330. Chrysostom himself actively promotes evangelism, sending missionaries to the Goths and the Scythians along the Danube and sustaining their ministry by frequent letters of encouragement (Theodoret, *HE* 5.31).

331. *Hom. John* 17.1; *Hom. 1 Cor.* 6.7.

332. *Hom. Acts* 18. The development of the rural church is hampered by lack of clergy, and in 398 Theodosius passes an act permitting clergy to be ordained to serve their own state or village under the guidance of the local bishop.

333. *Hom. Eph.* 4.

334. *Hom. Matt.* 7.8; *Hom. 1 Tim.* 14.

335. *Hom. Heb.* 8.9; 24.1; *Hom. Rom.* 25.

336. *Hom. Statues* 15.3. In 387, the people of Antioch, enraged by excessive taxation, revolt against Theodosius and smash statues of the emperor and his wife Flacilla. Theodosius threatens to destroy the city but relents due to the intercession of Bishop Flavius.

337. *Hom. Eutropius.* Eutropius uses his great power to attack the churches, but when defeated by the Goths, he flees to the church for sanctuary, which Chrysostom grants. Eventually he is captured and beheaded.

338. *Hom. 1 Cor.* 12.9.

339. *Hom. Acts* 24; cf. *Hom. Rom.* 8.

340. *Hom. 1 Cor.* 9.9.

341. *Hom. 2 Cor.* 10.

342. *Hom. Matt.* 43.5; 26.7; 31.5; *Hom. Acts* 21.

343. E.g., *Hom. Statues* 14.2. Marcus Aurelius dismisses swearing as unnecessary (*Commun.* 3.5). H.-G. Link ("Swear, Oath," in *DNTT,* 3:739) also quotes Plato, Plutarch, the Pythagoreans, and the Stoics, who also condemn the practice of swearing. Alan Kreider (*The Change of Conversion and the Origin of Christendom* [Harrisburg: Trinity Press, 1999], pp. 51-52) emphasizes that the renunciation of swearing is an important aspect of the "conversion" of catechumens.

344. *Hom. Statues* 8.6; *Hom. Acts* 8; *Hom. Matt.* 11.10; *Hom. Statues* 4.12; 12.17.

345. *Hom. Statues* 10.12; 8.7; 11.14. Since references to swearing diminish in his later Antioch sermons, perhaps his efforts prove to be successful.

346. *Hom. Statues* 1.12; *Hom. Matt.* 57.5-6.

347. *Hom. 2 Cor.* 20.3; *Hom. Rom.* 24.

348. *Hom. Acts* 27; *Hom. 2 Cor.* 20.3.

349. *Hom. Acts* 27; *Hom. Matt.* 57.5; *Hom. Rom.* 24.

350. *Hom. Col.* 10; *Hom. Matt.* 7.8.

351. *Hom. Evil Comes of Sloth* 1; *Hom. Statues* 17.9.

352. *Hom. Matt.* 37.7-8; 68.4; *Hom. Acts* 42; *Hom. Matt.* 6.10.

353. *Hom. 2 Cor.* 13.

354. *Hom. Acts* 42.

355. *Hom. 1 Thess.* 5; *Hom. Statues* 14.

356. *Hom. Rom.* 7; 4; cf. 9; *Hom. Titus* 5. The fact that pederasty is specifically prohibited in the *Apostolic Constitutions* 7.18 suggests that such homosexual activity is present in the churches.

357. *Hom. Matt.* 37.9.

358. *Hom. Eph.* 20, a sermon on Christian marriage.

359. *Hom. Eph.* 20; *Hom. Statues* 14; *Hom. 1 Cor.* 19.2 (a sermon in which Chrysostom discusses at length the nature of sexual relations within marriage); cf. *Hom. Acts* 11, in which he also prohibits wives abusing their husbands.

360. *Hom. Matt.* 30.5; *Hom. Heb.* 20.8; *Hom. 1 Cor.* 26.8.

361. *Hom. Eph.* 21, on parents and children; *Hom. Eph.* 22, on servants.

362. *Hom. 1 Cor.* 12.13; *Hom. Acts* 54; *Hom. Matt.* 71.

363. *Hom. 1 Thess.* 9; *Hom. Acts* 26.

364. *Hom. Eph.* 22; *Hom. Matt.* 20.2; 59.6.

365. *Hom. Eph.* 15; *Hom. Those Not Attending* 3.

366. *Hom. John* 64.4; *Hom. Rom.* 7; *Hom. Heb.* 2.2; *Hom. 2 Cor.* 12.

367. *Hom. 2 Cor.* 19.3; *Hom. Matt.* 15.12; 23.10; 73.4.

368. *Hom. 1 Tim.* 13; *Hom. Acts* 7; *Hom. 2 Cor.* 23.

369. *Hom. 1 Tim.* 6; cf. "I am continually saying that I do not attack the character of the rich men but of the rapacious" (*Hom. Eutropius* 2.3).

370. *Hom. Matt.* 54.9; 23.2.

371. *Hom. Matt.* 88; *Hom. 1 Cor.* 43.

372. *Hom. Acts* 11; 45; cf. *Hom. 1 Cor.* 21.11. Chrysostom is deeply shocked to learn that some wealthy Christians are actually charging rent for accommodation provided for the poor (*Hom. Acts* 45; *Hom. Matt.* 56.9).

373. *Hom. Acts* 45; *Hom. 1 Thess.* 2; *Hom. 1 Tim.* 2. Similarly they are to visit prisoners and care for them regardless of their crime (*Hom. John* 60.6). The *xenon* is the name given to the room reserved in churches for the accommodation of "strangers."

374. P. Schaff, in NPNF, 1st ser., 9:5. The stages described are: his youth until his conversion and baptism (347-70), his ascetic and monastic life (370-81), his ministry in Antioch (381-98), his episcopate in Constantinople (398-404), and his exile and death (404-7).

375. Edwards, p. 191; cf. Foakes-Jackson, p. 435; D. F. Wright, "Chrysostom," in *NIDCC*, p. 225, whose article concludes with a useful brief bibliography. In the Roman Church Chrysostom is regarded as the patron saint of preachers.

376. *Hom. 1 Cor.* 7.14; *Hom. 2 Cor.* 15.

377. *Hom. Acts* 18. He sends out missionary preachers (Sozomen, *HE* 8.4; Theodoret, *HE* 5.31) and sustains their ministry by frequent letters of encouragement.

378. *De sac.* 5.8.

379. *De sac.* 4.3ff.

380. *De sac.* 5.5.

381. *De sac.* 5.1.

382. *De sac.* 5.3.

383. *Hom. Matt.* 88; 50.4.

384. *Hom. Matt.* 85.4.

385. *De sac.* 5.4, 6.

386. *De sac.* 5.5, 8.

387. *De sac.* 5.1.

388. *De sac.* 5.4.

389. *De sac.* 5.7, 4.

390. *De sac.* 5.3, 7.

391. *De sac.* 5.3, 7.

392. *De sac.* 5.5.

393. H. Bettenson, *The Later Christian Fathers: A Selection from the Writings of the Fathers from St. Cyril of Jerusalem to St. Leo the Great* (London: Oxford University Press, 1972), p. 18.

394. *De sac.* 5.5-6.

395. Socrates (*HE* 6.3; 5.2) shows that the abrasive relationship began early in Chrysostom's ministry.

Epilogue — "'Whither the Great Ship?'
Preachers, Congregations, and Pluralism"

1. One of the most imaginative recent attempts to predict the future course of religion is to be found in Woodhead and Heelas's *Religion in Modern Times: An Interpretive Anthology* (Oxford: Blackwell, 2000).

2. The last verse of the hymn "Thy Kingdom Come, O God," which appeared in *Hymns for Minor Sundays* (1867) and was written by Rev. Lesley Hensley (1824-1905), an Anglican clergyman and academic. It is typical of hymns sung at missionary meetings of that time in England.

3. See O. C. Edwards's précis of the idea ("History of Preaching," in *CEP,* pp. 226-27).

4. J. Moltmann, *Theology and Joy,* trans. R. Ulrich (London: SCM Press, 1973), pp. 27, 60ff.

5. Schleiermacher, *The Christian Faith* (Edinburgh: T. & T. Clark, 1928), pp. 429ff.; cf. the development of his ideas in his *Brief Outline on the Study of Theology* (1811) and *Practical Theology* (published posthumously in 1850). Moltmann, pp. 78ff., appreciates Schleiermacher's insights.

6. D. de Vries, "Schleiermacher, Friedrich D. E.," in *CEP,* p. 429.

7. Chrysostom, *De sac.* 2.2.

Bibliography

Homiletics and Evangelism

Abrahams, W. "Proclamation." In *The Logic of Evangelism,* pp. 40ff. London: Hodder and Stoughton, 1989.

Allmen, Jean-Jacques. *Preaching and Congregations.* London: Lutterworth, 1962.

Atkins, M. D. *Preaching in a Cultural Context.* Peterborough: Foundery Press, 2001.

Barth, K. *Homiletics.* Translated by G. W. Bromiley and D. E. Daniels. Louisville: Westminster, 1991.

———. "The Need and Promise of Christian Preaching." In *The Word of God and the Word of Man,* translated by D. Horton. London: Hodder and Stoughton, 1928.

Becker, O. "Faith, Persuade." In *DNTT,* 1:587ff.

Becker, U., et al. "Gospel, Evangelize." In *DNTT,* 2:107ff.

———. "Proclamation, Preach, Kerygma." In *DNTT,* 3:44ff.

Bolger, R. "Rhetoric." In *EB* (1970), 9:257ff.

Bosch, D. J. *Transforming Mission: Paradigm Shifts in Theology of Mission.* New York: Orbis, 1991.

Braumann, G. "Comfort, Encouragement." In *DNTT,* 1:328-29.

Broadus, J. A. *Lectures on the History of Preaching.* New York: Sheldon, 1886.

Brown, C. "The Structure and Content of the Early Kerygma." In *DNTT,* 3:57ff.

Brown, R. "Preaching and Spirituality." In *DCS,* pp. 319-20.

Buttrick, D. "Proclamation." In *CEP,* pp. 384-85.

Buttrick, G. A. *Homiletic: Moves and Structures.* London: SCM Press, 1987.

Christlieb, T. *Homiletics: Lectures on Preaching.* Translated by C. H. Irwin. Edinburgh: T. & T. Clark, 1897.

Coenen, L. "Witness, Testimony." In *DNTT,* 3:1038ff.

Dargan, E. C. *A History of Preaching.* Vol. 1, AD 70-1572. London: Hodder and Stoughton and G. H. Doran, 1905.

———. "Preaching." In *NSHE*, 3:158ff.

Davids, P. H. "Homily, Ancient." In *DNTB*, pp. 515ff.

Demaray, D. E. "Evangelism." In *CEP*, pp. 119ff.

Dodd, C. H. *The Apostolic Preaching and Its Development.* London: Hodder and Stoughton, 1950.

Edwards, O. C. "History of Preaching." In *CEP*, pp. 184ff.

Ellis, I. "Homily." In *DBI*, pp. 297ff.

Els, P. J. J. S. "*lqh.*" In *DOTTE*, 2:812ff.

Evans, C. F. "The Kerygma." *JTS*, n.s., 7 (1956): 25ff.

Friedenberg, R. V. "Jewish Preaching." In *CEP*, pp. 280ff.

Fuller, R. H. "Sermon." In *NDLW*, pp. 484-85.

Goldinghay, J. *Models for Interpretation of Scripture.* Carlisle: Paternoster Press, 1995.

Green, M. *Evangelism in the Early Church.* London: Hodder and Stoughton, 1970.

Greenhaw, D. M. "Theology of Preaching." In *CEP*, pp. 477ff.

Gregoire, R. "Homily." In *EEC*, 1:394ff.

Greidanus, S. "Preaching from Paul Today." In *DPL*, pp. 737ff.

Grogan, G. W. "Evangelist." In *NIDCC*, pp. 361-62.

Haensli, E. "Preaching." In *Sacramentum*, 5:8ff.

Harnack, A. von. "The Religious Characteristics of the Mission Preaching." In *The Mission and Expansion of Christianity in the First Three Centuries,* translated by J. Pelikan, pp. 86ff. New York: Harper, 1962.

Hatch, H. P. "The Primitive Christian Message." *JBL* 57 (1939): 1ff.

Hayward, P. A. "Suffering and Innocence in Latin Sermons for the Feast of the Holy Innocents c 400-800." In *The Church and Childhood,* edited by D. Wood, pp. 67ff. Oxford: Blackwell, 1994.

Hesselgrave, D. J., and E. Rommen. "Reflections from the History of the Church and Its Missions." In *Contextualization: Meanings, Methods, and Models,* pp. 12ff. Leicester: Apollos, 1989.

Howden, W. D. "Preaching." In *EEC*, pp. 747ff.

Ker, J. *Lectures on the History of Preaching.* London: Hodder and Stoughton, 1808.

Kraft, C. H. *Communication Theory for Christian Witness.* New York: Orbis, 1991.

Lang, B. "From Luke to Luther: The Beginnings and Aims of Christian Preaching." In *Sacred Games: A History of Christian Worship,* pp. 149ff. London: Yale University Press, 1997.

Le Grys, A. *Preaching to the Nations: The Origins of Mission in the Early Church.* London: SPCK, 1988.

Lloyd-Jones, M. *Preaching and Preachers.* London: Hodder and Stoughton, 1998.

Long, D. S. "Prophetic Preaching." In *CEP*, pp. 387ff.

Loscalzo, C. A. "Rhetoric." In *CEP*, pp. 409ff.

Lowry, E. *The Homiletical Plot: The Sermon as Narrative Art Forms.* London: Westminster John Knox, 2001.

Lyons, M. E. "Style." In *CEP,* pp. 457ff.

Marshall, I. H. "In Honesty of Preaching: An Assessment." *ET* 112, no. 2 (November 2000): 41ff.

McDonald, J. I. H. *Kerygma and Didache: The Articulation and Structure of the Earliest Christian Message.* SNTSMS 37. Cambridge: Cambridge University Press, 1989.

Morris, L. *The Apostolic Preaching of the Cross.* London: Tyndale Press, 1960.

Mounce, R. H. *The Essential Nature of New Testament Preaching.* Grand Rapids: Eerdmans, 1960.

———. "Preaching, Kerygma." In *DPL,* pp. 735ff.

Mundle, W., and G. Braumann. "Comfort, Encouragement." In *DNTT,* 1:327-28.

Perleman, C. "Rhetoric." In *EB* (1992), 26:758ff.

Reicke, B. "A Synopsis of Early Christian Preaching." In *The Fruit of the Vine,* edited by A. Friedischen, pp. 128ff. Westminster: Dacre Press, 1953.

Resner, A., Jr. *Preacher and Cross: Person and Message in Theology and Rhetoric.* Cambridge: Eerdmans, 1999.

Rice, C. L. "Preaching." In *ER,* 2:494ff.

Richardson, A. "Hermeneutics." In *DCT,* pp. 154f.

Runia, K. "Theology of Preaching." In *NDCT,* pp. 527-28.

Sanders, J. A. "Hermeneutics." In *CEP,* pp. 175ff.

Simonetti, M. *Biblical Interpretation in the Early Church: An Historical Introduction to Patristic Exegesis.* Translated by J. A. Hughes. Edinburgh: T. & T. Clark, 1994.

Sloyan, G. S. "Liturgical Preaching." In *CEP,* pp. 311ff.

Stott, J. "Jesus, the Apostles and the Fathers." In *I Believe in Preaching,* pp. 16ff. London: Hodder and Stoughton, 1992.

Thiselton, A. C. "Hermeneutics." In *WDCT,* pp. 250ff.

Thompson, J. W. "Preaching, Proclamation." In *EDB,* p. 1079.

Wallace, R. S. "Homiletics." In *NIDCC,* pp. 479ff.

Wegenast, K. "Teach, Instruct." In *DNTT,* 3:759ff.

Westerhoff, J. H. "Teaching and Preaching." In *CEP,* pp. 467ff.

Willimon, W. H. "Anti-Jewish Preaching." In *CEP,* pp. 11ff.

Wilson, P. S. *A Concise History of Preaching.* Nashville: Abingdon, 1992.

Winter, B. W. "Rhetoric." In *DPL,* pp. 820ff.

General Church History

Bickerman, E. J. "The Name of Christian." *HTR* 42 (1949): 109ff.

Chadwick, H. *Alexandrian Christianity.* Philadelphia: Westminster, 1954.

———. *The Early Church.* London: Penguin Books, 1978.

Davies, J. G. *The Early Christian Church.* London: Weidenfeld and Nicolson, 1965.

Dodds, E. R. *Pagans and Christians in an Age of Anxiety: Some Aspects of Religious Experience from Marcus Aurelius to Constantine.* Cambridge: Cambridge University Press, 1965.

Duschesne, L. *The Early History of the Christian Church.* 3 vols. London: John Murray, 1950.

Ehrman, B. D. *The Orthodox Corruption of Scripture: The Effects of Early Christological Controversies on the Text of the New Testament.* New York: Oxford University Press, 1993.

Ferguson, E. *Background of Early Christianity.* Grand Rapids: Eerdmans, 1987.

Fletcher, R. "The Challenge of the Countryside." In *The Conversion of Europe from Paganism to Christianity, 371-1386 A.D.*, pp. 34ff. London: Harper Collins, 1997.

Foakes-Jackson, F. J. *History of the Christian Church to 460 AD.* Cambridge: J. Hall, 1905.

Frend, W. H. C. "The Church in the Roman Empire, 313-600." In *The Layman in Christian History,* edited by S. C. Neil and H.-R. Weber, pp. 57ff. Philadelphia: Westminster, 1963.

————. *The Early Church.* London: Hodder and Stoughton, 1971.

————. *Martyrdom and Persecution in the Early Church.* New York: New York University Press, 1967.

————. "Town and Countryside in Early Christianity." *SCH* 16 (1979): 25ff.

————. "The Winning of the Countryside." *JEH* 18, no. 1 (April 1967): 1ff.

Gamble, H. Y. *Books and Readers in the Early Church: A History of Early Christian Texts.* New Haven: Yale University Press, 1995.

Gardner-Smith, P. "The Church in the Roman Empire." In *The Expansion of the Christian Church,* pp. 1ff. Cambridge: Cambridge University Press, 1934.

Gowans, A. "Catacomb." In *EB* (1970), 5:57ff.

Grant, R. M. *Augustus to Constantine: The Thrust of the Christian Movement in the Roman World.* New York: Harper and Row, 1970.

Haines-Eitzen, K. *Guardians of Letters: Literacy, Power, and the Transmitters of Early Christian Literature.* New York: Oxford University Press, 2000.

Harrison, E. F. *The Apostolic Church.* Grand Rapids: Eerdmans, 1985.

Hastings, A. "Independence and Prophetism." In *The Church in Africa, 1450-1950,* pp. 493ff. Oxford: Oxford University Press, 1996.

Hopkins, K. *A World Full of Gods: Pagans, Jews, and Christians in the Roman Empire.* London: Phoenix, 1999.

Kidd, B. J. *Documents Illustrative of the History of the Church.* London: SPCK, 1932.

Klauck, H. *Magic and Paganism in Early Christianity.* Edinburgh: T. & T. Clark, 2001.

Latourette, K. S. *A History of Christianity.* 1 vol. edition. London: Eyre and Spottiswood, 1955.

Lebreton, J., and J. Zeiller. *The History of the Primitive Church.* Translated by E. C. Messenger. 2 vols. New York: Macmillan, 1947.

Leitzmann, H. *The Era of the Early Church Fathers.* Translated by B. L. Woolf. London: Lutterworth, 1958.

MacMullen, R. *Christianizing the Roman Empire: AD 100-400*. New Haven: Yale University Press, 1984.

Neill, S. *A History of Christian Missions*. London: Penguin Books, 1986.

Parkes, J. "Jews and Christians in the Constantinian Empire." In *SCH* 1 (1964): 69ff.

Ramsay, W. M. *The Church in the Roman Empire before AD 170*. London: Hodder and Stoughton, 1904.

Schlatter, A. *The Church in the New Testament Period*. Translated by P. P. Levertoff. London: SPCK, 1955.

Schnackenburg, R. *The Church in the New Testament*. Translated by W. J. O'Hara. London: Burns and Oates, 1981.

Sternberger, G. *Jews and Christians in the Holy Land: Palestine in the Fourth Century*. Translated by R. Tüschling. Edinburgh: T. & T. Clark, 2000.

Stevenson, J. *The Catacombs: Rediscovered Monuments of Early Christianity*. London: Thomas and Hudson, 1978.

Streeter, B. H. "The Rise of Christianity." In *CAH*, 11:253ff.

Toon, P. "Catacomb." In *NIDCC*, p. 199.

Ware, K. "Eastern Christendom." In *OIHC*, pp. 123ff.

Weiss, J. *Earliest Christianity: A History of the Period, AD 30-150*. Translated by F. C. Grant. 2 vols. New York: Harper, 1959.

Wiles, M. "Eastern Christendom." In *CUHB*, 1:454ff.

Williams, G. H. "The Ancient Church AD 30-313." In *The Layman in Christian History*, edited by S. C. Neil and H. R. Weber, pp. 28ff. Philadelphia: Westminster, 1963.

Workman, H. B. *Persecution in the Early Church: A Chapter in the History of Renunciation*. London: Epworth Press, 1923.

Historical and Social Background

Barclay, J. M. G. *Jews in the Mediterranean Diaspora from Alexander to Trajan, 323 BCE–117 CE*. Edinburgh: T. & T. Clark, 1998.

Brice, W. C. "Antioch." In *EB* (1970), 2:73ff.

Bultmann, R. *Primitive Christianity in Its Contemporary Setting*. Translated by R. H. Fuller. London: Collins, 1960.

Bury, J. B. *A History of the Later Roman Empire: From Arcadius to Irene (395 AD to 800 AD)*. 2 vols. London: Macmillan, 1889.

Cameron, A. *The Later Roman Empire*. London: Harper Collins, 1993.

Carcopino, J. *Daily Life in Ancient Rome: The People and the City at the Height of the Empire*. Translated by E. O. Lorimer. London: Penguin Books, 1991.

Davis, J. G. *Daily Life in the Early Church: Studies in the Church Social History of the First Five Centuries*. London: Lutterworth, 1955.

Dill, S. *Roman Society from Nero to Marcus Aurelius*. London: Macmillan, 1904.

————. *Roman Society in the Last Century of the Western Empire*. London: Macmillan, 1898.

Gibbon, E. *The Decline and Fall of the Roman Empire*. Edited by C. A. Robinson. Abridged ed. London: Penguin Books, 1980.

Goodman, M. *Mission and Conversion: Proselytizing in the Religious History of the Roman Empire*. Oxford: Clarendon, 1994.

Grant, F. C. *Hellenistic Religions: The Age of Syncretism*. New York: Liberal Arts, 1953.

Hengel, M. *Judaism and Hellenism: Studies in Their Encounter in Palestine during the Early Hellenistic Period*. Translated by J. Bowden. 2 vols. London: SCM Press, 1974.

Hoffmann, H. "Baths." In *EB* (1970), 3:274ff.

Houston, J. M. "Antioch (Syrian)." In *NIDCC*, p. 49.

Jeremias, J. *Jerusalem in the Time of Jesus: An Investigation into Economic and Social Conditions during the New Testament Period*. Translated by F. H. Cave and C. H. Cave. London: SCM Press, 1996.

Klauch, H.-J. *The Religious Context of Early Christianity: A Guide to Graeco-Roman Religions*. Edinburgh: T. & T. Clark, 2000.

Markschies, C. *Between Two Worlds: Structures of Early Christianity*. Translated by J. Bowden. London: SCM Press, 1999.

Millard, A. *Reading and Writing in the Time of Jesus*. JNTS, no. 69. Sheffield: Sheffield Academic Press, 2000.

Nock, A. D. "The Development of Paganism in the Roman Empire." In *CAH*, 12:409ff.

Oertel, F. "The Economic Life of the Empire." In *CAH*, 12:232ff.

Price, S. R. F. *Rituals of Power: The Roman Imperial Cult in Asia Minor*. London: Oxford University Press, 1984.

Rowlatt, M. "Alexandria." In *EB* (1970), 1:582ff.

Rupprecht, A. A. "The Cultural and Political Setting of the New Testament." In *EBC*, 1:501ff.

Schale, F. C. "Reading." In *EB* (1970), 19:9aff.

Tarn, W. W. *Hellenistic Civilization*. New York: World Publishing, 1971.

Trebilco, P. R. *Jewish Communities in Asia Minor*. Cambridge: Cambridge University Press, 1991.

Wells, C. *The Roman Empire*. London: Harper Collins, 1992.

Congregation and Community

Banks, R. *Paul's Idea of Community: The Early House Churches in Their Historical Setting*. Grand Rapids: Eerdmans, 1980.

Bennett, D. W. *Biblical Images for Leaders and Followers*. Oxford: Regnum Books, 1993.

Braumann, G., et al. "Child." In *DNTT*, 1:280ff.

Brown, C. "Woman." In *DNTT*, 3:1055ff.

Campbell, J. Y. "The Origin and Meaning of the Christian Use of *Ekklesia*." *JTS* 49:130ff.

Chadwick, H. "The Early Christian Community." In *OIHC,* pp. 21ff.

Clark, G. "The Fathers and the Children." In *SCH* 31 (1994): 1ff.

Coenen, J. "Ecclesia." In *DNTT,* 1:291-92.

Cullmann, O. "Dissensions within the Early Church." In *New Testament Issues,* edited by R. Batey, pp. 119ff. London: SCM Press, 1970.

Danielou, J. "The Christian Community." In *The First Six Hundred Years,* translated by V. Cronin, pp. 115ff. London: Darton, Longman and Todd, 1978.

Davies, J. G. *The Making of the Church.* London: Skeffington, 1960.

———. "Matrimony in the Early Church." In *DLW,* pp. 256ff.

De Mause, L., ed. *The History of Childhood.* London: Souvenir Press, 1974.

Filson, F. V. "The Significance of the Early House Churches." *JBL* 58 (1939): 109ff.

Fisher, J. D. C. "Catechumens, Catechumenate." In *DLW,* pp. 122-23.

Gould, G. "Childhood in Eastern Patristic Thought: Some Problems of Theology and Theological Anthropology." In *The Church and Childhood,* pp. 39ff. Oxford: Blackwell, 1994.

———. "Women in the Writings of the Fathers: Language, Belief and Reality." *SCH* 27 (1990): 1ff.

Hall, S. G. "Women among the Early Martyrs." *SCH* 30 (1993): 1ff.

Heine, S. *Women and Early Christianity: Are the Feminist Scholars Right?* Translated by J. Bowden. London: SCM Press, 1987.

Hellerman, J. H. *The Ancient Church as a Family.* Minneapolis: Fortress, 2001.

Hill, D. *The Christian Ecclesia: The Early History and Early Conceptions of the Ecclesia.* London: Macmillan, 1900.

Judge, E. A. "The Early Christians as a Scholastic Community." *JRH* 1 (1960-61): 8ff.

———. *The Social Pattern of Christian Groups in the First Century: Some Prolegomena to the Study of New Testament Ideas of Social Obligation.* London: Tyndale Press, 1960.

MacMullen, R. "The Preacher's Audience (AD 350-400)." *JTS,* n.s., 40 (1989): 503ff.

Malherbe, A. J. *Social Aspects of Early Christianity.* London: Louisiana State University Press, 1977.

Malone, M. T. *Women and Christianity.* Vol. 1, *First Thousand Years.* Dublin: Columba Press, 2000.

Petersen, J. M. "The Education of Girls in Fourth-Century Rome." In *The Church and Children,* edited by D. Wood, pp. 29ff. Oxford: Blackwell, 1994.

Rawson, B., ed. *The Family in Ancient Rome: New Perspectives.* London and Sydney: Groom Helm, 1986.

Reimer, I. R. *Women in the Acts of the Apostles: A Feminist Liberation Perspective.* Translated by L. M. Maloney. Minneapolis: Fortress, 1995.

Schattenmann, J. "Fellowship." In *DNTT,* 1:639ff.

Stegemann, E. W., and W. Stegemann. *The Jesus Movement: A Social History of Its First Century.* Edinburgh: T. & T. Clark, 1999.

Strange, W. A. *Children in the Early Church: Children in the Ancient World, the New Testament, and the Early Church.* Carlisle: Paternoster Press, 1996.

Tasker, R. V. G. "Widow." In *NBD*, p. 239.

Tisdale, L. T. "Congregation." In *CEP*, pp. 87ff.

Walton, S. *Leadership and Lifestyle.* Oxford: Oxford University Press, 2000.

Watson D. E. "Romans' Social Classes." In *DNTB*, pp. 999ff.

Wiedermann, T. *Adults and Children in the Roman Empire.* London: Routledge, 1989.

Winter, B. W. *Seek the Welfare of the City: Christians as Benefactors and Citizens.* Grand Rapids: Eerdmans, 1994.

Witherington, B., III. *Women in the Earliest Churches.* Cambridge: Cambridge University Press, 1988.

Doctrine and Spirituality

Bethune-Baker, J. F. *An Introduction to the Early History of Christian Doctrine.* London: Methuen, 1951.

Bietenhard, H. "Fire." In *DNTT*, 1:653ff.

Bostock, D. G. "Osiris and the Resurrection of Christ." *ET* 112, no. 8 (May 2001): 265ff.

Bultmann, R. *The Historical Jesus and the Kerygmatic Christ.* Edited by C. E. Braaten and R. A. Harrisville. Nashville: Abingdon, 1964.

Daniélou, J. *Gospel Message and Hellenistic Culture: A History of Early Christian Doctrine before the Council of Nicea.* Translated by J. A. Baker. 2 vols. London: Darton, Longman and Todd, 1973.

Douglas, J. D. "Gnosticism." In *NBD*, pp. 415ff.

Fuller, R. H. *The Foundations of New Testament Christology.* London: Collins, 1972.

Grant, R. M. *Gnosticism.* New York: Harper, 1961.

————. *Gnosticism in Early Christianity.* New York: Harper and Row, 1966.

Hall, S. G. *Doctrine and Practice in the Early Church.* London: SPCK, 1991.

Hamman, A. "Purgatory." In *EEC*, 2:725.

Hanson, R. P. C. "Alexandrian Theology." In *DCT*, pp. 4-5.

————. "Tradition." In *DCT*, pp. 341ff.

————. *Tradition in the Early Church.* London: SCM Press, 1962.

Hardy, R. H., ed. *Christology of the Later Fathers.* LCC 3. London: SCM Press, 1954.

Heick, O. W. *A History of Christian Thought.* 2 vols. Philadelphia: Fortress, 1965.

Hooker-Stacey, M. D. "Jesus and Christology." *ET* 112, no. 9 (June 2001): 200ff.

Hordern, W. "Man, Doctrine of." In *DCT*, pp. 202ff.

Jacobs, P., and H. Krienke. "Foreknowledge, Providence, Predestination." In *DNTT*, 1:692ff.

Jellema, S. E. "Predestination." In *NIDCC*, pp. 797ff.

Kelly, J. N. D. *Early Christian Doctrines.* London: A. & C. Black, 1965.

Kreider, A. *The Change of Conversion and the Origin of Christendom.* Harrisburg: Trinity Press International, 1999.

Leaney, A. R. C. "Gnosticism." In *DCT,* pp. 133ff.

Link, H.-G. "Swear, Oath." In *DNTT,* 3:737ff.

Mattei, L. *Philosophy and Early Christianity.* Nairobi: Consolata Press, 1995.

McDonald, H. D. "Alexandrian Theology." In *NIDCC,* pp. 26-27.

————. "Antiochene Theology." In *NIDCC,* p. 49

McGiffert, A. C. *A History of Christian Thought.* 2 vols. London: Scribner, 1932.

Parker, T. H. L. "Predestination." In *DCT,* pp. 264ff.

Pilcher, V. C. *The Hereafter in Jewish and Christian Thought: With Special Reference to the Doctrine of Resurrection.* London: SPCK, 1940.

Richardson, A. *An Introduction to the Theology of the New Testament.* London: SCM Press, 1958.

Roukema, R. *Gnosis and Faith in Early Christianity.* Translated by J. Bowden. London: SCM Press, 1999.

Steinmetz, D. C. "Purgatory." In *NIDCC,* p. 814.

Weiss, J. *Earliest Christianity: A History of the Period, AD 30-150.* Translated by F. C. Grant. 2 vols. New York: Harper, 1959.

Wessels, A. *Europe: Was It Ever Really Christian?* London: SCM Press, 1994.

Wibbing, S. "σωφροσύνη." In *DNTT,* 1:501-2.

Young, F. *Biblical Exegesis and the Formation of Christian Culture.* Cambridge: Cambridge University Press, 1997.

Biblical Material and Commentaries

GENERAL

Barr, J. "Allegory and Typology." In *WDCT,* pp. 11ff.

Bietenhard, H. "Lord." In *DNTT,* 2:510ff.

Deissmann, A. *Biblical Studies.* Edinburgh: T. & T. Clark, 1901.

Dunn-Wilson, D. "The Biblical Background of Martys and Its Derivatives, with Special Reference to the New Testament." M.A. thesis, University of Birmingham, 1958.

Goldinghay, J. *Models for Interpretation of Scripture.* Grand Rapids: Eerdmans, 1995.

Hunter, A. M. *Introducing the New Testament.* London: SCM Press, 1972.

Kennedy, G. A. *New Testament Interpretation through Rhetorical Criticism.* Chapel Hill: University of North Carolina, 1984.

Moule C. F. D. *The Birth of the New Testament.* London: A. & C. Black, 1973.

Porter, S. E., and D. L. Stamps, eds. *The Rhetorical Interpretation of Scripture.* JSOT Supplement 180. Sheffield: Sheffield University Press, 1999.

Robinson, J. *Redating the New Testament.* London: SCM Press, 1976.

Simonetti, M. *Biblical Interpretation in the Early Church: An Historical Introduction to Patristic Exegesis.* Translated by J. A. Hughes. Edinburgh: T. & T. Clark, 2001.
Wakefield, G. S. "Song of Songs." In *DCS,* pp. 355ff.

The Gospels and Acts

Bauckham, R., ed. *The Gospels for All Christians: Rethinking the Gospel Audiences.* Edinburgh: T. & T. Clark, 1998.
Brawley, R. L. *Luke-Acts and the Jews: Conflict, Apology, and Conciliation.* SBLMS 33. Atlanta: Scholars Press, 1987.
Brown, C. "Apostleship in Luke-Acts." In *DNTT,* 1:135ff.
Brown, R. E. "The Kerygma of the Gospel according to John." In *New Testament Issues,* edited by R. Batey, pp. 210ff. London: SCM Press, 1970.
Bruce, F. F. *The Acts of the Apostles: The Greek Text with Introduction and Commentary.* London: Tyndale Press, 1952.
Caird, G. B. *The Apostolic Age.* London: Duckworth, 1993.
Conzelmann, H. *The Theology of Saint Luke.* Translated by G. Buswell. London: Faber and Faber, 1960.
Davies, J. G. "The Primary Meaning of *Parakletos.*" *JTS,* n.s., 4 (1953): 35ff.
Dibelius, M. *Studies in the Acts of the Apostles.* Edited by H. Greeven. Translated by M. Ling. London: SCM Press, 1956.
Ellis, E. E. *The Gospel of Luke.* London: Nelson, 1966.
———. "The Role of the Christian Prophet in Acts." In *Apostolic History and the Gospel,* edited by W. W. Gasque and R. P. Martin, pp. 55f. Exeter: Paternoster, 1970.
Gempf, C. "Acts." In *NBC,* pp. 1066ff.
———. "Public Speaking and Published Accounts." In *The Book of Acts in Its Ancient Literary Setting,* edited by B. W. Winter and A. D. Clarke, pp. 259ff. Carlisle: Paternoster Press, 1993.
Glasson, T. F. "The Speeches in Acts and Thucydides." *ET* 76 (1965): 165ff.
Haenchen, E. *The Acts of the Apostles.* Translated by R. McL. Wilson. Philadelphia: Westminster, 1971.
———. "The Book of Acts as Source Material for the History of Early Christianity." In *Studies in Luke-Acts,* edited by L. E. Keck and J. L. Martyn, pp. 258ff. London: SPCK, 1968.
Hengel, M. *Acts and the History of Earliest Christianity.* Translated by J. Bowden. London: SCM Press, 1979.
Hoskyns, E. "The Evangelist and His Readers." In *The Fourth Gospel,* edited by F. N. Davey, pp. 48ff. London: Faber and Faber, 1947.
Hurtado, L. W. *Mark.* Carlisle: Paternoster Press, 1995.
Jeremias, J. *The Parables of Jesus.* Translated by S. H. Hooke. London: SCM Press, 1955.
Johnson, S. E. *The Gospel according to St. Mark.* London: A. & C. Black, 1960.
Lampe, G. W. H. "Acts." In *PC,* pp. 882ff.

Lane, W. L. *The Gospel of Mark.* Grand Rapids: Eerdmans, 1988.

Longnecker, R. N. "The Speeches in Acts." In *EBC,* 9:229ff.

Macgregor, G. H. C., and T. P. Ferris. "The Acts of the Apostles." In *IB,* 9:3ff.

Marsh, J. *The Gospel of St John.* Harmondsworth: Penguin Books, 1968.

Marshall, I. H. *The Gospel of Luke: A Commentary on the Greek Text.* Exeter: Paternoster Press, 1989.

————. *Luke: Historian and Theologian.* Exeter: Paternoster Press, 1988.

Millard, A. "Reading and Writing in the Time of Jesus." *JSNT,* no. 69 (2000).

Morgenthaler, R. "Generation." In *DNTT,* 2:35ff.

Mounce, R. H. *Matthew.* Carlisle: Paternoster Press, 1995.

Munck, J. *The Acts of the Apostles.* New York: Doubleday, 1967.

Nineham, D. *Saint Mark.* London: Penguin Books, 1963.

Ridderbos, H. N. *The Speeches of Peter in the Acts of the Apostles.* London: Tyndale Press, 1962.

Robinson, W. C. "On Preaching the Word of God (Luke 8:4-21)." In *Studies in Luke-Acts,* edited by L. E. Keck and J. L. Martyn, pp. 131ff. London: SPCK, 1968.

Rohrbaugh, R. L. "The Jesus Tradition: The Gospel Writers' Strategies of Persuasion." In *ECW,* 1:198-99.

Satterthwaite, P. E. "Acts against the Background of Classical Rhetoric." In *The Book of Acts in Its Ancient Literary Setting,* edited by B. W. Winter and A. D. Clarke, pp. 337ff. Carlisle: Paternoster Press, 1993.

Schweitzer, E. "Concerning the Speeches in Acts." In *Studies in Luke-Acts,* edited by L. E. Keck and J. L. Martyn, pp. 208ff. London: SPCK, 1968.

Stendahl, K. "Matthew." In *PC,* pp. 769ff.

Taylor, V. *The Gospel according to Mark.* London: Macmillan, 1952.

Wickens, U., and P. Schubert. "The Final Sequence of Speeches in the Book of Acts." *JBL* 97 (1968): 1ff.

Williams. C. S. C. "The Speeches and Theology of Acts." In *A Commentary on the Acts of the Apostles,* pp. 36ff. London: A. & C. Black, 1957.

Wilson, R. McL. "Mark." In *PC,* pp. 799ff.

Witherington, B., III. *The Acts of the Apostles: A Socio-Rhetorical Commentary.* Carlisle: Paternoster Press, 1998.

Wood A. S. "The Apostolic Church." In *EBC* (1979), 1:577ff.

Jesus the Preacher

Davies, W. D. *The Setting of the Sermon on the Mount.* London: Cambridge University Press, 1964.

Dodd, C. H. *The Parables of the Kingdom.* New York: Scribner, 1936.

Dunn-Wilson, D. "The Portrayal and Significance of Judas Iscariot in Christianity." M.Phil. thesis, University of Sussex, 1983.

Garvie, A. E. "Jesus Christ, the Lord." In *The Christian Preacher*, pp. 40ff. Edinburgh: T. & T. Clark, 1920.

Hill, D. "Jesus, a Prophet Mighty in Deed and Word." In *New Testament Prophecy*, pp. 48ff. Basingstoke: Marshall, 1985.

Homringhausen, E. G. "Jesus as a Teacher." In *ERK*, 1:598.

Hunter, A. M. "The Interpreter and the Parables: The Centrality of the Kingdom." In *New Testament Issues*, pp. 71ff. London: SCM Press, 1970.

Jeremias, J. *The Parables of Jesus*. Translated by S. H. Hooke. London: SCM Press, 1955.

Klappert, B. "King, Kingdom." In *DNTT*, 2:372ff.

Küng, H. "The Preaching of Jesus." In *The Church*, pp. 43ff. London: Search, 1978.

Marshall, I. H. "Jesus in the Gospels." In *EBC*, 1:515ff.

Mounce, R. H. "Sermon on the Mount." In *NBD*, pp. 1078ff.

Müller, D. "Apostle." In *DNTT*, 1:126ff.

———. "Disciple." In *DNTT*, 1:483ff.

North, R. "How Loud Was Jesus' Voice? Mark 4:1." *ET* 112, no. 4 (January 2001): 117ff.

Palmer, H. "Seeking Verdicts for Parables." *ET* 111, no. 8 (May 2000): 262ff.

Pannenberg, W. *Jesus: God and Man*. Translated by L. L. Wilkins and D. A. Priebe. London: SCM Press, 1968.

Peisker, C. H. "Prophet." In *DNTT*, 3:83.

Ridderbos, H. N. "Kingdom of God." In *NBD*, pp. 649ff.

Sanders, E. P. *Jesus and Judaism*. London: SCM Press, 1985.

Stanton, G. N. *The Gospels and Jesus*. Oxford: Oxford University Press, 1989.

———. *Jesus of Nazareth in New Testament Preaching*. SNTSMS 27. 1974.

Stott, J. *The Message of the Sermon on the Mount*. Leicester: Inter-Varsity, 2000.

Theissen, G., and A. Merz. *The Historical Jesus: A Comprehensive Guide*. Translated by J. Bowden. Minneapolis: Fortress, 1998.

Via, D. O. "The Parables of Jesus." In *CEP*, pp. 358ff.

PAUL AND THE EPISTLES

Bauckham, R. J. *Jude, 2 Peter*. Waco: Word, 1983.

Betz, H. D. *Galatians*. Philadelphia: Fortress, 1979.

Black, M. *Romans*. London: Marshall, Morgan and Scott, 1982.

Blaiklock, E. M. "The Epistolary Literature." In *EBC* (1979), 1:545ff.

Blum, E. A. "Jude." In *EBC*, 12:381ff.

Boobyer, G. H. "Jude." In *PC*, pp. 1041-42.

Bruce, F. F. *The Epistle to the Hebrews*. London: Marshall, Morgan and Scott, 1977.

———. *Romans: An Introduction and Commentary*. London: Inter-Varsity, 1974.

Chester, A. "The Pauline Community." In *A Vision for the Church: Studies in Early Christian Ecclesiology*, edited by M. Bockmuehl and M. B. Thompson. Edinburgh: T. & T. Clark, 1997.

Dodd, C. H. *The Johannine Epistles*. London: Hodder and Stoughton, 1947.

Donfried, K. P., and J. Beutler, eds. *The Thessalonians Debate: Methodological Discord or Methodological Synthesis?* Grand Rapids: Eerdmans, 2000.

Dunn, J. G. "Romans, Letter to." In *DPL*, pp. 838ff.

———. *Romans 1–8.* Dallas: Word, 1988.

Elliott-Binns, L. E. "James." In *PC*, pp. 1022ff.

Engberg-Pedersen, T. *Paul and the Stoics: An Essay in Interpretation.* Edinburgh: T. & T. Clark, 2000.

Hansen, G. W. "Rhetorical Criticism." In *DPL*, pp. 822ff.

Harrison, E. F. "Romans." In *EBC*, 10:1ff.

Harrop, J. "Epistle." In *NBD*, pp. 330ff.

Horrell, D. *The Epistles of Peter and Jude.* Peterborough: Epworth Press, 1998.

Kelly, J. N. D. *A Commentary on the Pastoral Epistles.* New York: Harper and Row, 1983.

Kennedy, H. A. A. *St. Paul and the Mystery Religions.* London: Hodder and Stoughton, 1913.

Kim, J. D. *God, Israel, and the Gentiles: Rhetoric and Situation in Romans 9–11.* SBL Dissertations 176, pp. 176ff. Atlanta: Society of Biblical Literature, 2000.

Kistemaker, S. K. *Exposition of the Epistles of Peter and the Epistle of Jude.* Welwyn, England: Evangelical Press, 1987.

Kreitzer, L. J. "Eschatology." In *DPL*, pp. 253ff.

Leon, H. *The Jews in Ancient Rome.* Philadelphia: Jewish Publication Society, 1960.

Longnecker, R. N. "On the Form and Function and Authority of New Testament Letters." In *Scripture and Truth,* edited by D. A. Carson and J. D. Woodbridge, pp. 101ff. Grand Rapids: Zondervan, 1983.

Marshall, I. *I Peter.* Leicester: Inter-Varsity, 1991.

Martin, R. P. *The Spirit and the Congregation: Studies in I Corinthians 12–15.* Grand Rapids: Eerdmans, 1984.

Meeks, W. A. *The First Urban Christians: The Social World of the Apostle Paul.* New Haven: Yale University Press, 1983.

Morris, L. "Hebrews." In *EBC*, 12:3ff.

Ramsay, W. M. *St Paul the Traveller.* London: Hodder and Stoughton, 1897.

Theissen, G. *The Social Setting of Pauline Christianity.* Translated by J. H. Schütz. Edinburgh: T. & T. Clark, 1999.

Wilson, R. McL. *Hebrews.* Basingstoke: Marshall, Morgan and Scott, 1987.

Winter, B. W. *After Paul Left Corinth: The Influence of Secular Ethic and Social Change.* Grand Rapids: Eerdmans, 2001.

Zeisler, J. *Paul's Letter to the Romans.* London: SCM Press, 1990.

THE PROPHETIC PREACHERS

Garvie, A. E. "Apostles, Prophets, Teachers." In *The Christian Preacher,* pp. 57ff. Edinburgh: T. & T. Clark, 1920.

Jewett, P. K. "Prophecy." In *NIDCC*, pp. 806-7.

Long, D. S. "Prophetic Preaching." In *CEP*, pp. 385ff.

Peisker, C. H. "Prophet." In *DNTT*, 3:74ff.

Von Campenhausen, H. "Prophets and Teachers in the Second Century." In *Ecclesiastical Authority and Spiritual Power in the Church of the First Three Centuries*, pp. 178ff. London: A. & C. Black, 1969.

The Fathers (General)

Relevant volumes of J. Migne's *Patrologia Latina* and *Patrologia Graeca* are indicated. Latin titles have generally been retained. Except where indicated otherwise, English translations of patristic texts are taken from The Ante-Nicene Fathers: Translations of the Writings of the Fathers down to AD 325, ed. A. Roberts and J. Donaldson (reprint, Grand Rapids: Eerdmans, 1994-97) and A Select Library from the Nicene and Post-Nicene Fathers, ed. P. Schaff (1st ser.) and P. Schaff and H. Wace (2nd ser.) (reprint, Grand Rapids: Eerdmans, 1991-97). When abbreviations of classical works, used in the notes, are not easily discernible from the titles of the works, they have been noted in the bibliographic entries.

PRIMARY SOURCES

Eusebius. *Historia ecclesiastica*. PG 20.

Gennadius. *De viris illustribus*. PL 160.

Jerome. *De viris illustribus*. PL 23.

Rufinus. *Historia ecclesiastica*. PL 21.

Socrates Scholasticus. *Historia ecclesiastica*. PG 67.

Sozomenus. *Historia ecclesiastica*. PG 67.

Theodoret. *Historia ecclesiastica*. PG 82.

ADDITIONAL MATERIAL

Altaner, A. S. *Patrology*. Translated by H. C. Graef. New York: Herder and Herder, 1960.

Bardenhewer, O. *The Fathers of the Latin Church*. Translated by M. Hoffmann. London: A. & C. Black, 1964.

————. *Patrology: The Lives and Works of the Fathers of the Church*. Translated by T. J. Shahan. Freiburg: B. Herder, 1908.

Bettenson, H. *The Later Christian Fathers: A Selection from the Writings of the Fathers from St. Cyril of Jerusalem to St. Leo the Great*. London: Oxford University Press, 1972.

Kidd, B. J. *Documents Illustrative of the History of the Church*. London: SPCK, 1932.

Payne, R. *The Fathers of the Western Church*. London: Heinemann, 1952.

Von Campenhausen, H. *The Fathers of the Greek Church.* Translated by M. Hoffmann. London: A. & C. Black, 1963.

Young, W. G., ed. *Handbook of Source Material for Students of Church History.* Serampore, India: Christian Literature Crusade, 1969.

The Post-Apostolic Preachers and Pseudo-Clementine Literature

PRIMARY SOURCES

Anon. Διδαχὴ τῶν Ἀποστόλων. *PG.* Abbreviated *Did.*

Anon. *Epistola ecclesiae Smyrnensis de martyrio S Polycarpi. PG* 5. Abbreviated *Mart. Pol.*

"Barnabas." *Epistola catholica. PG* 2. Abbreviated *Barn.*

Clement of Rome. *Epistola I ad Corinthos. PG* 1. Abbreviated *1 Clem.*

"Clement." *Epistola II ad Corinthos. PG* 1. Abbreviated *2 Clem.*

————. *Clementine Homilies. PG* 1.

————. *Clementine Recognitions. PG* 1 (ANCL 3).

————. *Constitutiones apostolicae. PG* 1.

"Hermas." *Pastor sanctus Hermas. PG* 2. Abbreviated *Herm. Man. (Mandates), Herm. Sim. (Similitudes), Herm. Vis. (Visions).*

Ignatius. *Epistolae. PG* 5. Abbreviated *Eph. (Letter to the Ephesians), Magn. (Letter to the Magnesians), Phld. (Letter to the Philadelphians), Pol. (Letter to Polycarp), Rom. (Letter to the Romans), Trall. (Letter to the Trallians).*

"Mathetes." *Epistola ad Diognetum.* Abbreviated *Diog.*

Papias. *Fragmenta e quinque libris de expositione oraculorum Domini. PG* 5.

"Peter." *Epistle of Peter to James.*

Polycarp. *Pros Philippesious. PG.* Abbreviated *Phil.*

ADDITIONAL MATERIAL

Foster, J. *After the Apostles: Missionary Preaching of the First Three Centuries.* London: SCM Press, 1951.

Lightfoot, J. B., ed. *The Apostolic Fathers.* London: Macmillan, 1893.

Nixon, R. E. "Didache." In *NIDCC,* pp. 297-98.

Schoedel, W. R. *Ignatius of Antioch.* Philadelphia: Fortress, 1985.

Tugwell, S. "The Apostolic Fathers and Irenaeus." In *SS,* pp. 102-3.

The Apologists

PRIMARY SOURCES

Arnobius. *Ad nationes. PL* 5.
————. *Contra Auxentium. PL* 5.
Athenagoras. *Legatio pro Christianis. PG* 6.
————. *De resurrectione mortuorum. PG* 6.
Clement of Alexandria. *Paedagogus. PG* 9.
————. *Quis dives salvetur. PG* 9.
————. *Stromateis. PG* 9.
Commodianus. *Instructiones adversus gentium deos. PL* 5.
Cyprian. *Ad Donatum epistola. PL* 4.
————. *Ad Perpetuam (attrib.). PL* 3.
————. *De bono patientia. PL* 4.
————. *De habitu virginum. PL* 4.
————. *De lapsis. PL* 4.
————. *De unitate ecclesiae. PL* 4.
————. *Epistolae. PL* 4.
————. *Testimoniorum libri tres adversus Judaeos. PL* 4.
Gregory Thaumaturgus. *Epistola canonica. PG* 10.
————. *Homiliae 1-3 in annunciationem Virginis. PG* 10.
————. *Homilia 5 in omnes sanctos. PG* 10.
————. *Homilia 4 in sancta theophania. PG* 10.
Hippolytus. *Demonstratio adversus Judaeos. PG* 104.
————. *Exegetica. PG* 10.
————. *Narratio de virgine Corinthica. PG* 8.
————. *Philosophoumena. PG* 16.
————. *Refutatio omnium haeresum. PG* 10.
————. *Sermo in sancta theophania. PG* 16.
————. *Sermo in sancta trinitate. PG.*
Irenaeus. *Contra haereses. PG* 7.
Justin Martyr. *Apologia I pro Christianis. PG* 6.
————. *Apologia II pro Christianis. PG* 6.
————. *Cohortatio ad Graecos. PG* 6.
————. *Contra haereses libri 1-5. PG* 6.
————. *Dialogus cum Tryphone Judaeo. PG* 6.
————. *Protrepticus. PG.*
Melito of Sardis. *Ex oratione de passione Domini. PG* 5.
————. *Ex apologia. PG* 5.
Origen. *Commentarius in Matthaeum. PG* 13.
————. *Contra Celsum. PG* 11.

————. *De oratione libellus. PG* 11.

————. *De principiis. PG.*

————. *Exhortatio ad martyrium. PG* 11.

————. *Homilia. PG* 13.

Pontius. *Vita et passio Cypriani. PL* 95.

Tatian. *Oratio adversus Graecos. PG* 95.

Tertullian. *Ad martyras. PL* 1.

————. *Ad nationes. PL* 1.

————. *Ad uxorem. PL* 1.

————. *Adversus gnosticos Scorpiacae. PL* 3.

————. *Apologeticus adversus gentes pro Christianis. PL* 1.

————. *De baptismo. PL* 1.

————. *De corona militis. PL* 2.

————. *De cultu feminarum. PL* 1.

————. *De modestia. PL* 1.

————. *De patientia. PL* 3.

————. *De poenitentia. PL* 1.

————. *De praescriptionibus adversus haereticos. PL.* 2.

————. *De spectaculis. PL* 1.

————. *Liber de velandis virginibus. PL* 2.

Theophilus of Antioch. *Ad Autolycum libri* 1-3. *PG* 6.

————. *De resurrectione. PG.*

ADDITIONAL MATERIAL

Behr, J. *Asceticism and Anthropology in Irenaeus and Clement.* Oxford: Oxford University Press, 2000.

————. *St. Irenaeus of Lyons on the Apostolic Preaching.* Crestwood, N.Y.: St. Vladimir's Seminary Press, 1997.

Cerrado, J. A. *Hippolytus between East and West.* Oxford Theological Monograph. Oxford: Oxford University Press, 2002.

Chadwick, O. *Early Christian Thought and the Classical Tradition: Studies in Justin, Clement, and Origin.* Oxford: Clarendon, 1987.

Droge, A. J. "Justin Martyr and the Restoration of Philosophy." *CH* 56, no. 3 (September 1987): 303ff.

Garvie, A. E. "Apologists and Fathers." In *The Christian Preacher,* pp. 59ff. Edinburgh: T. & T. Clark, 1920.

Grant, R. M. *Greek Apologists of the Second Century.* Philadelphia: Westminster, 1988.

Hanson, R. P. C. "Allegory." In *DCT,* pp. 4-5.

Kelley, J. N. D. "Tertullian." In *SS,* pp. 115ff.

Meredith, A. "Clement of Alexandria." In *SS,* pp. 112ff.

————. "Tertullian." In *SS,* pp. 115ff.

Wiles, M. F. "Origen as Bible Scholar." In *CUHB* (1970), 1:454ff.
Wright, D. F. "Tertullian." In *NIDCC*, pp. 960-61.
Yarnold, E. "Tertullian." In *SS*, pp. 109ff.

The Ascetics and Mystics

PRIMARY TEXTS

Aphrahat. *Demonstrations*. NPNF, 2nd ser., 13.
Athanasius. *De incarnatione et contra Arianos*. PG 26.
———. *De titulis psalmorum*. PG 26.
———. *Epistolae*. PG 25.
———. *Epistolae heortasticae*. PG 26.
———. *Oratio cive liber contra gentes libri*. PG 25.
———. *Vita S. Antoni*. PG 26.
Bardesan. *The Books of the Laws of the Countries*. ANF 8.
Ephrem the Syrian. *Homiliae tres*. PG 86.
Etheria. *The Pilgrimage of Etheria*. In *DIHC*, 2:116ff.
Evagrius. *Vita S. Antonii*. PG 26.
Jerome. *Interpretatio lehum et monitorum S. Pachomi*. PL 23.
Mar Jacob. *Homily on Habib the Martyr*. ANF 8.
Palladius. *Historia Lausiaca*.
Pseudo-Macarius. *Homilae 1-50*. PG 34.
Rufinus. *Historia monachorum*. PL 21.
Theodore of Mopsuestia. *Epistolae*. PG 83-84.

ADDITIONAL MATERIAL

Baltensweiler, H. "Discipline." In *DNTT*, 1:494ff.
Birdsall, J. N. "The Acts of Thomas." In *NIDCC*, p. 971.
Brock, S. "Macarius the Egyptian." In *DCS*, pp. 255-56.
Chadwick, H. "The Ascetic Ideal in the History of the Church." *SCH* 22 (1985): 1ff.
Daley, B. E. *On the Dormition of Mary: Early Patristic Homilies*. Crestwood, N.Y.: St. Vladimir's Seminary Press, 1998.
Didomizio, D. "Sexuality." In *DCS*, pp. 353ff.
Fanning, S. *The Mystics of the Christian Tradition*. London: Routledge, 2001.
Finkenrath, G. "Secret, Mystery." In *DNTT*, 3:501ff.
Gould, G. "Pachomius of Tabennesi and the Foundation of an Independent Monastic Community." *SCH* 23 (1986): 1ff.
Grutzmacher, G. "Pachomius." In *NSHE*, 8:297.
Gwynn, J. "Ephraim the Syrian and Aphrahat the Persian Sage." In NPNF, 2nd ser., 13.

Inge, W. R. *Christian Mysticism: Considered in Eight Lectures Delivered before the University of Oxford.* London: Methuen, 1899.

Ling, B. "Monastic Spirituality, Monasticism." In *DCS*, pp. 267ff.

Louth, A. "Mysticism." In *DCS*, pp. 272ff.

Maloney, G. A., ed. *Intoxicated with God: The Fifty Spiritual Homilies and the Great Letter.* New York: Paulist, 1992.

McGuckin, J. A. "Christian Asceticism and the Early School of Alexandria." In *Monks, Hermits, and the Ascetic Tradition,* edited by W. Sheils, pp. 25ff. Oxford: Blackwell, 1985.

McVey, K. E. "Ephrem the Syrian." In *ECW,* 2:1228ff.

Rader, R. "Asceticism." In *DCS*, pp. 24ff.

Robertson, A. Introduction to "Athanasius." In NPNF, 2nd ser., 4.

Rousseau, P. "Anthony and Pachomius." In *SS*, pp. 119-20.

Schönweiss, H. "Desire, Lust, Pleasure." In *DNTT,* 1:456ff.

Stewart, C. "Anthony of the Desert." In *ECW,* 2:1088ff.

Toon, P. "Diodore of Tarsus." In *NIDCC*, p. 300.

Underhill, E. *The Mystic Way: A Psychological Study in Christian Origins.* London: Dent, 1913.

Ward, B. "Monastic Spirituality, Monasticism." In *DCS*, pp. 267ff.

Wright, D. F. "Pachomius." In *NIDCC*, p. 741.

The Liturgists

Primary Sources

Cyril. *Catecheses ad illuminados et mystagoicae. PG* 33.

Lactantius. *Divinarum institutiones. PL* 6.

————. *Lucii Caecillii de morte persecutorum. PL* 7.

Prudentius. *Contra Symmachum. PL* 60.

Additional Material

Burtchaell, J. T. *From Synagogue to Church: Public Services and Offices in the Earliest Christian Communities.* Oxford: Oxford University Press, 1992.

Carroll, T. K., and T. Halton. *Liturgical Practice of the Fathers.* Wilmington: Michael Glazier, 1988.

Catherall, G. A. "Niceta." In *NIDCC*, pp. 707-8.

Crighton, J. D. "Paschal Vigil." In *DLW*, p. 309.

Cullmann, O. *Early Christian Worship.* London: SCM Press, 1973.

Delling, G. "Worship in the New Testament." *ET* (1962): 92ff.

Feree, B. "Architecture, Ecclesiastical." In *NSHE* (1908), 1:264ff.

Fisher, J. D. C. "Baptism, Patristic." In *DLW*, pp. 44-45.

Gamble, H. Y. *Books and Readers in the Early Church.* New Haven: Yale University Press, 1995.

Hardman, O. *A History of Christian Worship.* London: Hodder and Stoughton, 1937.

Harris, R. "Penitence." In *DCS*, pp. 294-95.

Harrison, A. "Exorcism." In *DCS*, pp. 140-41.

Hurtado, L. W. *At the Origins of Christian Worship.* Carlisle: Paternoster Press, 1999.

Jungman, J. A. *The Early Liturgy to the Time of Gregory the Great.* Translated by F. A. Brunner. London: Darton, Longman and Todd, 1972.

Lawton, G. "The Lineage of the Lectors." In *Reader-Preacher: A Model for the Lay Ministry.* Worthing: Churchman's Publishing, 1989.

Levertoff, P. P. "Synaogue Worship in the First Century." In *Liturgical Worship: A Companion to the Prayer Books of the Anglican Communion,* edited by W. K. L. Clarke and C. Harris, pp. 60ff. London: S.P.C.K., 1950.

Macdonald, A. B. *Christian Worship in the Primitive Church.* Edinburgh: T. & T. Clark, 1934.

Martin, R. P. *Worship in the Early Church.* Grand Rapids: Eerdmans, 1974.

Newns, B. "Exorcism." In *DLW*, pp. 174-75.

Norman, J. G. G. "Penance." In *NIDCC*, p. 762.

———. "Serapion of Thumis." In *NIDCC*, p. 897.

Peaston, A. E. "Unction." In *DLW*, pp. 358ff.

Pocknee, C. E. "Cathedra." In *DLW*, pp. 123-24.

———. "Paschal Candle." In *DLW*, pp. 308ff.

Schmithals, W. "Worship in the Early Church." In *The Theology of the First Christians,* translated by O. C. Dean, pp. 180ff. Louisville: Westminster, 1989.

Sloyan, G. S. "Liturgical Preaching." In *CEP*, pp. 311ff.

The Theologians

PRIMARY SOURCES

Basil of Caesarea. *De Spiritu Sancto. PG* 32.

———. *Epistolae. PG* 33.

———. *Hexaemeron. PG* 30.

———. *Homiliae. PG* 30-32.

———. *Regulae brevius tractatae. PG* 31.

———. *Regulae fusius tractatae. PG* 31.

———. *Sermo asceticus. PG* 21.

———. *Sermo de asceticia disciplina. PG* 31.

Gregory of Nazianzus. *Apologeticus de sacerdotio. PG* 35.

———. *Epistolae. PG* 37-38.

————. *Orationes. PG* 36.

————. *Orationes theologicae. PG* 36.

Gregory of Nyssa. *De anima et resurrectione. PG* 46.

————. *De baptismo Christi. PG* 46.

————. *De beatitudinibus orationes. PG* 46.

————. *De hominis opficio. PG* 46.

————. *De infantibus qui praemature abripiuntur. PG* 46.

————. *De peregrinis.*

————. *De virginitate. PG* 46.

————. *De vita S. Macrinae. PG* 44.

————. *De vita Mosis. PG* 44.

————. *Epistolae. PG* 44.

————. *Orationes. PG* 44.

————. *Oratio catechetica magna. PG* 45.

Hilary of Poitiers. *De Trinitate libri duodecim. PL* 10.

————. *Tractatus super Psalmos. PL* 9.

Leo the Great. *Epistolae et tractatus. PL* 54.

————. *Sermones. PL* 54.

ADDITIONAL MATERIAL

Arnold, F. "Zeno of Verona." In *NSHE*, 12:505.

Balas, D. L. "Gregory of Nyssa." In *EEC*, pp. 400ff.

Clarke, W. K. L. *St. Basil the Great: A Study in Monasticism.* London: Cambridge University Press, 1913.

Clouse, R. G. "Leo I, The Great, St." In *NIDCC*, p. 590.

Ferguson, E. "Preaching at Epiphany: Gregory of Nyssa and John Chrysostom on Baptism and the Church." *CH* 66, no. 1 (March 1997): 1ff.

Gribomant, J. "Gregory of Nyssa." In *EEC*, 1:363ff.

Kelley, J. N. D. "Cappadocian Fathers." In *DCS*, pp. 68ff.

————. *The Cappadocians.* Crestwood, N.Y.: St. Vladimir's Seminary Press, 1995.

————. *Gregory of Nyssa.* London: Routledge, 1999.

Milbank, J. "Gregory of Nyssa: The Force of Identity." In *Christian Origins, Theology, Rhetoric, and Community,* edited by L. Ayres and G. Jones. London: Routledge, 1988.

Stancliffe, C. E. "Hilary of Poitiers." In *DCS*, pp. 190ff.

Telfer, W., ed. *Cyril of Jerusalem and Nemesius of Emesa.* LCC 4. Philadelphia: Westminster, 1955.

Watson, E. W. "Introduction to the Works of Hilary." In NPNF, 2nd ser., 9:xliiiff.

Williams, D. J. "Hilary of Poitiers." In *NIDCC*, p. 470.

Wright, D. F. "Cyril." In *NIDCC*, pp. 277-78.

The Homileticians

PRIMARY SOURCES

Ambrose. *Commentarius in Cantico Canticorum*. PL 15.
————. *De Abraham*. PL 14.
————. *De Cain et Abel*. PL 14.
————. *De Elia*. PL 14.
————. *De Excessu fratris sui Satyri*. PL 15.
————. *De Isaac et anima*. PL 14.
————. *De mysteriis*. PL 16.
————. *De Nabuthe Jezralita*. PL 14.
————. *De obitu Theodosii oratio*. PL 16.
————. *De officiis ministrorum*. PL 16.
————. *De poenitentia libri duo*. PL 16.
————. *De SS Gervasii et Protasi*. PL 47.
————. *De Spiritu Sancto*. PL 16.
————. *De Tobia*. PL 14.
————. *De viduis*. PL 15.
————. *De virginibus libri tres*. PL 15.
————. *Enarrationes in Psalmos*. PL 12.
————. *Epistolae de fide*. PL 16.
————. *Epistolae variae*. PL 15-16.
————. *Expositio in Lucam*. PL 15.
————. *Hexaemeron*. PL 14.
————. *Hymni*. PL 16.
Augustine. *Contra duas epistolas Pelagianorum*. PL 44.
————. *De catechizandis rudibus*. PL 40.
————. *De civitate Dei*. PL 41.
————. *De doctrina Christiana IV libri*. PL 24.
————. *De gestis Pelagii*. PL 44.
————. *De gratia Christi et de peccato originali contra Pelagium*. PL 44.
————. *De musica sex libri*. PL 32.
————. *De praedestinatione sanctorum*. PL 44.
————. *De sermone Domini in monte secundam Matthaeum*. PL 24.
————. *De symbolo ad catecumenos et sermones tres de eodem*. PL 40.
————. *Enchiridion: liber unus*. PL 11.
————. *Epistolae dogmaticae*. PL 11.
————. *Epistolae ecclesiasticae*. PL 26.
————. *Epistolae exegeticae*. PL 22.
————. *Epistolae variae*. PL 33.
————. *Libri confessionum*. PL 33.

————. *Sermones. PL* 16, 17, 38, 41.

————. *Tractatus decem in epistolam Joannis. PL* 35.

————. *Tractatus evangelium sancti Joannis. PL* 35.

John "Chrysostom." *Ad populam Antiochenum. PG* 49.

————. *De non evulgandis fratrum peccatis. PG* 49.

————. *De Pentecostes. PG* 59.

————. *De sacerdotio libri 1-6. PG* 48.

————. *Demones non gubernare mundum. PG* 49.

————. *Evil Comes of Sloth.*

————. *Homiliae XXI de statuus ad populam Antiochenum habitae. PG* 49.

————. *Homiliae in Acta Apostolorum. PG* 60.

————. *Homiliae in epistolas. PG* 42.

————. *Homiliae in Genesim. PG* 53-54.

————. *Homiliae in Joannem. PG* 49.

————. *Homiliae in Mattheum. PG* 57-58.

————. *Homiliae in Psalmos. PG* 55.

————. *In Eutropium. PG* 52.

————. *Those Not Attending the Assembly.* In NPNF, 1st ser., 9:359ff.

Possidius. *Vita sancta Augustini. PL* 50.

ADDITIONAL MATERIAL

Bonner, R. "Augustine of Hippo, St." In *DCS*, pp. 33ff.

Broadus, J. A. "St. Chrysostom as a Homilist." In NPNF, 1st ser., 13:4ff.

Carey, G. L. "Ambrose." In *NIDCC*, pp. 32-33.

Deems, M. M. "Augustine's Use of Scripture." *CH* 14 (1945): 188ff.

Doye, G. W. "Augustine's Sermonic Method." *WTJ* 39 (1976-77): 213ff.

Dudden, F. H. *The Life and Times of St. Ambrose.* 2 vols. Oxford: Clarendon, 1935.

Ford, D. "Chrysostom, John." In *CEP*, pp. 70ff.

Hill, E. "St. Augustine as a Preacher." *Blackfriars* 35 (1954).

Kelly, J. N. D. *Golden Mouth: The Story of John Chrysostom, Ascetic, Preacher, Bishop.* London: Duckworth, 1995.

Lawless, G. "Augustine of Hippo." In *CEP*, pp. 19ff.

Mayer, W. "John Chrysostom and His Audiences: Distinguishing Different Congregations at Antioch and Constantinople." *Studia Patristica*, 31:70ff.

Mayer, W., and P. Allen. *John Chrysostom.* London: Routledge, 2000.

Pellegrino, M. *The True Priest.* New York: Philosophical Library, 1968.

Riddle, M. B. "St. Chrysostom as an Exegete." In NPNF, 1st ser., 10:xvff.

Rowe, T. *St. Augustine Pastoral Theologian.* London: Epworth Press, 1974.

Schaff, D. S. "Augustine as an Exegete." In NPNF, 1st ser., 7:viiff.

Schaff, P. "Chrysostom as a Preacher." In NPNF, 1st ser., 9:39ff.

————. "The Life and Work of Chrysostom." In NPNF, 1st ser., 9:3ff.

Van der Meer, F. *Augustine the Bishop: Church and Society at the Dawn of the Middle Ages.* Translated by B. Battershaw and G. R. Lamb. New York: Harper and Row, 1961.

Wright, D. F. "Chrysostom." In *NIDCC*, pp. 225-26.

Yarnold, E. "Ambrose." In *SS*, pp. 131ff.

Translations of Some Subsidiary Texts

Anon. *Apostolic Constitutions.* ANF 7 (1994).

———. *The Story of the King of Edessa.* ANF 8 (1995).

Narsai. *Liturgical Homilies.* J. A. Robinson, ed., *The Liturgical Homilies of Narsai* (London: Cambridge University Press, 1909).

Non-Christian Texts

References are given for the Loeb Classical Library edition, from which most English translations are taken.

Aelius Lampridius. *Severus Alexander, Antoninus Elagabalus. Scriptores historiae Augustae.* Vol. 2. Loeb 1931.

Aelius Spartianus. *Hadrian. Scriptores Historiae Augustae.* Vol. 1. Loeb 1931.

Aeschylus. *Eumenides.* Loeb 1957.

Ammianus Marcellinus. *Rerum gestarum.* 3 vols. Loeb 1939.

Aristotle. *The Art of Rhetoric.* Loeb 1936.

———. *Magna moralia.* Loeb 1935.

Cicero. *De oratore.* Loeb 1942.

Diogenes Laertius. *The Lives of Eminent Philosophers.* Loeb 1925.

Flavius Vopiscus. *The Deified Aurelian. Scriptores Historiae Augustae.* Vol. 3. Loeb 1931.

———. *Firmus Saturninus, Proclus and Bonosus. Scriptores Historiae Augustae.* Vol. 3. Loeb 1931.

Isocrates. *Epistles.* Loeb 1945.

Josephus. *Works.* Loeb 1930-63.

Julius Capitolinus. *Opellius Magnus. Scriptores Historiae Augustae.* Vol. 2. Loeb 1931.

Juvenal. *Satires.* Loeb 1961.

Lucian. *The Death of Peregrinus (De morte Peregrini).* Loeb 1936.

Marcellinus. *Chronicles.*

Marcus Aurelius. *Communings.* Loeb 1916.

Martial. *Epigrams.* 3 vols. Loeb 1933.

Pausanius. *Descriptions of Greece.* Loeb 1918.

Persius. *Satires.* Loeb 1961.

Petronius. *Satyricon.* Loeb 1916.

Philo. *The Journeying of Abraham (De migratione Abrahami)*. Loeb 1932.

————. *On the Embassy to Gaius*. Loeb 1962.

Philostratus. *The Life of Apollonius (Vita Apolloni)*. 2 vols. Loeb 1912.

Plato. *Philebus*. Loeb 1925.

————. *Republic*. 2 vols. Loeb 1930.

————. *Theaetetus*. Loeb 1921.

Pliny. *Natural History*. Loeb 1952.

Pliny the Younger. *Epistles*.

Quintilian. *Institutio oratoria*. 4 vols. Loeb 1953.

Seneca. *Ad Lucilium epistolae morales*. 3 vols. Loeb 1907.

Strabo. *Geography*. 8 vols. Loeb 1917-32.

Suetonius. *The Lives of the Caesars*. Loeb 1914. Penguin Books, 1966.

Tacitus. *The Annals of Imperial Rome*. Translated by M. Grant. London: Penguin, 1996.

Thucydides. *History of the Peloponnesian War*. 4 vols. Loeb 1919-23.

Trebellius Pollio. *The Deified Claudius*. *Scriptores Historiae Augustae*. Vol. 3.

————. *The Two Gallieni*. *Scriptores Historiae Augustae*. Vol. 3.

Virgil. *The Aeneid*. Translated by J. Jackson. Ware: Wordsworth Classics, 1995.

Miscellaneous

De Vaux, R. *Ancient Israel: Its Life and Institutions*. London: Darton, Longman and Todd, 1998.

De Vries, D. "Schleiermacher, Friedrich D. E." In *CEP*, pp. 428ff.

Moltmann, J. *Theology and Joy*. Translated by R. Ulrich. London: SCM Press, 1973.

Schleiermacher, F. *The Christian Faith*. Edinburgh: T. & T. Clark, 1928.

Souter, A. *A Pocket Lexicon to the Greek New Testament*. Oxford: Clarendon, 1953.

Wesley, J. *The Letters of John Wesley*. Edited by J. Telford. London: Epworth Press, 1960.

————. *Notes on the New Testament*. London: Wesleyan Conference Office, 1887.

————. *The Works of the Rev. John Wesley, A.M*. Edited by T. Jackson. London: Methodist Publishing House, 1831.

Woodhead, L., and P. Heelas, eds. *Religion in Modern Times: An Interpretive Anthology*. Oxford: Blackwell, 2000.

Index